WE ARE I

VICTORIA PRESTON

# We Are Pilgrims

*Journeys in Search of Ourselves*

HURST & COMPANY, LONDON

First published in the United Kingdom in 2020 by
C. Hurst & Co. (Publishers) Ltd.,
41 Great Russell Street, London, WC1B 3PL
© Victoria Preston, 2020
All rights reserved.

The epigraph to Chapter 7 ('Untitled haiku', translation © Jane Hirshfield,
in 'Seeing Through Words: An Introduction to Basho and Haiku',
*Ten Windows: How Great Poems Transform the World*, New York:
Knopf, 2015) is used by kind permission of Jane Hirshfield.
All rights reserved.

A Cataloguing-in-Publication data record for this book
is available from the British Library.

ISBN: 9781787383036

This book is printed using paper from registered sustainable
and managed sources.

www.hurstpublishers.com

Printed in Great Britain by Bell and Bain Ltd, Glasgow

*For Tony—long may we share the path*

# CONTENTS

# ACKNOWLEDGEMENTS

The band of players who helped bring these notes into some sort of harmony, through their expertise, insight and careful consideration of the material, include Kathy, Chelsey, Tony, Nicholas, Michael, Karin, Vivien, Miriam, Charles and, not least, my exacting editor Lara. Special thanks are due to Ina, Helen, Jo, Avi, Malik, Christopher, Malcolm, Jen, David, Musa, Constance, Bep and others along the road who generously shared their personal stories. At every step of the research and writing process, I have been traversing the sacred terrain of the beliefs of others, and have proceeded with caution and respect in my heart. If anything between these pages should cause offence, I apologise unreservedly. Notwithstanding rigorous fact-checking by a handful of experts, any inaccuracies are entirely my own.

# PROLOGUE

August 2019, Suffolk, and two years into a journey to understand why we are pilgrims, I pause for a moment and unfurl the map to get a view of the road ahead.

The path itself is many thousands of years old and, for every cycle of the seasons, 200 million pairs of pilgrim feet will pass this way, each person with a unique reason for their pilgrim journey. This track of faith and kinship, hope and redemption, solace and gratitude winds through a landscape of sacred rocks, trees, rivers and waterfalls. There are holy mountains too, and from their peaks you can see the heavenly bodies above and a field of stars below. Signposts point out the places where heaven and earth are closer, where God resides, where gods once fought, where lotus petals fell into blue lakes, where mystical rivers converge with living streams; places where it is possible for people to attain freedom from desire, including the desire for that very freedom.

This meandering human journey flows through time and space, across land and sea; and, despite the distance, the horizon seems ever close in this world that has 'no vestige of a beginning, no prospect of an end'.[1] On this journey we will swim across the north Pacific with migrating salmon, struggling against the current to find their way to the pebbled beds of their natal streams on Sakhalin Island. Back on dry land we will follow herds of

xi

Persian gazelles as they return to the lush grasslands of southern Turkey. There beneath a pot-bellied hill, we will find their buried bones and their images inscribed onto monolithic stones that marked a ritual gathering place, older than the hill itself. And as we trace the criss-cross tracks of fish and birds, and mammals following the cycle of the Sun and Moon, we will see in the imprint of our once-nomadic footsteps the tread of pilgrims everywhere and in every age.

We will warm our spirits around the campfires of the camel herders of Rajasthan who come to venerate Brahma on the Kartika full moon, and in April we will follow the European travellers who left India over a thousand years ago. We will watch while they carry their black-skinned Saint Sara-la-Kali into the Mediterranean, held aloft above the waves with wild white horses of the Camargue providing the guard.

Travelling onwards, we will encounter the warrior Alexander the Great, for whom pilgrimage to Delphi or Siwa was the necessary precursor to any battle, and when he dies, quite suddenly, in spite of his greatness, we will turn our steps to Alexandria, where his successor, Ptolemy I Soter, built a temple so magical that a new empire might be anchored by its magnetic power.

We will look over the shoulder of Nehru who writes from his prison cell about his love for the Ganga, the symbol of an ancient nation about to be reborn into freedom; and with Mark Twain, will watch from the *ghats* of Varanasi as departed souls make their way across from this world and into the next—the final liberation.

Unfolding a letter from Malcolm X, sent from Mecca to his people back home in New York, we can read how, at this great Hajj festival, he feels so good to be in a place where unity prevails amongst people of all colours and nations. Once an extremist, now tempered by pilgrimage, the freshly renamed El-Hajj Malik El-Shabazz will soon return home, only to be assassinated precisely because of his newfound moderation.

# PROLOGUE

We will fall into step with Richard Burton and Gombozhab Tsybikov, a British and a Russian spy who both used the guise of a pilgrim to enter sacred cities and in so doing gained power and advantage for their masters. And while in Tibet with Tsybikov, we will watch as the monks stir butter and spices into a great cauldron of tea made for the deities before pouring the contents into a pit as a punishment for their negligence.

We will take the Fitchburg Railroad to Concord, Massachusetts to visit the hut on Walden Pond where Henry David Thoreau once read the *Bhagavad Gita* as he sought to understand the meaning of life, and, like the great Scottish-American naturalist John Muir, we will wonder why this little plot on the outskirts of a Boston suburb could ever be considered a hermitage.

We will stand in awe as the Jewish diaspora come together in Jerusalem to celebrate Passover at the Second Temple, while it still stands; and, centuries after it has fallen, we will watch the flow of Muslims, Jews and Christians who continue to congregate in this city which was once thought to be the centre of the Earth.

We will watch as a procession of Shia Muslims, together with people of all faiths, pass by on their way to Karbala for the Arbaeen festival, their needs for food and water met by local people along the route. And in Amritsar we will wait in line at the Guru ka Langar as the spicy steam rises from the huge pots of vegetable curry and dahl that will feed over 50,000 pilgrims a day, free of charge.

We will wander through the Quantock Hills with Wordsworth and Coleridge as they conceive of the Ancient Mariner, the eternal wanderer in search of salvation, and we will join the writers and activists of the Refugee Tales project on their pilgrimage across Kent, looking for a story that might save us all.

High in the clear air of the Cascade Mountains of Washington State, we will hear the keening voice of Jack Kerouac lamenting the solitude of Desolation Peak, and down in Lebanon's Bekaa

Valley, with Mars hanging like a night light overhead, we will hear the fading chords of a concert ring out from the Temple to Jupiter. Later, as the summer grows tired and the season turns, we will climb Croagh Patrick following a path first trodden by the Neolithic people of Ireland's west coast. At the summit, we will give thanks for the harvest and pray that we all survive the winter ahead. And, as the new year dawns, we will join the hundreds of millions of Chinese making their pilgrimage to their ancestral villages in the biggest annual migration of our species.

Amongst the many pilgrim days marked by festivals and music, there will be times of sorrow as we turn off the path of our inner journey to follow women whose lives have been marked by grief; join a widow on the camel train from Damascus and a distraught mother on the pilgrim vessel from Venice; and, in that rumpled fold of rock that is the Andes, weep for the thousands of Bolivian wives making a pilgrimage of despair to the Virgin of Urkupiña to ask for her help.

Later, we will trace the activists walking the watercourse that runs from Owens Lake to Los Angeles in the hope of finding an answer to the water crisis in California. Reaching the shore, we will recross the wide Pacific Ocean to Japan and wander through the grove of sacred trees that shrouds the Shinto shrines at Ise. And from this place, where humans and deities and the natural world are held to be indivisible, we will float out beyond the Earth's pull and, looking back at this blue marble hurtling through space, protected only by the misty caul of its atmosphere, we will wonder what awaits us.

# INTRODUCTION

This small volume is a journey into the question of why we are pilgrims. The book's narrative travels through the epic landscape of human journeys of purpose and meaning, along a path of ten possible motives, from survival to enlightenment. If you have ever been on a pilgrimage, or are contemplating one now, you will no doubt recognise the ten motives in the Table of Contents, but will want to protest that it is not so clear-cut—that we act through a cocktail of reasons, never just one, and that a myriad of other possible drivers have been omitted from my list of ten. What of humility or simple curiosity? What of walking with purpose to get fit, or to spend time with a close friend? I agree. Pilgrimage is a highly individual experience. Even where two or more people take to the road together, each is on their own personal journey, and the purpose of that journey might be three- or four-fold, or even a complete mystery to the individual themselves. In exploring why so many of us are drawn to this timeless human activity, this book is intended not as a prescription of what does or doesn't constitute pilgrimage, but as an aid to private contemplation: 'Why am I considering going on a journey of meaning?' Or even, 'Why did I just do that and what did it mean?'

# WE ARE PILGRIMS

Every journey starts from where we stand, and this one began for me when, on returning to London from two years in Canada, I reflected on what to do next. Out of the haze of uncertainty an idea slowly took shape: perhaps a pilgrimage could create a space for proper consideration of the question. It wasn't clear where this idea had come from or why the prospect so magically lifted my spirits, but thus began the quest to understand why we are pilgrims.

The obvious place to start was to ask what we actually mean by 'pilgrimage'. Its very ubiquity as an expression of human society means that there is inevitably no single definition that adequately encapsulates the rich variety of the practice. So where are the edges? The term 'pilgrimage' is often used to describe visits to historic places, like the night club behind the London Library where Jimi Hendrix once played or beloved trips to see the Christmas lights on London's Regent Street, which a friend once described as a pilgrimage; such outings, however uplifting or profound, are not the subject of this inquiry. Rather, I have focussed on journeys which have a spiritual, religious or philosophical purpose and are directed towards a place of shared meaning. With this in mind, the definition which kept me on the straight and narrow path in this process is 'a ritual journey to a place of shared spiritual meaning'.

While helpful, this simple definition prompted many other questions, including whether such journeys must extend beyond the immediate boundaries of our home town; and, if not, what distinguishes them from everyday acts of devotion. There are, it seems, many local pilgrimage sites that are quite separate from local places of worship, and which serve a different ritual function. Intent rather than distance is the critical factor here. By way of example, the seventh-century St Peter's on the Wall in Essex lies only a mile from Bradwell, but that village's parish church of St Thomas observes a pilgrimage to it each July. This procession marks the cohesion of the community and a reaffirmation of shared faith, and so in every sense can be considered a pilgrimage.

By contrast, the Via Francigena runs to almost 1,200 miles and the Camino Way from St Jean Pied de Port almost 500 miles. Medieval pilgrims were often sent on months-long journeys to these and other shrines as penance for crimes or breaches of ecclesiastical law, and had to bring back the evidence that they had reached their destination. This paperwork of proof continues today in the pilgrim passports and completion certificates common to many major Christian routes. Travellers along the Camino de Santiago must complete the last 60 miles or so on foot in order to secure the coveted 'Compostela' certificate; at the end of my own journey along the Via Francigena I queued with others at a small Vatican office in St Peter's Square for the Testimonium. But faith does not rest on proof, so why does this physical evidence matter?

In part because it is a mark of intent and distinguishes the pilgrim from the casual visitor. I first visited St Peter's as a young child on a cultural trip to Italy with my parents and have returned to Rome many times, but these were not pilgrimages, and of the scores of other visits I have made to pilgrim sites in the intervening decades, not least during the research for this book, very few can truly count as such. Yes, where we go is a consideration in defining pilgrimage, but why we go is even more important. Stepping off the path of daily life with the intention of creating space for meditation, reflection, connection with the bigger picture; being nowhere, however briefly—this is part of the spell of pilgrimage that reels us in and what in part defines it.

The scale of pilgrimage, both in time and space, is truly epic. Pilgrim trails can be found right around the world, from China to Ireland and Norway to South Africa. The nature of routes and shrines are diverse, with some being close to home and others remote; some widely accessible to tourists, others reserved solely for the devout. The number of sites is incalculable, and estimated annual pilgrim numbers vary from 200 million to 300 million. New routes are regularly added to the map, with religious bodies, tourist boards and economic policy-makers recognising the social value of reviving ancient routes or creating new paths towards important sites. St Olav's Way through Sweden and Norway to Trondheim is one such example, and now draws thousands of walkers with spiritual purpose to these northern lands. The Via Francigena, which has carried travellers from Canterbury Cathedral to St Peter's in Rome since the time of St Augustine (sixth century) has been revived over recent years with help from EU funding, recognising that the pilgrim trade is of value to rural communities eviscerated by the marching mechanisation of agriculture. For whatever reason, it seems that more and more of us are making the choice to embark on a journey of purpose to a place of shared meaning, and the pilgrim economy continues to grow.

While considerations of public safety mean that there is a natural upper limit to how many can safely attend the Hajj at Mecca during any given year, other Islamic pilgrim sites are able to accommodate burgeoning demand. Amongst these is Karbala in Iraq, where the annual Arbaeen pilgrimage commemorating the martyrdom of Husayn ibn Ali (grandson of the Prophet Muhammad) now regularly attracts over 15 million participants, many of whom are non-Muslims. Seemingly undeterred by the security issues in Iraq, the high levels of participation in the procession from Najaf to Karbala point to the appeal of pilgrimage more generally: the experience of being part of a much greater humanity, and with it a sense of kinship beyond your immediate family or tribe.

Added to the scale of pilgrimage worldwide is its immense historical reach. Otherwise warring peoples once travelled under truce to Arabian and Hellenic festivals, to take part in seasonal rites—a reminder that, for thousands of years, cyclical migration was a matter of survival. The origins of pilgrimage are so early in the human story that we cannot know for certain where or how the practice began, but the very earliest site which we can examine today is Göbekli Tepe in southern Turkey, which dates back around 12,000 years. This recently revealed temple complex is located on what would have been the grazing lands of migratory herds on which these Neolithic humans depended for food.

At this distance in time, we can only speculate about the ritual purpose of the immense stone structures at Göbekli Tepe, but it seems that such places may have been created through acts of co-operation between small groups or individuals. Collective action between small bands would have enabled the corralling of wild animals at a scale providing benefits to all. Looking to more recent ritual landscapes for clues, the collective hunts led by Blackfoot tribes of North America up until the nineteenth century equally fostered social cohesion amongst warrior bands that competed for resources at other times of the year. This principle of shared sanctity amongst otherwise warring peoples recurs many times in history, placing pilgrimage firmly at the heart of human social evolution; these 'common grounds' helped us avoid mutual annihilation and allowed the emergence of societies, beyond the confines of the family, the band, or the tribe.

Pilgrim sites are often crowded and the intensity of feeling that can be stirred at such mass gatherings, however peaceful, is well known to those with an eye to law and order. But the one-mindedness of crowds also allows for a sense of unity and freedom from self. For some pilgrims this sensation translates into a profound connection with their faith and with their God. Many of the Hajj Stories recorded by the eponymous British Museum project testify to this. In sharing her experience of the Hajj, Saadia tells how, in coming face to face with the Kaaba, nothing else in the world mattered—for her, time stopped, and in this exact moment she felt she had finally arrived at home.

The idea of a place far from home standing for 'home' raises another big question around the practice of pilgrimage. Namely, wherein lies the mysterious pull of certain places? Mountains reaching up to the heavens feature in the location of Daoist temples in China, the Maronite monasteries of Lebanon and the 5,000-year-old pilgrimage up Croagh Patrick in Ireland, to name but a few. Sometimes we want to get as close to the heavens as we can in this life but many ancient sites do not share these features; nor were they established on major trading routes, even if trade at these places often grew later. So what is it that led our ancestors to choose one place rather than another? One of the strands of belief that emerges at many sites, including Jerusalem, Glastonbury and Prayagraj (formerly Allahabad), is that the veil between this and other worlds is more transparent at these places, allowing for a deeper connection between our temporal existence and what lies beyond our knowing.

More prosaically perhaps, despite our deep nomadic roots, once attachment to a location has formed it holds us fast. In behavioural terms this is known as 'confirmation bias', our preference for information that confirms and strengthens what we already know, irrespective of the advantages of any alternatives. Jerusalem is the poster child for this phenomenon, with Judaism, Roman paganism, Christianity and Islam all layered one over the other in this pilgrim city, but with no clear rationale for why here, rather than, say, Jaffa or Byblos along the coast.

Our preference for pre-existing sacred sites raises the question of how new sites ever become established. In pursuing this question, I found that the one topic which arose over and over again in my research was that of relics: those meaningful objects that connect place, person, and narrative. Santiago de Compostela, St Peter's in Rome, the Temple of the Sacred Tooth Relic in Sri Lanka and thousands of other Buddhist and Christian sites were all founded on relics, thus helping spread these religions to new followers. In seeking to explain this phenomenon, I looked to my own array of souvenir objects, some of which have the power to transport me to places I visited decades ago and to evoke the feelings I experienced in the very moment I was there. Admittedly, religious relics are invested with a different kind of potency, but the two share their power to communicate meaningful human experience, across time and space.

Once a coveted relic had been secured, the human propensity for embellishment often came into play. Valuable relics were typically encased in more worldly treasure, like a reliquary or tomb made of precious materials, this then being enshrined in a great architectural edifice, designed to further elicit the awe of the faithful. Chaucer's pilgrims on their way to Canterbury might have been drawn as much by their worldly appetite for wonder as by their spiritual need for reflection or penance. In Ancient Greece this same cocktail of motives translated into the evolution of pilgrimage as a multi-dimensional festival, with sacred rituals taking place alongside theatre and sporting contests. The site at Delphi, which no doubt began as a simple oracle, evolved over time to include a hippodrome, a stadium and a gymnasium. Why did the ancients come here? Was it to ask of the Pythia what lay ahead, or to see the spectacle of chariot racing and bathe in the spa, or to discuss philosophy along the pathways of this sprawling site? The answer is likely some or all of these: as with so many other aspects of human behaviour, our impulses toward pilgrimage are a brocade of interwoven strands, some glimmering clearly, others invisible even to ourselves.

Notwithstanding the human instinct to embellish, we are also reductive by nature. In the twenty-first century, our image of the typical pilgrim might derive from video coverage of the Hajj, or from films such as *The Way* (Emilio Estevez, 2010), which follows a group of characters walking the Camino to Santiago de Compostela. These two sites seem to dominate our idea of what pilgrimage means in this age, but however apposite these examples may be, they have simply replaced older and equally potent shorthand visualisations. One older stereotype is replayed in Werner Herzog's 2001 documentary *Pilgrimage*. The film comprises footage of pilgrims crawling on their knees as they approach the Basilica of Guadeloupe in Mexico, intercut with scenes of pilgrims kneeling and sliding across the frozen landscape towards the Tomb of St Sergei in northern Russia. It is intentionally painful to watch and highlights the transactional nature of pilgrimage, the supplicant offering up their efforts in return for something of immeasurable value to them. Possibly deliverance from physical or mental suffering, forgiveness of wrongdoing or perhaps the hoped-for blessing of a child? The requests of these and other such pilgrims are inevitably deeply personal, and for those whose prayers have been answered, their act of suffering stands as expression of gratitude for whatever favour has been granted. After all, if not personal sacrifice, what else can we offer up to the divine in exchange for mercy or redemption?

The narrative of suffering and self-sacrifice in service of a higher cause threads through the religious texts of Judaism, Islam and Christianity, and Buddhism is born of it. The central story of Buddhism hinges on the eponymous protagonist renouncing the comforts of his domestic environment in exchange for the privations of the road: a deliberate transition from princeling to wanderer in the quest for enlightenment. When the Buddha finally comes to see how things really are, and in so doing quenches desire and is delivered from suffering, the lexicon describing how his followers might arrive at this same point is framed in terms of a journey, more precisely an 'eightfold path'. This promise of enlightenment or journey towards self is amongst the many factors that continue to attract pilgrims irrespective of faith. Here comes the human instinct for simplification: what better place than the road, that somewhere which is nowhere, to face those eternal questions of why we are here and what life means?

Herzog's dictum that 'the world reveals itself to those who travel on foot' is as true for the pilgrim as it is for the film-maker, and there can be little doubt that whether we are searching for meaning or for answers we might usefully go out into the natural world to find them. This thinking informed the Walking Water project in California, which brought competing interests together on a pilgrimage in the hope of finding a solution to an environmental crisis. At stake was the wetland habitat of Owens Lake, one of the most important bird migration sites in the United States, under threat from expanding human water consumption. The scale of Walking Water relative to the scale of the problem in hand might be considered 'a drop in the ocean', but this project embodies one of the fundamentals of pilgrimage. On the road, on foot, with our minds fully open, we come to the realisation that we are nothing more than a speck of dust in the great scheme of things, but that what we do as individuals always matters. This duality gives a clue to the almost universal appeal of pilgrimage and why so many of us return to it time and again. Stepping outside of our lives to walk or just 'be' for a few days or even hours allows for both our individual insignificance and our common humanity.

What began in the Neolithic era, when our ancestors paid homage to the forces of nature, continues in the Anthropocene: as we awaken once again to our dependence on this planet that sustains us all, it seems reasonable to conclude that pilgrimage will continue to serve its timeless purpose. In setting out to explore what that purpose might be, I considered many alternative routes towards an answer, and could equally have chosen another; but—to paraphrase Robert Frost—though each way looked just as fair, I chose this one. It begins over the page...

1

# SURVIVAL

*'Grain within grain successive harvests dwell,*
*And boundless forests slumber in a shell.'*

Erasmus Darwin, *The Botanic Garden*

August 2005, and in a hotel room on Sakhalin Island, many time zones from home, I lay awake as the grainy TV screen showed relentless scenes of devastation. Hurricane Katrina had smashed into the southern coast of the US, ending the lives of hundreds of citizens and washing away the homes of many thousands more. Immediately after the event a helicopter, hovering above the devastation, relayed images of storm waters flowing through the streets and highways of New Orleans. In another clip from the same bulletin, President George W. Bush was shown waving and smiling to waiting TV crews as he strode across the tarmac to climb aboard Airforce One. The news narrative implied that the US had failed its most vulnerable in their hour of need. But, over the coming weeks, the world would see what this land of migrants was made of. The collective will to survive that first brought so many to America's shores was reignited, and communities in Texas and beyond quickly mobilised to offer displaced families much more than emergency food and water, providing free lodging in their own homes and places in their children's schools.

I was in Sakhalin to discuss survival of a different kind, and in particular, how two species of non-human migrants might or might not be affected by an oil and gas project. On day one, our focus was the gray whale. When the thick pack ice of the north-western Pacific has melted away in the summer months, these immense mammals can be found off the coast, lying on their sides in the shallow waters as they sift tons of protein-rich plankton soup through the bristles of their baleen palates. They are fattening up for a long trip and in early autumn, as water temperatures begin to fall, the whales head south. Although the migratory pattern of this group is still unclear, their close cousins in Alaska make an epic journey to Baja California, Mexico, hugging the coast as they go. It is here that they will mate and where, after a more than year-long gestation, the females will give birth to their young. Scientists have been working for years to understand gray whales and word has got out amongst Sakhalin's relatively poor fishing community about the cost of that research, which runs to millions of dollars. The local media has dubbed them 'the golden whales' and they are precious indeed. Almost hunted to extinction and once on the critically endangered species list, Sakhalin's gray whale population is now recovering. What's more, as the Earth's climate changes and melting ice opens up new channels, the gray whale has begun to migrate to parts of the ocean where it has been extinct for many hundreds of years.

On day two of the Sakhalin trip, we drove down to a narrow point in the river where tens of thousands of salmon were competing to make their way upstream. These ardent travellers were heading back to the natal rivers where they themselves had hatched: those successfully completing the journey would spawn the next generation, which in time would return to the sea. The salmon have had millions of years of experience of this annual cycle, helpfully encoded in every single pink egg deposited in the gravelly riverbeds.

The salmon and the gray whales of Sakhalin are amongst thousands of species, including *homo sapiens*, that make a seasonal migration for the purpose of feeding, breeding or both. Some, like the tiny 'painted lady' butterfly, make an annual round trip of up to 9,000 miles from the heat of Africa to the edge of the Arctic Circle.[1] Others, like American bighorn sheep, travel relatively small distances between lowland winter pasture and highland summer breeding grounds. We don't fully understand what prompts the start of these migrations, or how myriad creatures large and small navigate the vast distances across and between continents, but we can reasonably assume that these epic undertakings are worth the effort—spurred by a deeply imprinted instinct to survive.

As apex predators, we humans have long since learned how to make the most of this moveable feast, following in the migratory wake of the species with which we fill our bellies. As with the whales and the butterflies, this practice flows from something truly fundamental to our survival, a behavioural equivalent of the mitochondrial DNA that has been carried deep inside our cells down the ages, since the first female of our species gave birth to her first daughter. Underneath the wafer-thin carapace of modernity that cloaks our animal selves, we too are pre-programmed for survival, and perhaps this offers a clue as to why, when spring arrives, so many of us are pricked by the impulse to take to the road. As Chaucer observed:

> When the sweet showers of April have pierced
> The drought of March, and pierced it to the root,
> And every vein is bathed in that moisture
> Whose quickening force will engender the flower;

And when the west wind too with its sweet breath
Has given life in every wood and field
To tender shoots, and when the stripling sun
Has run his half-course in Aries, the Ram,
And when small birds are making melodies,
That sleep all the night long with open eyes,
(Nature so prompts them, and encourages);
Then people long to go on pilgrimages.[2]

Chaucer wrote his *Canterbury Tales* in the fourteenth century, but the story of pilgrimage itself—the act of travelling to a place of shared meaning—is infinitely older. Its origins are so early in the human story that we cannot know for certain where or how the practice began, but one possible explanation is that it emerged from the seasonal migration of bands of nomads, going to and returning from places where food was more abundant, breeding conditions more favourable, survival more assured; following in the wake of herds, flocks and schools on their own seasonal journeys. One of the earliest sacred sites we know of is Göbekli Tepe, or Pot-Bellied Hill, in south-eastern Turkey—and it is truly ancient. It is thought that here, close by the summer grazing pastures of migrating herds, hundreds of hunter-gatherers came together for the purpose of collective rituals some 12,000 years ago.[3]

Over the past twenty years or so, German archaeologist Klaus Schmidt and his team worked with great care and wonder at Göbekli Tepe to reveal a complex series of temple-like structures, buried beneath tons of earth for millennia. Some of the T-shaped stone pillars that sit within the circular enclosures are richly inscribed with depictions of gazelles, birds, snakes, foxes and other wild animals. At the centre of one of these monumental rings is a pair of standing stones over 5 metres tall, inscribed with a face, arms and hands, and a belt or loincloth. Each of these monoliths weighs many tons; while the slabs of rock of which they are made were quarried nearby with the use of primitive technology, it would have taken a considerable collective effort to move them into position. We cannot know whether this collaboration was achieved willingly or under duress, but in either event, it would have required significant endeavour in both the planning and the execution, and this begs the question of why these elaborately decorated structures were built at all.

Given both its great antiquity and its relatively recent discovery (Schmidt's excavation only began in 1996), theories about the site's exact nature are both abundant and as yet unresolved. Was it, as some have suggested, built following the appearance of a new star—Sirius, the dog star that appears on the horizon at the break of summer's dawn?[4] Or did it begin as a shared place where funerary rites took place, providing a big send-off for the departing Neolithic soul? Whatever the precise underpinning of its creation, it seems that a great deal of feasting occurred at Göbekli Tepe, and excavations have unearthed evidence that high on the menu were Persian gazelles, summer visitors to these parts.[5] Work continues on decoding what took place at this complex nine-hectare site, with its multiple temples and giant anthropomorphic monoliths, but there is an even greater mystery at the heart of Göbekli Tepe. There are no signs here of habitation, suggesting that co-operation to construct places for shared rituals may have preceded the dawn of agriculture and fixed human settlement. Or as Klaus Schmidt once so starkly stated, 'First came the temple, then the city.' If this assumption proves to be correct, it places pilgrimage at the very foundation not only of our belief systems, but of human social evolution. We are, it seems, pilgrims to our very roots.

While we might lack information on how our Neolithic ancestors behaved at ritual sites such as Göbekli Tepe, it is not hard to imagine what drove their behaviours. Let us close our eyes for a moment and travel back through time to stand shoulder to shoulder with those nomadic bands, hunting game in the summer pastures of the Fertile Crescent. As we wait our turn to drink at the shared watering hole, as animals so often do, let us consider how such protocols might evolve into something more elaborate, with the same groups arriving at more or less the same time each year to take advantage of spring grazing. Competition for sparse game may be a matter of survival in the barren winter months, but at times of abundance, co-operation between small groups offers singular advantages. Hunting on foot with spear or slingshot is hard. It requires a great deal of energy and a lot of luck. Better to work together in a pack, like jackals or wolves, surrounding the herd and driving off the weakest, the youngest, the oldest.

Such corralling of wild animals requires strength in numbers, but most of all, a tried and tested method in which each member of the team knows their role. On an assignment in Swaziland (now Eswatini), I met Ted Reilly, the man responsible for reintroducing wild game into his native land in the late twentieth century. By sleight of hand I was inveigled by Ted into helping with a roundup of wildebeest on the reserve, an event that required every available hand. In our case a small helicopter overhead was steering them into a corral as we conspired to close off any possibility of retreat. Ritual communal hunting offers bounty for all and the promise of a feast at the end of it. The most common depictions of the human form found on objects unearthed at Neolithic sites across southern Europe and the Near East are of dancers. Dating from the eighth to the fourth millennia BCE,[6] such artefacts suggest that music and dance have been important expressions of shared purpose and communal effort since our earliest days: 'We have enough to survive the winter, let's give thanks, let's celebrate, let's do it again next summer.'

Stretching back at least 5,000 years, and only coming to an end relatively recently, the traditional rituals of North American hunter-gatherers offer a wormhole into the distant past and perhaps some clues to the social value of ritual sites such as Göbekli Tepe. The UNESCO-listed Head-Smashed-In Buffalo Jump, a sheer escarpment in the foothills of the Canadian Rockies, is a well-documented example of a ritual landscape, and its somewhat self-descriptive name gives an indication of its purpose. The Blackfoot tribes' annual bison hunt long culminated here, only dying out with the arrival of European settlers in the late nineteenth century. By then, the pedestrian hunters of old had long since been superseded by horseback-riding hunters with guns; but oral tradition and the landscape itself tell of herds of bison driven over long distances by men on foot, with the ultimate goal of driving them over the Buffalo Jump to their deaths.

So far, so good. But bison are large and fast, and men working on foot are comparatively small and slow, so how did the Blackfoot succeed in driving vast numbers of bison over these dead-drops? Recent research indicates that, over the course of many generations, the Blackfoot tribes developed highly specialised knowledge about bison movements and, importantly, their psychology—in some respects mimicking the hunting tactics of wolves.[7] This enabled the Blackfoot to lure migrating herds to a particular area and then, using a combination of songs, shouts, grass-fires and other means, they would start moving the herd in the desired direction. Enormous collective effort and fine coordination was required for this and for what followed. 'Drive lanes' were constructed, with smouldering bison dung, small piles of rocks and other obstacles forming boundaries on either side of a funnel, which started wide and became ever narrower as it led irrevocably towards the cliff edge. The herd was encouraged into the entrance of the drive lane and pushed onwards; as it gathered momentum, it became a single flowing stream of stampeding muscle. There was now no looking to left or right and, as they thundered on, no hope of turning back. Over the jump the bison fell, limb upon limb, heads smashed in. And here was the bounty for every man, woman and child involved: the meat and skins that would be shared by all, with plenty of surplus to see them through the winter and into spring, and even to trade.

This communal hunt was a way of reinforcing social cohesion amongst a tribe more inclined to fighting than feasting; the Jump was their shared ritual site for a unique annual event. The secret of how to achieve it was held by elite warrior societies, a highly valued asset. The Blackfoot comprised three interconnected tribes, each made up of small bands of 80–120 individuals, any one of whom could leave and freely join another band. This social flexibility offered a helpful means of avoiding conflict within bands, and of building bonds between them. Warrior societies existed in which young men could buy their way in at the lowest level, trading up throughout their lives, while selling their old positions to the new generation.

These warrior societies had a number of governance functions, including holding the special knowledge of how to round up and run the hunt. The Blackfoot bands were nomadic,[i] living in settled camps in winter as they waited for the bison to move from the shelter of the forests onto the grassy plains. When spring arrived and the snows had melted, each band would set out to hunt alone. But later, in mid-summer, as the wild serviceberries used to preserve meat were ripening in the woods, the loosely organised tribal bands came together for their only collective ceremony: the Sun Dance. The communal bison hunts that formed part of these rites provided food for the feast, not least the bulls' tongues, which were used as ritual offerings.

---

[i] In 1877 the Blackfoot signed Treaty 7, in which they gave up some ancient hunting grounds and settled on reserves in southern Alberta. By this time the bison were almost extinct due to overhunting, largely as a result of European settlement in the southern borderlands of what is now Canada.

At the centre of the Sun Dance rites was a tree, felled with great ceremony in the woods, stripped of all but its top branches and dragged into the centre of the festival grounds, where it was re-erected. The Sun Dance involved the elite warriors undergoing days of thirst, fasting and ritual piercing of the flesh—demonstrating their willing self-sacrifice on behalf of the tribe. The women danced too but were spared the self-torture, in recognition of their courage in facing the pain and danger of childbirth. In Canada these trials of resilience are being revived today (although without the flesh piercing) as a means of treating drug and alcohol addiction amongst First Nation people; this revival gives testimony to the earlier value of such practices in building social order and cohesion.

The days- or weeks-long trek on foot to round up the bison, the coordinated rituals of the hunt and the tortuous sweat lodges where the hunter's will was tested are not the stuff of hiking boots and EU-sponsored routes, or charter flights to religious shrines and pilgrim festivals, but they do share many of the same characteristics. Notably, participants coming from far and wide to take part in shared rituals in a sacred landscape, a voluntary trial of endurance rewarded—a recognition that we are each part of something bigger. It is more than a century since the last herd of bison were driven over the cliff of Head-Smashed-In Buffalo Jump, and at least 10,000 years since Persian gazelles were roasted over a spit at Göbekli Tepe, but even when settled communities were established in many parts of the world, humans continued to travel to communal sites to mark important moments in the annual cycle, to give thanks for what had passed, and to pray for what lay ahead.

Following humanity's discovery of agriculture, collective action around sowing and harvesting crops gave rise to celebratory festivals, and the ritual sacrifices of firstborn livestock provided the food for the feast: a reward and a thanksgiving for Earth's bounty; a recognition of the favour of those forces that control our destiny. Shifting these festivities from the local level where the sowing and harvesting took place, instead centralising activity around more broadly shared temple sites, offered many advantages. Naturally there was a big incentive for the spiritual centres themselves: they were able to reinforce their power and wealth through the offerings brought by pilgrims, and also through the indirect benefit of great numbers of visitors wanting food and lodging. There were singular advantages for the pilgrims too, many of whom would have travelled for days or weeks to attend the festival. These gatherings provided the opportunity to trade goods and exchange ideas, to learn new ways of doing things, and to broaden the gene pool of livestock and human stock. Pilgrimage rites were evolving from feasts around communal hunting and harvesting activities into multi-layered events that embraced both the sacred and the mundane.

In this sense, pilgrimage was a very early social networking 'platform', and the night sky the 'app' which provided the crucial data on when to travel. The scheduling of these early gatherings depended on the lunar and solar cycles. Lunar festivals were common to nomads who depended on the moon cycle to measure the passage of time and who, in hotter climates, would have travelled largely by night. By contrast, sedentary farming peoples depended on the solar cycle, which determined when to sow and when to reap. And then there were the stars, guiding us across land and sea and marking the seasons as they revolved above our heads. For many faith groups today, the pilgrimage calendar remains largely determined by the cosmos, whose infinite nature somehow has the ability to shrink time. The Nobel Physics laureate Isidor Isaac Rabi, who helped develop the atomic clock in the twentieth century, would nevertheless have celebrated the Jewish festival of Passover according to the ancient lunisolar calendar—which embraces the lunar cycle while ensuring it remains aligned with the seasons of the agricultural year. The Islamic Hajj, on the other hand, is scheduled solely according to the moon, always beginning on the eighth day of the twelfth month of the lunar calendar. Yet more complex than both of these, the Hindu Kumbh Mela rotates across four different locations according to a twelve-year calendar cycle determined by the positions of the Sun, the Moon and Jupiter.

\* \* \*

The Ancient Greeks, those great stargazers, did not have a word equating to the more modern term of 'pilgrimage', but the practice of 'going to the rites' was deeply woven into the fabric of society. Across the Greek world, the near-dawn rising of the Pleiades constellation, also known as the Seven Sisters, heralded the arrival of spring, and the beginning of the seafaring and farming year. The onset of spring also marked the start of the festival season, in which Greeks travelled by land and sea to worship the gods at gatherings that might also include taking part in or watching sporting games and other entertainments, such as theatre, music and dancing.

Then, as is now the case for cities hosting the modern Olympic Games, enormous prestige flowed to the states that mounted these major regional or Panhellenic events. Special amphitheatres and stadia were constructed, and some sites became noted for theatre, sport or music, but whatever else was on offer, all the festivals had Greek religious practice at their centre. At Olympia the great temple of Zeus dominated all and within it could be found one of the Seven Wonders of the World, the giant statue of the king of the gods created by the sculptor Phidias. Around 13 metres high, the seated figure was covered in ivory and gold, and looked down from a throne adorned with precious stones, woods and metals. Pythagoras compared life to a *panegyris*, or festival, in which some of us are competitors, some traders, and others simply spectators.[8] In this regard, the immense statue of Zeus was most definitely part of the spectacle.

Despite or perhaps because of the great wealth that allowed such wonders to be created, the ancient world was a dangerous place, and for centuries war was waged on a number of fronts between, amongst others, the Athenians, Egyptians, Persians, and Spartans. But such was the status of these Panhellenic festivals that war was not allowed to disrupt them. In 480 BCE, when the Persian ruler Xerxes invaded Greece, the Olympic festival and its contests went ahead all the same. These events were a means of keeping diplomatic channels open even in the face of long-term strife between hostile powers. The competition between athletes to demonstrate who was fastest or strongest, the displays of prowess in music and theatre, the gracious hospitality of the host nations, and the trust of the visiting dignitaries were proxies for the strength, power, pride and fearlessness of the nations taking part. Akin to the seasonal displays of strength and beauty we see amongst so many other animals, these festivals were a tool for social order and survival for all concerned.

These demonstrations of prowess and dominance were nothing without broad participation, and the Greeks created elaborate protocols to ensure that pilgrims could travel with impunity to take part in seasonal rites. Official truce-bearers, known as *theoroi* (observers) or *spondophoroi* (truce-bearers), went out to states where a truce was being offered, often many months in advance of a festival, inviting the state to send delegations and encouraging their people to attend. Although the average pilgrim came from the higher socioeconomic orders, (almost) all were welcome, and sacred journeys offered a rare opportunity for ordinary people to travel outside the immediate confines of their local village or town.

Athens and Sparta fought each other long and hard during the Peloponnesian War (431–04 BCE), but the briefly effective treaty known as the Peace of Nicias (signed in 421 BCE) included a clause guaranteeing the safe passage of pilgrims to important Panhellenic sanctuaries, such as Olympia and Eleusis. Such guarantees were essential, as pilgrims often travelled great distances by sea and land; with all the risks entailed in such journeys, it must have helped to know that you wouldn't be caught up in the crossfire between two warring armies. Indeed, the word sanctuary has come to stand for an inviolable place of safety, and the conditions of truce around pilgrim travel even extended to ancient Greek pirates, the *leistai*, who held off robbing pilgrims, presumably for fear of antagonising Poseidon and his friends. But not all were able to resist the temptation of a pilgrim ship full to the brim with offerings for the gods. One known victim was Phrynon, an Athenian visiting Olympia under the period of Nician truce. On his way to the games, he was unfortunately kidnapped by *leistai*, only being released on payment of a ransom. Turning to the rule book on these matters, on his return to Athens Phrynon sent an invoice to Phillip II of Macedon, who duly paid him back the ransom sum in full.

Outside the big setpiece events of the Panhellenic festivals, there were many shrines and oracles across the Aegean and Mediterranean to which individuals could journey for guidance in a world of great uncertainty. Warrior or farmer, fisherman or merchant, their concerns for survival and prosperity were timeless. Will I succeed in battle? Should I marry? Will I have a son? This idea that a pilgrimage might somehow provide a key to what fate has in store for us is precisely where my own journey had begun. At a certain point, a trip to Delphi became inevitable.

It was around noon when I checked into the Artemis Hotel at the tail end of town. Dropping my rucksack with this daughter of Zeus, I emerged back into the bright, silent street and headed out to the ruins.[9] 'Why is it here, Delphi? Why is it here, far from everything?' I asked the woman in the ticket booth. She didn't hesitate to answer: 'There is a special energy.' It was the same reply I had heard in Glastonbury and Avebury, but in that moment it didn't feel special. Not yet. It was hard to make sense of anything in the unfamiliar heat, and as I clambered up the steeply sloping site in the full glare of Helios I began to wonder what I was really up to. The maxim 'Know Thyself' (*gnothi seauton*) was reputedly inscribed in the *pronaos*, the forecourt of the Temple of Apollo that sits at the heart of Delphi. 'Know Thyself'—easy to say, hard to achieve, but a worthwhile ambition nonetheless. Onwards and upwards I climbed, zigzagging towards the arena: a long narrow oval stadium squeezed into the last possible sliver of flat ground at the apex. The amphitheatre and the temple, the treasury and the Castalian spring, where Apollo killed Python, all rolled out below, a carpet of myth and mystery. The view down the valley was shrouded in haze, flattening the distance between Mount Parnassus and the Gulf of Corinth: space and time both distorted and disorienting.

This had been a sacred site long before the pillars were erected for the Temple of Apollo in the fourth century BCE. At a time distant beyond our knowing, Gaia (Mother Earth) and Uranus (Father Sky) had a daughter, the Titan Rhea. Rhea was in an unimaginably terrible union with her brother-husband Kronos, who, believing a prophecy that his own child would surpass him, swallowed each of their children as soon as they were born. Finally, when baby Zeus arrived in the world with a healthy bawl, Rhea hid him, instead swaddling a rock to trick Kronos, who swallowed it down. Thus surviving his father's violent jealousy, the prophecy came good and Zeus became king of all the gods. Wanting to find the centre of the world, Zeus set two eagles flying, one from the east and another from the west. And this is where they met, in Delphi—the *omphalos*, the belly button of the Earth itself. And there on the slopes of Mount Parnassus it still sits, that smooth, grey cone of stone: either the swallowed rock of Kronos, or the omphalos, or both. You decide.

This hillside is thought to have been a centre for cult activity since around 1500 BCE, the Minoans having sailed here with their stories of Zeus and Kronos, but the rock of Delphi may have been a fetish object even before then. Earth itself was a primordial power and its spirit was seen in its very fabric. Rock, water, trees: these elements appear over and over again at pilgrim sites, invested with ritual or spiritual potency. At a certain point, our ancestors took a small step from worshipping a natural feature in situ to constructing around it a dedicated home for the divine. As we saw with the Blackfoot Sun Dance, trees were the mightiest of all vegetation, and amongst the most notable tree pilgrimage sites is the oracle of Dodona.

Thought to date back at least as far as the second millennium BCE, Dodona was mentioned by Homer in the *Iliad* (c. 750 BCE) and centres around an oak tree. Here the *Peleiades*, the priestesses of Dione, and the *Selloi*, the priests of her male equivalent Zeus Naios, 'god of the spring below the oak', interpreted the prophecies given by the rustling of the leaves. This simple and direct approach developed over time, and in due course the priestly intermediaries drew lots in response to a question inscribed on a strip of lead. Inspired by the deity's advice, the medium delved a hand into a pouch containing two types of stone: one white, one black, for 'yes' or 'no'.[ii] Many of the lead strips have been recovered and we can learn much from them about what bothered the Bronze Age pilgrim to Dodona: 'Lysanias asks Zeus Naios and Dione whether the child which Nyla is carrying is really his.' Or, more prosaically still, 'Agis asks Zeus Naios and Dione whether he lost the blankets and pillows

---

[ii] This method remains in use today in the gentlemen's clubs of London. Voting on new joiners, every voter drops a ball unseen into the deal box, either white or black. If, when you lift the lid, you've been 'blackballed', it's a 'no' to membership.

himself, or whether they were stolen by someone outside the household.'[10] Dodona is remote, and it seems a long way to go to ask about bedding. Perhaps some nuance or subtext has been lost in translation, or in the chasm of elapsed time? In any event, these lead strips offer a clue to the highly personal motives behind each individual act of pilgrimage, then as now.

At Delphi, pilgrims looked to the Pythia, the Oracle, for answers. Typically priests were the same gender as the deity they served, but at Delphi's Temple of Apollo, the Pythia, the oracle's human vector, was female. Named for Python whom Apollo slew, she was typically chosen from the local community, was beyond childbearing age and had to remain celibate; the fate of great empires depended on her. Some anthropologists have described pilgrimage shrines as 'pre-eminent centres for dealings between human beings and the divine', focal points of influence where the shrine deities act as mediators.[11] The Oracle at Delphi was one such marketplace, and those with power and wealth were not shy to leverage those assets in an attempt to sway divine influence in favour of their own survival. This was especially true of Croesus, King of Lydia.

Writing in the 440s BCE, Herodotus left us a detailed description of Croesus' dedications to Delphi over a century earlier.[12] High on the list was a lion of pure gold weighing 600lbs; this standing on four half-bricks of pure gold each weighing 150lbs; all atop a pile of 113 half-bricks of white gold (an alloy of gold and silver) each weighing around 120lbs. Rich as Croesus was, he was mean in every sense of the word. This heap of gold and silver was the product of a burnt offering made in Lydia to honour Apollo. Some 3,000 human victims were sacrificed, and Lydian subjects were strongly encouraged to contribute offerings of their own precious metals to the pyre.

What did Croesus want? More power? Yet more wealth? All of this and more. He wanted to extend his empire over the Greek cities on the coast of Asia Minor, and hoped that a favourable pronouncement from Delphi might persuade some Greeks from the mainland to back him against the Persians. He sent to Delphi for advice and here's what came back: 'If Croesus goes to war he will destroy a great empire.' Croesus felt encouraged, and went to war; he misjudged the enemy's strategy and was ultimately dragged before the Persian King Cyrus the Great in chains. The Oracle had proved right. A great empire had been destroyed— but, sadly for Croesus, it was his own. We all hear what we want to hear when seeking answers and meaning about the highest stakes of our lives. Now, as then, it pays to 'know thyself'.

Not all questions are as historically decisive as war, not all oracles as influential as Delphi. Hermes is an emissary moving between earthly and divine worlds and many oracles were dedicated to this messenger of the gods. The second-century Greek traveller and writer Pausanias tells of one in the marketplace of Pharae: a statue of a bearded Hermes, 'called Hermes Agoraios' (Hermes of the Market).[13] Pausanias goes on to describe how this stone oracle worked. Coming at eventide, the inquirer would burn incense in a small adjacent hearth, light the nearby oil lamps, and, after giving some money, depart with his hands over his ears. Once he was safely outside the marketplace, he would uncover his ears and whatever he immediately heard he could consider oracular. Hermes Agoraios is an early example of a local pilgrimage site, raising yet again the question of what makes a pilgrimage. The answer is surely that the location of the special place is not what matters; the important thing is what makes it special. There is something about stepping outside the bounds of normal routine or ritual that differentiates pilgrimage from other forms of devotion or meditation.

In the way that religions, cults and deities often overlap and morph from one to the next (as with the Minoan cult of Zeus migrating to Delphi), the Egyptian god Amun is closely associated

with the Greek Hermes. One of the eight deities of Egypt's primordial pantheon, the Ogdoad, Amun shares Hermes' quality of
unboundedness, making him an ideal messenger between this
world and the unseen forces that govern our fate. An influential
oracle was founded in his name at the oasis of Siwa, in the desert
that lies between Egypt and Libya. Such was the authority of
this Oracle of Amun that, in the sixth century BCE, Persia's
King Cambyses II sent an army to destroy it after the priests
there refused to legitimise his claim to Egypt. All 50,000 of the
king's men perished in the attempt. Centuries later, in 331 BCE,
Alexander the Great and his men made a huge detour to Siwa
before heading off to pursue the Persians, driving King Darius III
to defeat and death at the hands of his own soldiers. The power
and influence of such oracles is hard to grasp today, but at this
time, going to war without seeking their advice was considered
an act of hubris, leaving you a hostage to fortune. The authority
of leaders and the confidence of their soldiers were underpinned
by these prophecies, making pilgrimages to an oracle a matter of
life or death.

The cautionary tales of greed and folly that describe the
downfall of both Croesus and Cambyses II are not just history:
they are folk wisdom appealing to the ears of the everyman,
reminding us of human fallibility and that even powerful leaders
cannot control everything through force or wealth. The Pythia
of Delphi famously gave her answers while in a state of intoxica-
tion; perhaps due to gases leaking up through the rock beneath
the tripod on which she sat, or maybe from chewing the leaves
of oleander, a flowering shrub that grows in abundance in the
nearby hills. Theories abound, but the essential point is not how
she entered her trance-like state, but that her prophecies represented the intuitive rather than the rational. It was this which
was valued by even the most powerful or most enlightened
thinkers in the land. Plato himself was a huge fan of the oracles

of Amun, Delphi and Dodona, and insisted that the religious life of his ideal city-republic be based on their instinctive revelations, even though his philosophical system was based on reason and science: then as now, both faith and pilgrimage occupied a place beyond the pragmatism of the everyday.

* * *

It may be hard to place ourselves in the minds of our Neolithic or Bronze Age ancestors, but it seems that in many respects they were little different from ourselves: worrying about the big issues, like the consequences of war, as well as domestic issues, like misplaced household goods, or whether to marry. The future and the day-to-day: humans, as ever, seek assurance about both, and this gives another clue regarding the ubiquity of pilgrimage as a favoured route to an answer. Traces of ancient pilgrimage sites can be found almost everywhere and it is impossible here to do justice to the rich web of historical evidence from across the world. What of Stonehenge or Carnac, or the mysterious Cave of Swimmers in the Libyan desert? What of Nineveh, or the millennia-old citadel of Erbil, which still stands today?

In August 2015, on a work assignment to Erbil, I sidestepped the security protocols and took a taxi from my hotel-fortress into the city. The taxi driver spoke good English, having recently returned from two years of living in England. I asked him why he had come home, and he told me he preferred the uncertain jeopardy of war-torn Kurdistan to the certain misery of life as a 'modern slave' washing cars in Manchester. A wave of shame washed over me. Together we climbed the cobbled ramp that runs up the side of the citadel, to look out across the newer city below.

There is evidence that the citadel of Erbil was already occupied in the fifth millennium BCE. At a height of between 25 and 32 metres, its commanding position over the surrounding landscape gives a clue to why. From this elevated plinth, one could have seen an enemy coming hours if not days in advance. Beneath Erbil's dusty deserted streets lie the remains of a once great empire dating back to Antiquity. It was to Erbil, or Arbela, that Alexander pursued Darius III and it was here, after his adversary had fled, that he assumed leadership of the Persian Empire. This is the place where Ishtar, the ancient goddess of love, fertility and war, had her temple, which rose above the walls of the citadel, its electrum coating flashing across the land like a beacon.[14] Rulers and warriors came to her for guidance, and the temple drew offerings from across Mesopotamia as Arbela became home to people of all races—Babylonian, Assyrian, Scythian, Palestinian. It was a rich melting pot and the basic recipe of its appeal can be found at many other pilgrim sites: temple, homage, trade, wealth, power.

Erbil's tale is an ancient one and its leading character, mighty Ishtar, goes on to feature in many later pilgrim traditions. But well before Alexander the Great came to lay offerings in her temple, she played a critical role in the oldest story we know, namely the *Epic of Gilgamesh*. Inscribed onto stone tablets around 4,000 years ago, the epic tells of Gilgamesh's love for his friend Enkidu and how, by their snubbing of Ishtar, Enkidu is killed. Devastated by this loss, Gilgamesh embarks on a journey to find the secret of life, and in the end, discovers that there is no secret; that life is to be lived and that death is inevitable. This very first epic, which has at its heart the quest for meaning, shows that pilgrimage as a human impulse is as old as human storytelling itself.

What emerges from dashing back and forth between Homer and Ishtar, Hellenic kings and Blackfoot warriors, Neolithic nomads and Bronze Age Minoans is that, from its very earliest beginnings, pilgrimage has been wrapped up with the survival and evolution of our species. Like the downy parachute of a dandelion clock, or the whirling helicopter of a sycamore seed, the impulse to follow the wind is somehow encoded within our

DNA. Whilst we may not fully understand why we go, we go, nevertheless. Being human, we have naturally developed elaborate rites and rituals, stories and structures, power and wealth around this instinct, as we have around so many other aspects of social organisation. And in this regard, Croesus at Delphi is the poster child. A 600lbs pure gold lion? Really? I forgot to mention the life-sized gold statue of a woman who, they say, resembled his baker. Seriously Croesus, it was bound to end badly. Perhaps, like so many other characters in our long human history, the king of Lydia missed the other Delphic maxim: *meden agan*, 'Nothing to Excess'.

On the day I was due to leave Delphi, I wanted to truly feel this place and, like the Pythia, to sense it beyond reasoning; to be entranced. In the cool of the early morning, I struck out once again on the road out of town. The sun remained hidden by the pink and grey escarpment of the mountain; in its shadow, the Temple Athena Pronaia lay in solitude, lower down and apart from the main site. Many of this temple's monumental stones have long since rumbled down the grassy slope into the valley that leads to the wine-dark distant sea, but a few resilient pillars still stand. Behind me, Delphi's ruins clung to the hillside interspersed with the tawny gold of dried grasses and yellow limestone columns, dark green cypress trees boasting a muscular continuity. And, as the rosy-fingered dawn broke over Mount Parnassus, I finally felt it in my core: the potency of this place at the belly button of the world.

# 2

# KINSHIP

*'But such desire is in him merely to see the hearthsmoke leaping upward from his own island, that he longs to die.'*

Homer, *The Odyssey*[1]

In January 2018 I travelled to Singapore, where Chunyun was well underway. Signs of this new year festival were everywhere and red was the colour. The Year of the Dog was coming and in the foyer of the shopping centre huge storyboards told of what lay in store for dogs, rats, tigers and a whole host of other animal signs. The monkey board indicated things were not looking good for me, but I was born on the cusp of two years, so how about roosters? No, not looking good for roosters either. I read each text in turn, looking for a positive word, but it seemed that 2018 didn't hold much promise for any of us.

Outside in the empty street, two immense lion dogs adorned with red scarves were reassuringly guarding the entrance to a bank, as I descended into the cool order of the metro. Twenty minutes later, re-emerging into the humid hustle of Chinatown, the nose-to-tail traffic and crowds of pedestrians came as something of a shock. Here in the narrow streets, the market stalls were a blizzard of red. Scarlet and crimson lake, cardinal, ruby and rich maroon. Racks of dried sausages, piles of little stuffed dogs, price labels stuck into sacks of nuts, the silky suits of small children. All were red.

I was here to visit the Buddha Tooth Relic Temple. The historian Jonathan Sumption has observed that 'Relics are the milk teeth of the Christian faith, of value in the early years but of little use in maturity.'[2] But while this may be so for Christianity, it is clearly not true for Buddhism. Built to serve the Republic's 1 million or so Buddhists and to attract many more, the temple was only completed in 2007 and houses a tooth of the Buddha, reportedly recovered from a collapsed stupa in Myanmar almost thirty years earlier. Scores of translucent tasselled lanterns hung in rows beneath the eaves of this robust landmark; as I passed through the dark lacquered doors, a sudden peacefulness descended, despite the crowds.

I joined a snaking stream of visitors, and we all shuffled past the scores of Buddhas that sit serene and cross-legged in the gold and red niches lining the walls. The position of the hands are different for each statue—a forefinger pinched with a thumb, an open palm, fingertips facing the earth or the sky, all of them gestures or *mudras* reflecting aspects of the life of Buddha, his teachings and his journey. Something adorned each niche—a candle, an orange, a shell, a flower—and, in front of all, a continuous row of little slotted moneyboxes offered those who passed by the chance to give a few coins. In the centre of the temple, under the gaze of an immense and golden-seated Maitreya, the Buddha of the Future, shaven-headed monks in their saffron cotton workwear were busy arranging seating, flowers and fruit in preparation for the new year ceremonies.

The temple might have been almost as busy as the market, but I found the business district in Singapore eerily quiet. Where was everyone? At this time of year, the city is hollowed out, as all those who have the means and freedom to travel head back to their ancestral homes. What was at one time a local affair is now truly epic in scale, with the diaspora both within and beyond China's borders harking the call of their rural roots. According to World Bank figures, between 1990 and 2005, China's economic progress accounted for more than three-quarters of all poverty reduction globally; China has become the world's second largest economy in a matter of decades. A rising tide lifts all boats, so they say, and to a large extent reform in China has helped raise hundreds of millions of Chinese out of poverty. Since the 1980s, when China established Special Economic Zones and fourteen coastal cities were completely opened to direct foreign investment, there has been a steady flow of internal migration from the countryside to urban centres, as people take advantage of the opportunities for work.

In 2015, the number of passenger journeys over the course of the forty-day festival was estimated at around 3.6 billion: the equivalent of almost three trips per head in China, making Chunyun the largest annual human migration on Earth. For many workers, the journey back to their natal villages may take several days on plane, train, bus or bike before they are finally reunited with their beloved families. While Chunyun has no single destination or shrine, the festival shares many characteristics with other seasonal pilgrim traditions in which members of a community travel somewhere fundamental to their identity. At the heart of ancient Chinese culture are the dual pillars of the cult of ancestry and reverence for nature. These concepts are expressed through the six great festivals, three of which honour the dead and three of which celebrate life. The most important and joyous of these is Chinese New Year, and Chunyun—this time of mass return to the ancestral home at the end of winter—can be seen as a confluence of both respect for nature and respect for ancestry.

The timing of Chunyun is determined by the lunisolar calendar and, like many other spring festivals, symbolises both the end of the old and the start of the new. It begins fifteen days before New Year itself, in the month of the twelfth moon, also known as the 'Bitter Moon'. This period has special foods and rituals of housecleaning. One popular and very ancient dish is a congee made of dried fruit, nuts, sugar and whole grains. By tradition, a bowl of this eight-treasure porridge is offered first to the ancestors before the family takes their share, with any surplus then distributed among other relatives and friends. Towards the end of the month, a symbolic offering is made to Tsao Wang (Prince of the Oven), the kitchen god, before he leaves for Heaven, where he will report on the conduct of the family during the year past. Tsao Wang is one of the oldest deities in the ancient Chinese pantheon. Identified with fire, Heaven's great gift to mankind, he personifies the hearth or home and, like Hermes or the Hindu fire divinity Agni, he is a messenger between men and the gods. During Chunyun, debts are typically settled in a bid to start the new year with a clean slate, and talismans hung about the home to attract *fu* or luck.

An account dating from the 1920s describes how 'At Midnight on the *San Shih Wang Shang* (the last night of the dying year) members of a family present New Year's wishes to one another. Among old-fashioned people this is done with much ceremony. The master and mistress of the house seat themselves, rigid as Buddhas, on two stiff chairs in the reception hall where all those living under the roof appear and *k'o t'ou* before them.'[3] The literal meaning of *k'o t'ou*, or kow-tow, is to 'knock the head'; the ritual involved kneeling and then bowing before the seated parents or grandparents.[i] Later, during the Hour of the Tiger (between 3

---

[i] This act of deference took on a much darker meaning when Chinese indentured labour replaced African slave labour after the abolition of

a.m. and 5 a.m.), before the cock crowed, cypress and pine branches would be spread in the courtyard of the home before the head of the house broke the seals on the front door or gate, placed there the night before. Prayers were given in honour of Heaven and Earth, of the Ancestors, and of the returning household gods, led by the kitchen god Tsao Wang. Things have moved on since this account, which predates the cultural tsunami of Chinese communism, but in the twenty-first century, the principle of continuity—from one year to the next, and across the generations—remains at the heart of the festivities. As they celebrate the new year just beginning, family members young and old acknowledge their duty to the dead, paying homage to their ancestors at household shrines set up for this purpose.

After visiting the Buddha Tooth Relic Temple, I headed for Chinatown's food court. On the top floor of this sparse concrete block people were queuing patiently at their favourite stands, waiting to buy whole roast ducks and slabs of pork belly, all shining in a rosy slick of chilli, honey and hoisin sauce. This food was destined for the big family feasts taking place all over the city. Many Chinese families in Singapore are the descendants of the free and indentured workers who settled on the island under British rule over a century ago; for them, Singapore is their home and hearth. As I made my back to the street, a banner slung across the dusty staircase reminded customers that the food court would close for cleaning later in March. This clean-up heralds both the spring and another pilgrimage closely bound up with celebration of kinship.

The Qingming or Tomb-Sweeping Festival typically falls on 4 or 5 April, 106 days after the winter solstice. This is the date

---

slavery in the nineteenth century. Then, 'kow-towing' came to mean deferring or pandering to someone in power.

when families return home to mourn their dead, sweeping their tombs and saying prayers for relatives who have passed from this life.[4] Qingming is said by some to have arisen from the earlier Hanshi 'Cold Food Feast', which—as tradition has it—originated sometime in the first millennium BCE, when a Duke Wen of Jin (given name Chong'er) was exiled from his homeland and accompanied only by a small band of followers. The feudal lord and his men wandered for many years and, at a moment of near starvation, the Duke's most loyal servant, Jie Zhitui, cut a piece of meat from his own leg to feed his master. But this very personal sacrifice was not rewarded and Jie soon retreated to the remote seclusion of the mountains with his mother. Later, when the Duke gained power, he called on Jie to serve him once again; when Jie refused, the angry aristocrat ordered that he be flushed out of his wooded hiding place by fire. With the forests ablaze all around, both Jie and his mother were trapped and burned to death. By now filled with remorse, Chong'er declared that at a certain point each year all fires were to be extinguished—hence the Cold Food Feast.

The practice of eating only cold food on this festival appears to have largely died out, but another aspect of Hanshi is central to the Qingming festival today: sweeping the tombs of one's ancestors. As rural Chinese families traditionally buried their dead on their own land, the task of tomb-sweeping and the ritual meal that went with it would take place under a grove of trees, left standing as a mark of respect, and to create shade and comfort for the departed souls. After the day of Hanshi, a new flame was sparked by rubbing two willow sticks together and money burnt in offering to the dead, that they might be appeased and not harm the new season's crop. Those unable to make the pilgrimage to the tombs burned paper money at home, and after due ceremony took the smouldering currency out into the street before dousing it in wine.[5] The tomb-sweeping festival of

Qingming is marked by a public holiday in mainland China, Hong Kong and Taiwan.[ii]

Aside from the fun of feasts shared with family, the pull of *chia*, the ancestral home, has helped shape China's history. It is a manifestation of the Confucian social doctrine, which priorities the family above the personal and collectivism above individualism: a principle of reciprocity also known as *guanxi*. Whereas the English adage holds 'neither a borrower nor a lender be', the Chinese principle of *guanxi* values the strength of interdependence; rather than a risk to harmonious relationships, personal loans and favours between family members are seen as reinforcing the bonds of collective interest over the longer term. This high-trust ethos is in part what makes all merchant societies successful, and there can be little doubt that, reinforced by kinship festivals dating back many millennia, *guanxi* has played a part in China's economic re-emergence since the 1990s.

\* \* \*

While Qingming involves each returning to his or her own ancestral village, in other parts of the world, the opposite direction is the more common pattern of pilgrimage festivals held in celebration of spring: going out from our individual homes to places of more broadly shared significance. Historically, kinship was often an important dimension here too. One only has to think of the May Day and Whitsuntide festivals that were once so familiar across Europe. Here amongst the flowers and the feasting, traditional dances afforded men and women the oppor-

---

[ii] On Qingming in 1976, protesters gathered in Tiananmen Square to mourn not their ancestors, but Premier Zhou Enlai, who had died earlier that year—the first 'Tiananmen Incident', marking opposition to the Gang of Four (the second 'incident', of course, took place in 1989).

tunity to connect with the greatest number of potential marriage partners. Dancing in unison and swinging through the line, hand to hand (traditionally) from boy to girl and girl to boy, there was the promise that a spark of electricity might pass through finger-tips touching, or the crooks of arms briefly linked.

As with Chunyun, people often travelled far to attend these spring festivals; for highly atomised rural communities living in isolated farmsteads, hamlets or villages, this was a rare moment in the year when young people could find partners beyond their immediate gene pool. Tying the prospect of flirting with fun and faith created an irresistible menu of incentives to join the festivities. In some parts of the world, these traditions continue today and, as ever, perform a rich mix of social functions. One such pilgrim festival is the Pushkar Camel Fair in Rajasthan. Pushkar Lake is known as the *tirth raj*, the king of pilgrimage sites, and is one of the most sacred places in the Hindu faith. There are hundreds of temples here and festivals throughout the year, but the full moon day of the month of Kartik, known as Kartik Poornima, is especially important, marking Brahma's *yajna* or fire-sacrifice. The Kartika Mela festival, held in the days leading up to the full moon, attracts tens of thousands of pilgrims, who come to bathe in the holy waters of the lake. By descending from one of the many *ghat* staircases into the waters of the lake, the faithful can wash away the sins of a lifetime.

In Hinduism, the whole of creation is considered to be the work of the Trimurti, a triad of fundamental forces, each represented by a god: Brahma, the Creator; Vishnu, the Sustainer; and Shiva, the Destroyer. Accounts of Brahma's origins vary, but in one version he is self-born out of a lotus flower that grew from Vishnu's navel. At a certain moment, Brahma saw the demon Vajranabha trying to kill his children and slew him with his weapon, the lotus flower. Where the blue lotus petals fell, three lakes sprung up, of which Pushkar Lake is the greatest. Of the Trimurti, Brahma is these days the least prominent, and Pushkar marks the only major temple dedicated to him. It is considered very sacrosanct and only *sadhus* (holy men) are permitted to enter the temple, making offerings on behalf of the devotees outside. Pushkar is also a destination for Sikh pilgrims. There are gurdwaras, or temples, dedicated to Guru Nanak, the first guru and founder of Sikhism, as well as to the tenth and final guru, Guru Gobind Singh, who took refuge in Pushkar when, aged nine, his father was publicly beheaded in Delhi by Aurangzeb, the seventeenth-century Moghul emperor.

The *mela* (festival) at Pushkar is an important event for Indian politics too. Some of the ashes of Mahatma Gandhi and Pandit Nehru are scattered in the lake, and the *mela* is an opportunity for politicians to demonstrate their Hindu credentials. Hindu nationalism has been an important part of the political scene in India since well before independence in August 1947, and today the country is ruled by a Hindu nationalist government and senior politicians make a point of being photographed attending major pilgrim festivals. While their attendance is typically rather brief, dropping in for a few hours by helicopter for the chance of a photo call (onto the helipad constructed for just that eventuality), the Kartika Mela also coincides with an important camel fair, and pastoralists from far and wide can travel for many days or weeks to get here.

India has one of the largest camel populations in the world, and the majority of these beasts are to be found in the northern state of Rajasthan. At the time of the *mela*, livestock breeders and pastoral herders from across the region come together in Pushkar, along with some 50,000 camels and many thousands more cattle, sheep and goats. Circus performers and folk dancers, snake charmers and magicians are there to entertain; aside from the serious business of visiting the temples, washing away sins in the lake, or sealing contracts for livestock, there are plenty of opportunities to sing, dance and be merry.

Amongst the noise and dust of this melee are the Rabari or Raika: the noted dromedary breeders of Rajasthan, put on earth by Shiva to tend the camels owned by Parvati, goddess of fertility, marriage, devotion, and much more. In other accounts, it is thought that the Raika initially took up camel breeding in the fourteenth century to supply the Maharajas with mounts and pack animals for desert warfare. As peace settled over the region and market demand changed, the Raika refocussed their efforts, producing strong male draft animals for use in farming and transportation, much as cart horses or oxen were used elsewhere. Traditionally, the breeding females are never sold, and the Raika themselves never buy camels. The main mechanism of exchanging breeding stock is through marriage, with camels changing hands as dowry payments.[6] The Raika divide into two distinct groups, the Chalkia and the Maru. This latter group are considered to be of superior status and observe strict protocols on lineage: who may leave the fold and who may join. While Maru men can take Chalkia women in marriage, Maru women cannot marry Chalkia men. In this sense, marriage is the primary means of introducing new female bloodlines into the Maru and their herds, with the *mela* providing the perfect setting for these contracts to be agreed.

Until relatively recently, camels were a common sight in the streets of Rajasthan, often pulling eye-wateringly heavy loads on two-wheeled carts amidst the chaos of trucks and cycle rickshaws, taxis and wandering sacred cows. This traffic was imprinted forever on my retina during a hair-raising trip to Jodhpur railway station on the back of a motor scooter in 1993, with my daughter Clare, then aged nine, wedged between me and the driver. But the boom in India's economy in the twenty-first century has made motorised transport increasingly affordable, and the Raika camel breeders are now facing something of a crisis. And political interference, no doubt designed to protect tradition, has made things considerably worse.

In 2016, the camel was declared the state animal of Rajasthan, and the slaughter or export of camels across the state border now carries the threat of a long prison sentence. With the general use of camels as draft animals dying out and their trade as livestock now severely constrained, it is not clear how long the Kartika Mela can continue as an authentic festival which marries religious pilgrimage, kinship, and meaningful commerce beyond simple tourism. For groups like the pastoralists of Rajasthan that are widely dispersed or live outside the mainstream, such fairs offer the rare opportunity for individuals and small family groups to connect with a larger collective identity; one such group in Europe is the Roma people, also known as Travellers in the British Isles.

\* \* \*

Each June an estimated 10,000 Travellers gather at a small town in the north of England for the annual Appleby Horse Fair. Many will arrive by horse-drawn trailers and caravans, and the stars of the show are the characteristic brown and white Vanner ponies, valued for their soft temperament and, like the Raika dromedaries, for their strength as draft animals. The piebald ponies are washed and brushed in the shallows of the River Eden in the centre of Appleby before being shown off (or *flashed*) by trotting at speed along a particular lane in the town. For many, it is the main social event of the year and a chance to see friends and members of the wider family. Like the Pushkar *mela*, the Appleby fair also carries the chance for young people to find a spouse—many will have saved for months to buy clothes that they hope will enhance their chances of meeting a prospective husband or wife.

Aside from the Travellers themselves, around 30–40,000 non-Travellers, or *Gorgios*, come to see the horse trading and, perhaps even more than that, to enjoy the rare sight of a distinctive traditional culture and the spirit of joyous kinship, so hard to find in the fog of modern urban life. Appleby claims to be the largest Traveller gathering in Europe, and each year families will make their way from Ireland, Scotland, Wales and across England—unlike the *mela* at Pushkar, Appleby is a solely secular festival, a time of coming together as a people for its own sake. For English Travellers at least, the pilgrimage of faith must wait until 15 August. This is the time when Traveller communities from across the country congregate at the shrine of Our Lady of Walsingham in Norfolk.

According to tradition, in the year 1061, a widowed noble-woman, Richeldis de Favarches, had a series of visions of the Virgin Mary. Through these visions Richeldis was requested to build a place of pilgrimage: a replica of the house in Nazareth where the Annunciation took place—the Angel Gabriel coming to Mary to tell her that she would bear the Son of God. Within a few decades, a priory was also founded here, and Walsingham became established as one of the most important pilgrim sites in Christendom. Europe was beset by many periods of war and political uncertainty in the Middle Ages, often making the roads to Rome and Santiago de Compostela perilous. By contrast, the rural tranquillity of this Marian shrine contributed to its appeal, not least amongst the many kings and queens of England who made pilgrimage here, including Catherine of Aragon and her husband Henry VIII (before he had a change of heart about such things, of which more anon).

Despite the ravages of the Reformation in England, which saw shrines like this closed down, Walsingham has risen once more from the ashes and here, on the Feast of the Assumption, Travellers congregate to celebrate their shared Catholicism and kinship. In one personal account we get some insight into the role that pilgrimage plays in the religious lives of this community: 'Our Lady, who held her own child dead in her arms, has a very special place in Travellers' hearts. We feel she is very close to us and [is] our second mother, who can share our thoughts, pains and joys because she understands life and so we have a great love for her [and] places of pilgrimage like Lourdes and Knock hold a great attraction for us.'[7] This articulates the popularity of the Virgin Mary across the Catholic community, which has given rise to a great number of dedicated Marian shrines and pilgrimages worldwide. It also provides a link between the devotional practices of the Roma and their history of persecution and suffering.

Thought at one time to be itinerant Egyptians (*Gypsy* derives from the old English *Gypcian*), recent linguistic and DNA evidence suggests that the Roma are in fact related to the Dom or Domba people of north-western India. Travelling through Persia and Turkey, the Dom reached Europe around the tenth century CE, gradually radiating northwards and westwards. Despite their dispersion over time and space, it is now thought that all Roma people are descended from one small group that left India at the same time. Theories abound as to why they did so. Were they, as some legends suggest, a group of musicians given as a gift from an Indian king to his Persian neighbour? Or were they escaping from famine, conflict or persecution? We don't yet know and may never find out, but what is clear is that for centuries the Roma have been simultaneously romanticised and persecuted. The very strength of their bonds of kinship are somehow perceived as a threat to parts of the settled population. To this day they remain a source of fear and suspicion, curiosity and admiration. Long valued for their skills as craftsmen, musicians and soldiers, there are also records of their enslavement dating back to the eleventh century CE. The Roma's unique skills as metalsmiths were particularly valued by the military and many were held captive for this reason alone. This practice continued in various Balkan states until it was curtailed in the middle of the nineteenth century, but the reprieve when it came was short-lived. Under the direction of Nazi Germany, the Romani Holocaust led to the death of an estimated half a million men, women and children across Europe.

Skilled artists and artisans, or irresistible seducers and thieving magpies? Take your pick. When it comes to outsiders, we all bring our prejudices to bear. Bizet's Carmen embodies all of these stereotypes: a Rom woman who holds all men in her thrall and leads them into peril, using her sexual allure to distract soldiers on the lookout for smugglers. Carmen's literary male equivalent is Emily Brontë's Heathcliff: the 'gypsy' foundling hero of *Wuthering Heights*, whose raw masculinity holds the book's heroine, Catherine, spellbound until her last dying breath, along with many of its readers. It is this same sense of enchantment which brings the crowds of *Gorgios* or *Gadjes* (Rom terms for non-Roma people) to see the spectacle at Appleby, and to the annual Roma pilgrimage at Saintes-Maries-de-la-Mer.

Towards the end of May each year, Roma people from across Europe gather on the outskirts of this small village in the Camargue to celebrate their patron saint Sara la Kali (Sara the Black). Situated on the southern edge of France, this is where the Rhône River meets the warm Mediterranean after its long flow down from the icy Swiss Alps, and the estuarine marshes here are noted for the white horses that roam wild and the pink flamingos that flock here to breed. Like Appleby, most of the year this is a quiet backwater with a small resident community of around 2,500, but at the time of the pilgrimage, locals are outnumbered fivefold by the *Gens du Voyage*, the Travellers. Like many other places freighted with spiritual significance, Saintes-Maries-de-la-Mer is not easy to get to—so what is it that draws them here in particular?

According to tradition, around the year 42 CE, a group of Christ's followers arrived on these shores, forced to flee from persecution in the Levant. Amongst their number was Mary

Magdalene, Mary Salome (mother of Apostles James and John) and Marie Jacobé (or Mary of Clopas), a sister of the Virgin Mary. These women are credited with helping to carry the message of Christianity to Europe, and both Mary Salome and Marie Jacobé lived, died and were buried in the small church of Les Saintes Maries de la Mer—their relics now rest in a small casket perched high above the altar. The third and far more mysterious female figure venerated here is the dark-skinned St Sara, or Sara la Kali, who shares her name with the ancient Hindu goddess Kali, destroyer of evil forces and mother of the universe.[8]

Sara is variously attributed with being the abbess of a convent in Libya, a Persian martyr, or the handmaiden of the two Marys, who sailed with them and helped their small boat to land safely here on the coast of France in the early part of the first century CE. In other accounts she was a Rom camped on the shore when the two Marys arrived.[9] At the time in which the legend is set, the Roma practised a polytheistic religion, and once a year they carried a statue of Ishtar, the Bronze Age deity we met in Chapter One, into the sea for ritual cleansing. One day Sara, the leader of this community, had visions informing her that the saints who had been present at the death of Jesus would come, and that she must help them. Sara stood on the shore and watched them approach, but the sea was rough, and the small boat threatened to capsize. Quickly Sara threw her cape onto the waves and, using it as a raft, floated out towards the saints and brought them safely in.

In the weeks and days leading up to the main rituals of the May festival, the Gens du Voyage begin arriving on the outskirts of Saintes-Maries-de-la-Mer, setting up camp in specially designated areas according to their origins (some French, some Italian, others Swiss). Each group has their own chaplain and Mass is celebrated daily, delivered from camper vans and tents—makeshift arrangements that test the boundaries of Catholic orthodoxy. Each evening a prayer vigil is held in the village church,[iii] and then, on the evening of 23 May, the statue of St Sara is dressed in clothes, capes and jewellery in readiness for her procession the next day. Carried through the streets by Roma men, and flanked by *gardians*, local men mounted on Camargue horses, the statue is held aloft as her entourage wades into the sea. The crowds follow, hoping to touch her skirts. Horses and riders splashing, jostling and crying out salutations to St Sara; tourists straining arms in the air, attempting to catch the spectacle on camera—all contribute to the exuberant atmosphere that marks this pilgrim tale. On the following day, with due ceremony and rejoicing, the relics and a carving of the two Saintes Maries in their small boat are taken from the church to the shore. Clergy climb into a boat to perform a benediction, before all head back to the church. Here, as the reliquary is raised once more into its usual place above the altar, the faithful stretch out their hands, hoping for one last chance to touch it. This marks the end of the pilgrimage, until next year.

In the absence of an identifiable ancestral home or even, for some, a permanent place of residence, Saintes-Maries-de-la-Mer is a spiritual home of sorts for the Roma. Many come here outside the festival period to pray for sick family members, sometimes placing an item of the person's clothing behind the statue of St Sara. Candles bought during the pilgrimage may be taken home to be lit in the event of family problems later in the year, and water from the well here is bottled and given to the sick. More than this, for the duration of Sara's festival, Roma people who might feel marginalised in other settings are no longer on

---

[iii] Organised by members of France's Catholic Chaplaincy for Traveller People, which has a presence at this and other pilgrim sites, such as Lourdes, that attract large numbers of Roma pilgrims.

the periphery, but right at the heart of the community. This is what home means: a place where we can truly be ourselves, amongst our own.

The notion of home as somewhere we do not abide may seem paradoxical, especially when we might know little about the place we set out to reach, but it is an ancient and powerful idea nevertheless. Almost inevitably, the pull of your people's spiritual homeland brings with it a sense of proprietary ownership, and this sentiment can and does lead to religious and cultural frictions at many pilgrim sites, including Appleby, Walsingham and Saintes-Maries-de-la-Mer—but in this regard, as in many others, Jerusalem stands out as exceptional.

* * *

For the outsider, the picture of contested rights in Jerusalem is almost too complex to understand, let alone describe. For Muslims it is the place where Muhammad made his night journey on the white steed Buraq to the 'farthest mosque', and from thence ascended the seven levels of heaven, meeting the prophets before returning to Mecca. For Christians, it is the place where Jesus of Nazareth rose as a prophet amongst the Jews and died on the Cross to save us all from our sins, and was resurrected on the third day. According to the Hebrew Bible, the Tanakh,[10] the place where Jerusalem now sits was first promised by God to Abraham and his descendants, the Children of Israel. (There is no consensus on when the Abrahamic story was first told, or in which era the events were set, or the exact boundaries of this 'Promised Land' and the terms on which it was promised.)

The struggle for control of land around and within the city has rolled on almost without pause for millennia. The tensions and rivalries between different peoples and faiths in the city are almost matched in intensity by intra-faith factionalism, particularly the various Christian sects. Competing claims between

Orthodox, Armenian and Roman Catholic, Coptic, Syrian and Abyssinian Churches have rumbled on for centuries. One notable example is the Church of the Holy Sepulchre, for many Christians the holiest of all churches. By tradition, the keys to the church are held by Muslims, with one family opening up in the morning and a second to lock up at night. It really is complicated, but the real friction at the Holy Sepulchre is not between Christian and Muslim. After an earthquake damaged this ancient building in 1927, the various Christian groups who use it were unable to agree on its repair; for decades it remained propped up with steel girders and stout timbers as it slid slowly towards an apparent destiny of disintegration. In 2015, almost at the eleventh hour, Israel's Antiquities Authority declared the building unsafe and the police kicked out the quarrelling monks, bolting the doors—a third-party intervention that broke the impasse over restoration. The paradox of Jewish authorities directly saving this important, Muslim-guarded Christian monument cannot have gone unremarked by any of the parties concerned. The universal intensity and importance of kinship—the sense of belonging to a place—is nowhere more plain to see than in Jerusalem.

Elsewhere in this city of spiritual homes, the Western Wall, a place of religious devotion for Jews, has also had its fair share of disputes, not least between factions with different views of women's right to worship there. Rivka Haut, the wife of a Brooklyn rabbi, had long fought for the dignity and rights of orthodox Jewish women at home in the US; in 1988, she took that same fight to Jerusalem, convening the Western Wall's first all-female prayer service with a Torah scroll. The action of these pilgrim-activists provoked immediate protest from ultra-Orthodox religious leaders in Israel, but it also sparked a flame amongst many multi-denominational women around the world who shared Rivka Haut's mission. The Women of the Wall movement was born and, thirty years later, the controversy continues with protests and arrests, legal battles and a little progress. These activists are determined to pursue their religious practice on their own terms, but more than that, they demand the right to share in this symbol of the Jewish spiritual homeland and the resilience of the Jewish people through the ages.

Jerusalem has been the focus of pilgrims' devotion and prayer for thousands of years, and the city's importance is due in part to its great antiquity: the city itself dates back to the Bronze Age. But the ancient city of Jericho, located around 30 miles away, provides evidence of habitation going back to Neolithic times.[11] So Jerusalem's significance for Jews is not about how old the place is, but about the religion that binds them together as a people and the long-awaited home that it represents. The Jews' account of their arrival here, the Exodus story,[12] centres on a pact between Moses and God or Yahweh, in which the Israelites were granted freedom from enslavement by the Egyptians in exchange for their covenant with God. According to tradition, following forty years wandering in the Sinai desert, they arrived into the land of Canaan, the 'Promised Land', under the leadership of Joshua. Some scholars hold that, for any religion, the place of origin for their belief system is regarded as both the centre of the earth and the place closest to God. For Jews, this place is Jerusalem because of what the Israelites brought with them when they came out of the wilderness and settled in the Promised Land: the Ark of the Covenant.

This chest contained tablets of stone on which were written the Ten Commandments, given from God to Moses on Mount Sinai. Sheltered within a tent or tabernacle along the way, the Ark was finally placed within the Temple, in the room known as the Holy of Holies, or *Kodesh haKodashim*, the place where God dwelt. Towards Jerusalem, then, is the *mizrah*, or direction of prayer for Jews wherever they may live: the Talmud, the book of

Rabbinic law, states that a Jew shall direct their prayers towards Israel; when in Israel, toward Jerusalem; in Jerusalem itself, toward the Temple; and inside the Temple, toward the Holy of Holies. When it is not possible to know the precise compass direction, the pragmatic rule is to direct one's heart towards Jerusalem.[iv] For many Jews, Jerusalem is a symbol of their 'peoplehood'—that sense of historic unity and common kinship that binds them beyond the diversities of race or religious practice. This, my friend Avi said, is what drove him to move there from North London in the 1970s. 'I wanted to live in a place where being Jewish was not a "thing", where I could be amongst my people and of my people.' He and his wife Helen named their firstborn Ariella, the feminised version of the Hebrew name Ariel, meaning Jerusalem.

When the Israelites reached the Promised Land, it marked their transition from life as nomadic pastoralists to a settled existence based around sedentary agriculture. King Solomon created their First Temple, where the Tanakh prescribed a pilgrim gathering three times a year, stipulating: 'All your males shall appear before the LORD your God at the place that He will choose; at the Feast of Unleavened Bread, at the Feast of Weeks, and at the Feast of Booths. They shall not appear before the LORD empty-handed. Every man shall give as he is able, according to the blessing of the LORD your God which He has given you.'[13] When it comes to establishing a community around a shared ethos and identity, calling a tribe or people together to take part in communal festivities is a good place to start. These three annual festivals marry important moments in the agricultural

---

[iv] Jerusalem was also briefly the target of the *Qibla*, the direction of prayer for Muslims, until 624 CE (see Chapter 3). Christian prayer is directed to the east and—notionally, at least—in the direction of Jerusalem.

calendar with elements from the story of the Israelites' long journey to the Land of Canaan from Egypt.

The first of the year and possibly the oldest is Pesach or Passover, which coincides with the first harvest and the arrival of new-born animals in the flock. The date is set for the full moon following the ripening of the barley.[v] Passover also celebrates the time when the Israelites were spared the tenth terrible plague of Egypt. The Pharaoh had earlier issued an edict that all Hebrew male babies should be killed, but Moses was saved by being placed in a basket on the river, from where he was rescued by Pharaoh's daughter. When Moses became an adult, he demanded that the Pharaoh allow the Israelites to leave Egypt; God, lending some weight to this request, caused ten plagues to be brought down on the Egyptians in order to persuade Pharaoh to release them. When it came to the tenth plague, the death of all first-born sons, God commanded Moses to tell the Children of Israel to daub lamb's blood on the doorposts of their homes, so that the plague would 'pass over' the doors marked with blood.

Passover is also known as the Feast of Unleavened Bread, which symbolises the haste with which the Israelites fled from Egypt, without enough time to wait for the bread to rise. By tradition Jewish families come together on the first night of Passover for a Seder dinner. Special foods are served and rituals observed, and during the meal the story of the Exodus from Egypt is retold, using a text known as the *Haggadah*. This ritual storytelling is the observation of a *mitzvah* (commandment) to tell each new generation of how the Jews came from slavery to freedom. As such, Passover is central not only to Jews' faith in the God who has chosen to save them, but also to Jewish identity and the Jewish people's connection to Jerusalem.

---

[v] The Hebrew calendar is based on lunar months and the solar year.

The second pilgrimage festival is the Feast of Weeks, Shavuot, which falls seven weeks after Passover. It gives thanks for the wheat harvest and commemorates the revelation of the Torah to Moses on Mount Sinai, marking the Israelites' Covenant with God: their pledge of allegiance after God had freed them from slavery. Finally, the Feast of Booths, Sukkot, is celebrated in the autumn and marks the last harvest festival of the year. According to the Torah, during this holiday, the Jewish people should live in tents or booths erected for that purpose. Today, observant families take their meals inside such booths or *sukkot*, with some still sleeping there too. The temporary nature of the shelters erected for Sukkot echoes the flight from Egypt, when the Jews camped out for forty years in the wilderness, but equally may be a layering of cultural meaning onto the practice of workers camping out during the harvest season. Success of the harvest means survival through the winter, and turning hard agricultural labour into a festival or holiday is a good way to motivate those doing the labouring—pulling together as a people for the common good. Well into the twentieth century, Travellers and poor working-class families from the East End of London would travel to Kent to pick hops in autumn, camping out by the side of the fields where hard days of toil were rounded off by campfires, singing and camaraderie, blurring the lines between work and holiday.

For several centuries before the fall of the Second Temple in 70 CE, pilgrims came to Jerusalem for these festivals from across the Jewish world, which at the time included Crete, Libya, Parthia (in modern-day Iran) and Babylon (now Iraq). Over time the city became firmly established as a nexus for faith, commerce and politics. There is no reliable data on how many undertook the pilgrimage to Jerusalem during the festivals at this time. The first-century historian Josephus suggested that as many as 2.5 million came for Passover. He arrived at this figure through a calculation of how many people were likely to share in the sacrificial Passover feast, in which 'not less than ten belong to every sacrifice, (for it is not lawful for them to feast singly by themselves), and many of us are twenty in a company.' Finding that the number of animals sacrificed was 256,000, he deduced that there could therefore be no fewer than ten times that number of pilgrims.[14]

These figures are now considered highly exaggerated, but archaeological evidence indicates that seasonal pilgrimage took place at scale and was an important part of the city economy. The archaeologist David Gurevich suggests that the remains of a large number of open-water pools are a manifestation of the widescale pilgrimage movement to Jerusalem during the later Second Temple period.[15] Designed to capture and store spring rains, these cisterns would have been essential sources for both potable water and for the ritual baths or *mikveh* required to purify those wishing to enter the sacred areas of the Temple Mount complex. The Second Temple, built in the sixth century BCE, had been relatively modest in design, but in the first century BCE Herod the Great expanded it on a truly epic scale. Immense beams of Lebanese cedar were floated down the coast; monolithic ashlars over 40 feet in length and weighing up to 600 tons were prepared before being slotted into position; and, when the Temple was complete, its gold cladding shone at sunrise in such fiery splendour that visitors were forced to look away.[16]

This golden glory was to be short-lived. In 70 CE the Second Temple was completely destroyed by the Romans under their leader Titus: an act of retribution for Jewish rebellion. Worst of all, the inner sanctum, the Holy of Holies, was obliterated. After the fire and the fury, pilgrimage to Jerusalem ceased to be a religious obligation for Jews, and almost all that remained was the monumental Western Wall. Over time this has become the focus of Jewish devotion in Jerusalem, a symbol of the enduring link between a people and a place; or as the Chinese might say, *chia*.

Setting aside the complex political questions of contested rights and governance in this troubled and ancient city, there can be no doubt that for the Jews, Jerusalem's significance extends beyond faith, nationality or ethnicity, and their longing for the place they believed was promised to them has never wavered. This can be heard in the last line of the Passover Seder service: '*L'Shana Haba'ah B'Yerushalayim*'—next year in Jerusalem.

3

# FAITH

On 6 March 632 CE, the ninth day of Dhu al-Hijjah (the month
of pilgrimage), the Prophet Muhammad ibn 'Abdullah had travelled from Medina for his first and last Hajj, his farewell pilgrimage. On this second day of the rites, he was on a camel atop
Mount Arafat. All around him, as far as the eye could see, were
tens of thousands of pilgrims, expectant, waiting. He began,
clearly and deliberately setting out his vision and hopes for all
Muslims. He enjoined them to profess their faith, to pray five
times a day, to fast during Ramadan, to give a portion of their
wealth in alms and, importantly, to perform the Hajj if they had
the means to do so. Criers were placed throughout the crowd to
repeat line by line what proved to be the Prophet's final sermon,
and so his words were carried to the very edges of the multitude
assembled on this dusty plain. The echo reverberated further

out, resounding through centuries and across continents to reach billions of Muslims worldwide.

Muhammad called on men and women to respect each other, reminding all present that God holds all races equal, and that 'All mankind is from Adam and Eve; an Arab has no superiority over a non-Arab nor any non-Arab any superiority over an Arab; also a white person has no superiority over a black person nor a black person any superiority over a white person, except through piety and good deeds.'[2] Some 1,332 years later in April 1964, in the same spot and during another Hajj, this true arrow found its mark in a pilgrim who had arrived in Mecca with a firm conviction that all white men were devils: Malcolm X. The US civil rights movement was in full flood and until recently X had been a leading spokesman for the radical Nation of Islam, a group that advocated bloody revolution to right the wrongs against black people everywhere. A month before he arrived in Mecca, Malcolm X had stepped down from this black supremacist movement, having become disillusioned with its leader Elijah Muhammad, and he had just created his own group, Muslim Mosque Inc. The Hajj changed Malcolm X, both radicalising him and moderating him. By his own account he was overwhelmed by the experience of being together with pilgrims of all races, participating in the same rituals, and by the spirit of unity and brotherhood that he had previously believed 'never could exist between the white and non-white.'

He penned a long letter to his assistants back in Harlem, in which he recognised that his allies might be shocked by his words, but insisted that he was shocked too. The pilgrimage to Mecca had caused him to change his mind about many things. He was the product of a segregated society, a society that went to great lengths to deny black people their voting rights, a society of entrenched racial inequality—yet, in Mecca he noted that 'here in the Muslim world, I have eaten from the same plate, drunk from the same glass, and slept on the same rug—while praying to the same God—with fellow Muslims, whose eyes were the bluest of blue, whose hair was the blondest of blond, and whose skin was the whitest of white. And in the words and in the deeds of the white Muslims, I felt the same sincerity that I felt among the black African Muslims of Nigeria, Sudan and Ghana.'[3]

Participation in the Hajj convinced Malcolm X that there might be a peaceful way of addressing the racism that he believed was 'plaguing America like an incurable cancer'. He travelled onwards to Africa in the hope of building an alliance with others struggling for freedom. By the time he arrived back in the US, he was no longer Malcolm X: now he was El-Hajj Malik El-Shabazz and a convert to Sunni Islam. Nine months later he was alive no more, shot dead by Nation of Islam assassins as he was about to give a speech in the Audubon Ballroom, New York.

Malcolm X came to Mecca for reasons of faith, and participation in the collective rituals gave him a new, additional faith in the possibility of equality through an all-embracing community. He was not alone in becoming more tolerant as a consequence of his pilgrimage. Research by a team at Harvard suggests that, while the Hajj may help forge a common Islamic identity, it does not do so at the expense of non-Muslims. The study, carried out amongst Pakistan's Muslim community, found that participation in the Hajj also appeared to extend 'notions of equality and harmony to adherents of other religions'.[4] The festival provides what is, for many pilgrims, their only experience of living within a broad multi-ethnic and multinational group, where Sunni and Shia participate together and rich and poor are briefly levelled by their simple white pilgrim garb (*ihram*).

Another special thing about the Hajj and its ability to bring the faithful together is that men and women are not segregated here as they are in the mosque, and the opportunity to interact across the gender divide in a religious context is for many both novel and inspirational. The Harvard study on Pakistan's Muslims found that those who had made the Hajj were more likely to support girls' education and female participation in the professional workforce. Such a shift of attitude is truly meaningful in a country where only 13 per cent of girls are still in school by the age of thirteen.[5] While there are inevitably some whose radical views are not tempered through pilgrimage, for many who travel to Mecca for their faith, the experience seems to increase a desire for peace and tolerance towards others, both Muslims and non-Muslims. Do such pilgrims set out in search of community or to embrace tolerance, or do they stumble across it along the way?

In April 2017, I set off with my old friend Constance to walk through Italy along the Via Francigena, that ancient pilgrim track running from Canterbury to Rome. Constance and I have known each other since our time as teenaged art students back in the 1970s, but our common bond predates our first meeting, stretching back to early childhood years spent in Jamaica, a time when we were strangers; one black, one white, broadly speaking. On the long road to Rome we were enriched by the great spirit of friendship and common endeavour amongst the strangers we met, but this was in no measure the same as the unifying spirit of the Hajj: Constance and I did not share an identity of faith with our fellow travellers and throughout our journey remained more bonded to each other than to the confraternity of the road.

Many of the travellers we met were making their pilgrimage singly or in pairs, and the only coherent group we encountered was made up of troubled youngsters from Paris. Sometimes we passed one or other of them, each walking their own walk, thinking their own thoughts; sometimes they passed us, striding angrily across the undulating Tuscan fields, fleeing their demons. Under the guidance of a valiant young female leader, their pilgrimage to Rome was a means of taking time out from difficult lives framed by parental neglect, crime, self-harm or all three.

For these kids the Via Francigena offered a chance to think, to breathe, to find their inner strength—healing rather than faith was the driving purpose here.

The Hajj is very different: it may be an equally individual and personal experience, and it may be a source of healing or solace, but faith is unequivocally at its centre and the rituals are entirely focussed on collective devotion rather than individual action. Aayesha Irani, one of many British Muslims who participated in the recent British Museum project on the Hajj, described how when she entered the Masjid al-Haram, the Great Mosque at the heart of Mecca, peace descended on her being as 'all the people of different colours, shapes, languages and nationality circle the Holy Ka'ba together, oblivious of everything but that they were all human and devoting their time to the worship of one God.'[6] Many of the other first-hand accounts captured by the British Museum project echo these same sentiments. Without doubt, being part of the *ummah*, the community of Muslim believers, is central to this pilgrimage.

For others among the faithful, the Hajj offers a chance for quiet meditation even in the middle of the crowd. Musa, a Sufi who has been on the Umrah (the pilgrimage to Mecca outside the Hajj festival period), tells me how, for him at least, pilgrimage is not a physical activity in which you visit a shrine, but a spiritual journey that offers the chance to connect with yourself and with your God. He describes how, in the anti-clockwise circumambulation of the Kaaba, one is turning again and again towards one's own heart. Here, he says, patting his chest with his right hand as he turns to his left. For Musa, the ritual throwing of stones against the pillars represents the symbolic castigation of his ego. He reveals that he was transformed by his Umrah, saying, 'Pilgrimage is like a mirror: through it you see some of the flaws in yourself that you are afraid to see, and it gives you the hope that you can fix them. You see how weak and vulnerable you are, and that you are nothing, and that allows you to be something.' As we sit talking together on a park bench in St James's Square, a man in a suit sitting next to us, eating his paper-bag lunch, is transfixed by Musa's account of his faith, and remains quietly listening long after his sandwiches are finished. It is almost impossible for me (and I suspect for the man in the suit) to digest the profound nature of Musa's pilgrim journey while the city buzzes around us—and really that is the point. We have to step outside daily life if we truly want to think about big ideas: faith, hope, humanity, self.

Mecca has been the pre-eminent destination for Muslim pilgrimage since the seventh century CE, but what of its beginnings? The tradition of a seasonal pilgrim festival in the Hijaz region,[i] timed according to the lunar calendar, began long before the advent of Islam, with some sources suggesting that certain Hajj rituals practised today also date back to pre-Islamic times. Some scholars suggest that the Kaaba, the 'cube'-shaped building, was at one time a shrine to the Nabatean deity Hubal. Islamic scholars believe that the Kaaba is the earliest place of worship on Earth—that it was founded by Adam and that he was the first pilgrim, and that the original shrine was destroyed by the Great Flood, then rebuilt by Noah.[7] Mystery also surrounds the origins of al-Hajar al-Aswad, the black stone housed within the Kaaba. One theory suggests that it could be a glassy impactite, a composite material resulting from heat generated by a meteorite that may have fallen to Earth some 6,000 years ago.[8] It is not hard to imagine how profound such meteoric events must have been for any community witnessing them, especially when set against the clear, star-spangled sky of the desert night.

---

[i] The Hijaz is the liminal territory of the western edge of the Arabian Peninsula, in which both Medina and Mecca are located.

We cannot know how the Kaaba came to be here, but whatever its origins, it is intriguing that one of the most magnetic places on Earth is somewhere so inhospitable to man. Historically this was a tough environment for herders and farmers alike, and carrying out raids on other tribes or trade caravans meant improving the chances of survival. For local tribes, violent vendettas and blood feuds were a fact of life. But, as was the case for ancient Hellenic pilgrim festivals, strict truces were in place for pre-Islamic pilgrims to travel freely and without fear to take part in rites at the Kaaba. By the sixth century CE, the shrine had become associated with the High God, *Al Lah* (literally The God), although it still retained 360 smaller shrines around its base. The evolving significance of the Kaaba meant that, in the time of the Prophet Muhammad, it was a destination both for northern tribes who had converted to Christianity and for tribes who were yet to embrace monotheism.

In Islamic tradition, the Kaaba is framed as having originally been built by Ibrahim (Abraham) and his son Ismael (Ishmael) and later restored to its original purpose by the Prophet. Islamic texts tell how, by the command of God, Ibrahim took his second wife Hagar and Ismael, the son she bore him, into the desert, where he entrusted them to God. First leaving her infant under a bush, out of the burning heat of the desert sun, Hagar ran back and forth seven times between the hills of Al-Safa and Al-Marwah, in search of water. They survived thanks to the intervention of an angel who dug his heel into the ground, causing water to spring forth from the Zamzam Well. At this same moment, the Yemenite Jurhum tribe were wandering in the desert and looking for water when they saw a bird circling above. They guessed that the bird had spied water and, arriving at the source, were persuaded to settle there. Sometime later, Ibrahim returned and constructed the shrine, which became known as *bayt Allah*, the House of God.

The Kaaba's special status as a sanctuary where all could safely meet created the conditions for Mecca to thrive as a mercantile city. But while some social groups became rich, others remained on the margins of existence. And, as with many social revolutions before and since, this discrepancy between rich and poor provided an opportunity for new ideas and new leadership. Muhammad regularly retired to a cave on Mount Hira outside the city for prayer and contemplation and it was here, in the year 609 CE, that he first began to receive the revelations that would come to be known as the Quran, literally the 'Recitation'. A couple of years passed before Muhammad felt empowered to recite these revelations, but with encouragement from his wife and others he began preaching on the need to create a fairer society. This Qurayshi merchant of Mecca became the Prophet of a religious movement that in time would spread out across the world.

The welfare of the wider community was at the heart of the new creed of Islam, and members of the poorer clans were amongst the first converts. Unsurprisingly, rich merchants were not quite so receptive to a message focussed on their obligations to distribute their wealth to weaker members of society, many of whom were not of the same tribal identity. Within a few years, Muhammad had become actively unpopular amongst the merchants, not least because he preached a message subversive to capitalists of any era: that, on the final day of Judgment, each will be tried not on his wealth, but on his merits.

Life in Mecca became increasingly uncomfortable for the Prophet and his followers, and when they were approached by a delegation from Yathrib, a settlement some 250 miles to the north, they saw a possible way out. Here was the opportunity for Muhammad to implement the social, political and religious principles of the Quran. One by one, Muslim families set out for Yathrib, later known as Medina. This moment of exile or *hijra* in 622 CE marks the starting date of the Islamic calendar. And, in the seventeenth month following this exile, the *Qibla* (direction of prayer) was reoriented from Jerusalem to Mecca: from this moment, the Kaaba became the primary focus of the Islamic faith.

The Muslims had settled in Medina, but they wanted control of Mecca. In 630 CE, after concerted military pressure, they got it. The Meccans had seen the ranks of Islam swell over the years, with one tribe after another giving their allegiance to the Prophet; the surrender, when it came, was peaceful. Within a few days Muhammad and his followers entered the city in a historic event known as *Fath Makkah*, the conquest of Mecca. The pagan idols were stripped away from the Kaaba, associated practices were banned, and it now stood simply and clearly as a shrine to Al Lah—then as now the most sacred site in the Muslim world.

The Farewell Pilgrimage that came two years later was important in part because it established the rites and rituals of the Hajj for all time.[9] The Prophet led a procession of around 90,000 followers from Medina to Mecca, stopping at various mosques along the route to pray and give thanks to God. All were dressed in the simple white garb of pilgrims. The convoy spent the night on the outskirts of the city and the following morning the Prophet went directly to the Sacred Mosque and made seven rounds of the Kaaba, after which he prayed at the Stations of Abraham. He ran seven times between the hills of Al-Safa and Al-Marwah and, a day or so later, rode to the valley of Mina. He stayed there for a day and a night; at sunrise on the following day, he proceeded by camel to the Mount of Mercy, Mount Arafat. Following his sermon there, the Prophet set off at sunset to Muzdalifah, where he spent the night sleeping under the open sky. On the tenth day, he returned to Mina, stopping to throw pebbles against a rock: a ritual attack on Satan still emulated by pilgrims today. He sacrificed sixty-three camels, one for each year of his life, and distributed the meat amongst the poor.

Finally, having shaved his head, the Prophet declared his pilgrimage to be complete.

Of the millions who travel to Mecca each year, either for the Hajj or at other times of the year, only a fraction have a common national or racial identity, but what brings them to this place is the shared identity of their faith, and the sense of *ummah* or community this implies. Malcolm X may have been an exceptional individual, but his experience of pilgrimage will be familiar to many: the opportunity to dwell a while amongst strangers and focus on what binds us together rather than what sets us apart. Religious reforms in the Middle Ages resulted in non-Muslims being forbidden to enter the holy cities of Mecca and Medina, and this seems unlikely to change in my lifetime, but once, on a trip to Syria—before the war tore the country to pieces—I was privileged to witness something of the collective joy of the Muslim faith.

* * *

In November 2008, I had been invited to Damascus to celebrate the opening of a world ceramics exhibition, on loan from London's Victoria & Albert Museum. On the second day of the trip, my compatriot Tim invited me to join him on a short car journey that proved revelatory. That afternoon we stood quietly on a hillside overlooking this ancient and once great city; as the sun began to set, a single call to prayer rang out from a mosque at the eastern limits of Damascus. Dusk arced its way across the sky and, as more and more *muezzins* joined in the call, mosque by mosque, street by street, a great wave of sound began to build, flowing up from the forest of minarets below. And then, as the evening light faded from east to west, so too did the call to prayer, until only a single voice was left, plaintively rising from the westernmost boundary of the city. As quietness descended once more, Tim and I walked slowly back to the car, stunned into a silence of our own.

Next day, in the 'dressing room for visitors' to the Umayyad Mosque, I slipped off my shoes and donned an abaya before being led by my guide Ali into the open courtyard. Over the centuries, the white paving here has been worn smooth by the feet of the faithful, the open expanse of stone now glimmering like water. Three young boys in their stockinged feet ran joyfully and silently across this stone pool as I stood transfixed by the serene beauty of this place. Inside the cool dark of the prayer hall a small group of women, clad from head to foot in black and heavily veiled, were huddled in prayer around a tomb. They were, Ali told me, pilgrims from Iran, coming to visit the final resting place of the head of St John the Baptist. Slain by Herod at the request of his vengeful wife and her daughter, Salome, John the Baptist's is a bloody tale and a cautionary one, resonating through the ages lest we forget the folly and weakness of those in power.

This Christian tomb within a Muslim mosque—built on the site of a more ancient temple to Jupiter, itself built over an even older Iron Age temple—illustrates something particular about the power of objects to create a locus for faith, encouraging pilgrimage. Shrines and relics create a focal point for devotion, but more than this, they carry a profound spiritual charge that can bring an individual closer to their God. The means by which an object can evoke feeling and connect us to a place is as complex and mysterious as any human emotion. But while it may be hard to pin down, this impulse has been recognised since the earliest times and harnessed in the cause of building a community of faith.

Storytelling was a great way to spread the word about Christianity in the early years, and pointing to the physical relics of the people, events and places that featured in its stories would undoubtedly have brought them to life in a much more real and tangible way. 'Here is a fragment of the True Cross', or 'Here is the cloth with which St Veronica wiped the sweat from the face of Christ as he carried his cross along the Via Dolorosa on the way to Calvary'. How powerfully emotive it must have been to see an image said to be formed from the blood, sweat and tears of the Son of God. Building a church above the burial site of relics, or placing them within a church, was the next step in bringing the story, the object and the believer together in one place of meaning.[ii] It was a potent combination. Relics did more than just illustrate the story: their ability to attract the faithful was such that they could act as a foundation stone on which to build new centres of religion, or power, or both.

Following his conversion to Christianity in 312 CE,[iii] the Roman emperor Constantine the Great was quick to recognise this as he set about imprinting his authority on important strategic locations. Rome provided a direct link with Christ through his disciple, St Peter. Many theological controversies swirl around the figure of Peter, beginning with his name. Previously known as Simeon, in Aramaic his nickname was said to be *cepha*, or rock. Translated into the Greek, this becomes *petra*, or the masculinised version Petros. Is Peter, then, the rock upon which Christ vowed to build his Church? Notwithstanding differences over this question, what seems indisputable is that the figure of Peter provided the foundation for the Church in Rome when in 318 CE Constantine commissioned the construction of the original Basilica of St Peter over the saint's tomb, and the Basilica of St

---

[ii] Even St Augustine, who complained of relic-mongers dressed as monks in the 5th century, acquired some relics of St Stephen to consecrate his church at Hippo (in modern Algeria), which became an important North African pilgrimage destination.

[iii] Constantine was only actually baptised on death's door in 337 CE. By that time, he had created an axis of power from Rome in the West to Constantinople in the East, with himself as emperor over both.

Paul over the tomb of that disciple, thought to have been beheaded in Rome on the orders of Emperor Nero in around 65 CE. The creation of these important churches, combined with Constantine's support for the Edict of Milan (which gave Christianity legal status across the Roman Empire), established Rome as a destination for pilgrimage almost on a par with Jerusalem.

Then, in 324 CE, Constantine sent his mother Helena on a pilgrimage to the Levant to uncover important Christian sites and to search for the True Cross, a powerful motif of his newfound faith. At this point Jerusalem had been under pagan Roman rule for over 200 years and there was much to be done. Helena founded the Church of the Nativity in Bethlehem and a church marking the site of Christ's Ascension, and then ordered the demolition of an important temple to Jupiter. It was here, according to tradition, that she discovered the tomb or sepulchre in which Jesus had been buried. Very soon afterwards, on the advice of an aged Hebrew called Jude, Helena ordered the demolition of another temple, this one dedicated to Venus. Here four nails and three crosses were found, indicating a connection to the story of Christ, who was crucified alongside two thieves. But how to determine which of the three was the 'True Cross'? A woman, suffering from some severe illness, was brought to adjudicate. This ailing woman reached out to each cross in turn, and as she touched upon the third, she was cured, thus providing the essential proof. Helena, despite her advancing years (she was about sixty-three when she started), oversaw the task of unearthing and restoring these sites and encompassing them within the Church of the Holy Sepulchre, also known as the Church of the Resurrection in Jerusalem.

With Christian shrines anchoring two points of the empire, Constantine now needed something to cement the link between Christianity and the new capital of the Roman Empire, Constantinople, formerly Byzantium, which the emperor had modestly renamed after himself. In the Christian story, three kings or magi had travelled to see the newly born infant Jesus in Bethlehem, guided there by a star first seen above the Hill of Vaws. By tradition, it was also here that they were buried, and Helena travelled to the site to recover their earthly remains. The relics of the three kings, Melchior, Balthazar, and Jasper, were placed into a single ornamented chest and transferred to Constantinople, the heart of her son's empire, and there, in the Church of Saint Sophia, they were laid to rest. For a while, at least.

The historical veracity of the ruins and relics enshrined in Rome, Jerusalem and Constantinople have been called into question many times by archaeologists and in some cases by competing faith groups.[iv] But whatever the facts, the act of endowing these places with a sacred status, either through the placement of relics or association with the story of Christianity, is what really mattered in the fourth century. These sacred places not only served to gloriously illuminate the narrative of this new faith, but also—more pragmatically—offered pilgrims an alternative to the old temples of Jupiter and Venus that had once commanded their devotion. The Church of the Holy Sepulchre in Jerusalem and St Peter's in Rome remain earthly focal points for the faithful and important centres of pilgrimage today.

---

[iv] The Protestants, for example, have argued that the Crucifixion and Resurrection of Christ happened in two separate locations and could not therefore be encompassed within one building. Equally, in December 1950 Pope Pius XII declared that none of the bones found in archaeological digs related to St Peter's could be verified as those of the saint himself. In 1953 another set of bones were found, and subsequent testing indicated these belonged to a man of around 60–70 years old. One renowned Italian archaeologist made the case that these were the remains of St Peter, while others working at the site remained unconvinced.

Beyond these foundation points of the new faith, saintly relics also proved a useful missionary aid in spreading Christianity more widely—ultimately swelling the numbers of pilgrims travelling from one relic site to another. A reliquary or shrine offered a focus point for devotion; the more important the saint, the greater the status of both the shrine and the town or city in which it stood. Centres of trade not only wanted the prestige that came with such relics; city fathers and merchants also recognised the significant economic value that derived from their power to attract pilgrims—then as now, visitors were prized for their deep pockets. In this regard, the Magi were a truly valuable asset. Around the middle of the fourth century, their relics were taken from Constantinople and transported to Milan, first by boat and then by ox cart[10]—but this was not their final resting place. In the twelfth century, faced with an anti-imperial insurrection in Milan, the Holy Roman Emperor, Frederick Barbarossa, called on the support of his ally, Rainald, the Archbishop of Cologne. Accounts vary, with some describing the relics as a gift from Frederick in recognition of Rainald's help; others frame the story in terms of looting. Whatever the case, when the fog of war had cleared, the relics were no longer in Milan, but in Cologne, signalling a shift of power from Italy to Germany. A century later, on the banks of the Rhine, an immense church was built to house them, and the Magi's three crowns became the symbol of Cologne, signalling the city's status as an important centre of both commerce and faith.

On Christmas Day 2017 I stood alongside my husband Tony and hundreds of others in Cologne Cathedral as the songs of praise rose up into the soaring Gothic nave on a cloud of incense. In this moment, feeling my spirit soar too, it was clear why pilgrims have been drawn here for centuries: this glorious church is a testament to the magnetic pull of relics. For outsiders like me, though, it can seem inexplicable that any object, however valuable or valued, can amplify the prestige of a city to this extent. Looking for a key to unlock this conundrum, I landed on Leonardo da Vinci's portrait *Lady with an Ermine*. When I worked on a project in Kraków in the late 1990s, the first question from everyone I met was, 'Have you seen the Leonardo yet?' Held by the city's National Museum and deemed one of Poland's national treasures, this small rectangle of oil-painted walnut board is beyond monetary value. A work by perhaps the most revered artist of the Western canon, the presence of this small picture raises Kraków's status, not least in the minds of those who live there.

Relics appealed to people of all classes: the poor travelled to see them, and the rich and powerful aspired to own them, often sending relic collectors off around Europe to track down choice items. The British monarchy's Royal Picture Collection, which includes works by da Vinci, Michelangelo, Vermeer and Rembrandt, is not simply an expression of princely covetousness, but a public demonstration that the monarch has not only power, but wealth. By presenting that wealth via objects that are and have always been widely valued, at home and abroad, the collection is a political statement that the royal family's authority has historical provenance extending far beyond the boundaries of its individual members. In the Middle Ages, relics embodied these same two characteristics of public prestige and immeasurable value; as such, they were potent tools of diplomacy, used as gifts by leaders of both Church and State. Collecting on the considerable debts of the Emir of Córdoba in 1047, Fernando, Count of Carreon apparently said, 'Of gold and silver I have enough already, give me the body of St Zoyl.'

Attracting pilgrims to see the bones of saints in a specially built shrine had the advantage of drawing followers together in a single location where they might all learn the same teachings and rites and build a community of faith. The question then was how to create an authentic connection between a relic, which typically had its origin in the Holy Land, and its new place of rest. This was sometimes resolved through a revelatory dream. The role of dreams and visions as a channel through which actions could be directed, or events predicted, had been central to earlier Greek beliefs and, as Christianity spread, they came to play an important role in the translocation of saintly remains to newly established centres for the faith.

Andrew, one of the Twelve Apostles of Christ, preached widely in Asia Minor before meeting a violent end in Patras, Greece, where he was crucified on an X-shaped crucifix or saltire. By tradition, a Greek monk, St Regulus (St Rule), was instructed in a vision to take St Andrew's bones to the 'ends of the earth' and there to build a shrine for them. After first translating the relics to Constantinople, St Rule reportedly removed a tooth, arm bone, kneecap and some fingers from the remains of St Andrew and then set off on what must have been an arduous journey by sea. Crossing the Mediterranean and then passing through the Strait of Gibraltar, St Rule and his cargo emerged into the hostile waters of the North Atlantic. Guided by the stars, and without the aid of the Shipping Forecast, he passed safely by the treacherous Bay of Biscay, Portland, White; Dover, Thames, Humber, Dogger, and Tyne; before running aground in the inshore waters of Rattray Head to Berwick on Tweed. Here, legend has it, St Rule alighted with the saint's bones at the remote Christian settlement of Muck Ross, later known as St Andrews.

The importance of St Andrews as a focal point for faith comes not only from St Rule's dream, but from a second vision, too. Legend tells how, in the year 832 CE or thereabouts, a Pictish army under King Angus MacFergus waited nervously together with a band of Scots for dawn to break on the day of battle. They were to fight the Northumbrians for the control of East Lothian, a strategic piece of land on the Firth of Forth, close to what is today Edinburgh. As he lay in his cot, Angus received a vision of St Andrew, and when the sun rose, as the two armies faced each other across the battlefield, a white saltire appeared against the blue sky. Buoyed by this sign from St Andrew that God was indeed on their side, victory was assured for King Angus and his men. St Andrew became Scotland's patron saint, and a white saltire on a blue background the nation's flag. Not for the first time, relics and visions were the seed corn of a pilgrim trade that in time brought wealth and power to a city. The saint's perceived role in the battle helped anchor Christianity in Scotland and gave his shrine added appeal. By the twelfth century, there was enough demand (and sufficient financial support) to commission a larger church to hold the relics. Work began on construction of a new cathedral that was designed to be larger than either York or Canterbury, both of which at the time claimed jurisdiction over the Scottish Church.

The power of faith to make or break kingdoms went beyond the imagination of the soldier on the eve of battle—relics and visions were potent symbols of a shared religious identity and were critical in forging political allegiances built on faith. Just a few years before King Angus saw off the Northumbrians, a dream about another saint far from Scotland had proved equally decisive.

* * *

In June 2003, I wandered alone through the Spanish town of Santiago de Compostela, not a pilgrim, just a curious visitor diverted from a conference nearby. The medieval nature of the scene was striking: the winding cobbled streets full of footsore travellers simply dressed, many carrying walking sticks or shepherd crooks, progressing slowly and deliberately towards the great cathedral. Stepping out of the bright sunlight into the church, I found myself in an almost foggy interior dappled with light and sat down to wait alongside scores of others, not knowing what might occur. There was a huddle of activity as many more congregants started to fill the church. As everyone settled into their seats, the smell of incense started to stroke across the noses of the assembled crowd.

Eight red-robed attendants, the *tiraboleiros*, were standing in the centre of the cathedral, and all became clear as they began to pull on ropes anchored high above. One of the great censers, perhaps the Alcachofa or the Botafumeiro, began to swing—first gently, and then at a terrifying rate, the frenetic pendulum dousing the faithful in smoke and not a little anxiety.[v] This fantastic and intoxicating ritual is typically carried out twice a day, a celebration for those who have completed the Camino pilgrimage to its destination here, and a taste of what that might feel like for casual onlookers like myself. As with Delphi, or Mecca, the question is: why here? Why does this exact place exert a mysterious and magnetic pull on pilgrims? The answer is in part historical, and while that can never be the whole answer, it offers a good place to start.

After he was brutally beheaded in 44 CE on the orders of King Herod Agrippa I, the body of St James was reportedly stolen away and transported aboard a small boat to the north coast of Spain. Here, so it is told, the remains were hidden in woodland, where they lay undisturbed for many centuries. All that changed in 814 CE when Pelayo, a wandering monk, received a vision; a bright star guided him to a secluded clearing in the wood. There, he discovered a marble sarcophagus containing the mortal remains of St James. This dream of Pelayo was to determine the path of Spain's history. A few years earlier, this part of

---

[v] Weighing around 60kg and measuring about 1.5m in height, the Botafumeiro is one of the largest censers in the world; in full swing it can reach speeds of up to 42 miles/hr.

Spain, Asturias, had come under attack by Umayyad forces. At the time, the greater part of the Iberian Peninsula was already under the control of Abd al-Rahman I, the Falcon of the Quraysh. By 794 CE, two of his finest generals, the Ibn Mugait brothers Abd al-Karim and Abd al-Malik, had made significant progress in outflanking the Asturian forces, and the Asturian King Alfonso II desperately needed help. He called first on his Basque neighbour, Belasco, and then, growing increasingly desperate, appealed directly to Charlemagne and his Frankish army. Together, they were successful in pushing back the Andalusian offensive. As a consequence of this victory, Alfonso II was acknowledged as a king by Charlemagne and the Pope, and Asturias became a kingdom within the Holy Roman Empire.

Alfonso's security was to be short-lived. In 814 CE, Charlemagne, who had done so much to establish Christianity in Europe, died. For Alfonso II, whose power and Christianity were inextricably linked, this political uncertainty left him vulnerable to Umayyad attack. In this respect, the discovery of the relics of St James not long after Charlemagne's death proved extremely timely. On examination by the local bishop Teodomir, it was attested that these were indeed the true remains of the saint; after visiting the site, King Alfonso II ordered that a church be built to house the relics and subsequently made the first peregrination to what has become one of Christianity's most enduring pilgrimage shrines: Santiago de Compostela, or St James of *campus stellae*, the 'field of the star'.

The new shrine proved to be as potent as any present-day defence treaty, ensuring that Christian allies would rally to the aid of the new Kingdom of Asturias to defend the faith and the faithful. St James' political value did not end there, and he was brought back into the fray of conflict on several occasions after his relics were reinterred. Around 844 CE, this included appearing in a vision and leading the Christian army to victory during the probably fictional Battle of Clavijo against the Muslim forces of the Emir of Córdoba. Through this legend, he became known as Santiago Matamoras (St James the Moor-Slayer), and thereafter earned his place as the patron saint of Spain.

Over the course of the Middle Ages, the numbers making their way along the Camino de Santiago grew as pilgrimage became an ever more popular way of demonstrating faith and as a means of carrying out penance, imposed by the Church for sins real or imagined. The cost of making such pilgrimages was high, in terms of both time and money, but the cost of not doing so was far more onerous: failure to repent might result in long years in purgatory or, worse, in Hell itself.[vi] This great era of Christian pilgrimage inevitably declined as religious reform rippled through Europe, and as revolution and war disrupted historic routes to Santiago, Jerusalem and Rome. The nineteenth century saw the first shoots of a revival as the European middle classes grew and grand tours of the Mediterranean and Holy Land became a marker of education and wealth. Shrines of more local or national relevance, like Canterbury and Walsingham in the UK, also enjoyed a revival in popularity. It was only a matter of time before Santiago de Compostela rose once more, helped yet again by the ever-active spirit of St James.

Under Spain's secular Second Republic (1931–6), St James' status as patron saint had been suspended, but during the subsequent Spanish Civil War he made a comeback to the advantage of the Nationalist cause. On the feast of St James, 25 July 1937, Franco's army won the decisive Battle of Brunete. This particular fracas between Republicans and nationalist Falangist forces had

---

[vi] Pope Urban II offered a 'plenary indulgence', a lifetime absolution of sin, in return for joining that most controversial of pilgrimages, the First Crusade to Jerusalem (1095–9).

been waging for weeks and, when the Republican forces were defeated, Franco announced that 'The Apostle has granted me victory on his feast day.'[vii] Despite this, pilgrim numbers to Santiago remained in the low thousands under Franco's regime, but as Spain democratised and strengthened its economy, pilgrim numbers began to climb once more. In 1986 there were 24,911 *peregrinos*, but in 2018 some 327,378 received their official Compostela certificate, rewarding their great personal efforts to complete the 100 kilometres or more of the journey on foot, bicycle or horseback, or in a wheelchair. Many millions more travelled straight to the shrine to visit as tourists.[11]

It is hard to pin down the precise cause of the rising popularity of the Camino de Santiago, but the available data for 2018 indicated that nearly half made the pilgrimage for 'religious and other reasons', with a further 43 per cent indicating that religion was their sole motivation for pilgrimage.[12] As one might expect, Spanish *peregrinos* make up the biggest single category, but each year scores of thousands of pilgrims make their way to Spain's remote north-western coast from places as distant as Afghanistan and Eswatini, Qatar and Congo. The numbers are small when compared to Lourdes, or Fatima in Portugal, each of which receives 6–8 million Christian pilgrims each year, but for many who complete the Camino, the journey rather than the destination is the defining experience.

My ever-generous sister-in-law Jen once travelled a great stretch of the Camino de Santiago, simply to keep company with

---

[vii] Having God on one's side has long been an aspiration in political, personal and sporting contests. When the Portuguese football team won the Euro 2016 Cup, the team's manager Fernando Santos told the waiting press, 'First of all I would like to thank God the Father for this moment.'

a friend who was wrangling with big changes in her life. For Malcolm, a barrister friend whose professional life is inevitably defined by conflict and friction, the Camino is an annual fixture in his calendar. Malcolm walks various sections of the route from southern Spain in two-week blocks every summer; having secured his Compostela years ago, arriving at the end point of the Camino is no longer an important goal. For this pilgrim at least, and for many non-believers, it is all about the space such a journey provides for quiet contemplation along the way of matters that might otherwise remain buried, unrevealed. Jen and Malcolm are amongst the statistical 9 per cent who indicate that faith is not part of their motive for pilgrimage to Santiago, but they nevertheless find personal and emotional value in an experience that has been created in large part by the faith of others. For the vast majority who are travellers of faith, their isolation from domestic matters can offer the chance to connect more deeply with their religious beliefs and bring them closer to God.

For secular pilgrims like myself, perhaps the nearest we can come to appreciating what pilgrimage means to those with faith is through their first-hand accounts. Malik is a native of Mecca and since his early childhood has witnessed the annual cycle of pilgrims arriving in his hometown and spiritual home. He and I became great friends through the topic of pilgrimage, and although there is no possibility for me to truly conceive of the profound nature of the Hajj, the nearest I could hope for was to see it through his eyes. And what eyes they are—he told me:

> When your home is God's land, when each year you are waiting and longing for the Hajj, you are in a perpetual state of transition. This is how it is to be Meccan. The call goes out to Muslims, from every place on Earth, and from every deep abyss, to come to God. You are waiting and longing, and the proof is that they always come; with their arrival, God comes. He is in every pilgrim. This is the greatest act of community and humanity. It expresses the fortitude of the

human spirit; you want to help them and give them what they need. All differences disappear in a common purpose, as the channel between Earth and Heaven opens up over the Kaaba.

4

# WONDER

'*Though a good deal is too strange to be believed,*
*nothing is too strange to have happened.*'

Thomas Hardy[1]

In September 1982, in a surreal turn of events I found myself sitting in a side room of the great Imam Ali Mosque in Najaf, Iraq. Our small party comprised half a dozen journalists and an equal number of army officers. The journalists had been invited by the authorities to cover the second anniversary of Iraq's war with Iran. I was there to make preparatory drawings and photographs for an exhibition scheduled to take place in London the following spring. For reasons of logistical convenience, our hosts had lumped us all together in a sightseeing tour that took in the archaeological ruins of Babylon, as well as the two great Shia mosques of Karbala and Najaf.

Outside in the busy streets the heat was fierce, but in the Imam Ali Mosque's anteroom all was cool and still. Through an interpreter, the journalists were asking the army officers some very difficult questions about local events. This was the city that had given sanctuary to Iran's Ayatollah Khomeini until the revolution in 1979 that brought him to power, and it seems that recently twelve Shia rabble-rousers had been publicly hanged here *pour encourager les autres*. The British and Americans, and their European friends, had been allied with Iraq in the Iran–Iraq War, and until this point I had been labouring under the illusion that this meant the Iraqis must be good guys. We're always on the side of the good guys, aren't we? Apparently not so simple, as would become very clear to me in the months and years that followed.

Fear liberates the imagination, and as the tension between the armed officers and the probing journalists grew, I was desperate to close my mind's eye. I turned my attention instead to our surroundings. The Imam Ali Mosque is an exquisite example of Islamic architecture, its golden dome shining over the city; I could see a great crystal chandelier inside the inner sanctum of the shrine (where we could look but not enter). Throughout the colonnades that led to the anteroom where we sat, honeycomb vaulting subdivided each arch and niche into ever smaller frag-ments in a mind-bending feat of three-dimensional geometry. Everywhere, intricate glazed ceramic tiles filled the eye with pat-tern and light. Out of nervousness I looked down at my hands, closing my eyes, willing the press interrogation to be over; finally, mercifully, silence descended. No more sharp questions, no more half-answers—we got back into the minibus and drove on to Karbala.

After Mecca and Medina, Karbala is Islam's holiest city, and when we arrived a pilgrim festival was in full flow.[i] In the streets surrounding the mosque, tents were pitched on every spare patch of ground. People flowed in and out of the arched entrance, and

---

[i] It is not clear whether this was Arbaeen or another festival, as the Arbaeen pilgrimage was suspended for a time under Saddam Hussein's Sunni Baathist rule.

in the courtyard beyond groups of men and women sat in sociable circles while the melee moved around them. The central shrine is dedicated to Imam Hussein, martyred during the Battle of Karbala in 680 CE and, as befitting the third imam and the grandson of the Prophet Muhammad, housed within a gleaming wonder. The mosque's gold dome and minarets are visible from beyond the city limits and, while believers come because of their faith, such magnificence is a statement of the shrine's importance. There can be little doubt that the splendour helps to draw pilgrims here. The annual Arbaeen pilgrimage to Karbala marks the end of forty days of mourning for the death of Imam Hussein; many make their journey on foot from Najaf, 55 miles away, and a significant number walk from the largely Shia city of Basra 300 miles to the south. The scale and diversity of this peaceful procession contribute to its appeal, and the estimated number of those taking part annually is reported to exceed 20 million.

Almost inevitably, given the ongoing friction between Sunni and Shia communities in Iraq, the pilgrimage has been subject to attack on several occasions, but the pilgrims seem undeterred. The Arbaeen is a testament to the potency of pilgrimage to inspire wonder in both those who take part and those who minister to them along the way. On the road into the city, local people clean the shoes of passing pilgrims as an act of piety, and thousands of *mawakibs* or tents are erected to provide shelter, medical help and free food for those in need. At its core, the Arbaeen is a Shia event, but pilgrims from other sects, faiths and nationalities join in as an expression of shared humanity. All are levelled by the road, and yet the mind's eye of each is focussed on the gleaming shrine that draws the procession onwards.

* * *

This rare opportunity to break through the barriers that normally divide society (class, race, gender, beliefs) is a feature of

many pilgrim journeys and in part what makes them so wondrous, both as a phenomenon, and for the individuals taking
part. Chaucer chose his storytellers from all walks of life, from
Knight to Nun, Miller to Physician, and not forgetting the
Merchant, or the Wife of Bath, who had thrice been to
Jerusalem. Rich and poor, masters and servants—all breathed
their share of dust along the road to Canterbury. The practice of
extending hospitality to pilgrims on the road to Karbala could
also be found along major Christian routes in medieval times,
and still exists along paths such as the Via Francigena. Simple
pilgrim menus are offered by cafes at key stopping points; many
hostels run a system of voluntary payment, and the mood of
equality and bare necessity echoes through the shared dormito-
ries. Packing up our modest rucksacks each morning to get back
on the trail underscored how little material wealth we really
need, especially when set against the backdrop of the commonwealth of comradeship on the road. All this simplicity and equality stirs another, less explicit and less comforting feeling: the
recognition that perhaps there is another way to live.

There are many accounts of how a pilgrim journey has been a
catalyst for change at the personal level, but time and again
throughout history it has also proved to be a powerful tool in
shaping society. The wonder of pilgrimage is not only in the great
monuments or landscapes to be contemplated, but also in the
social effects of being brought together to a place of shared significance. In late-fifteenth-century northern India, Guru Nanak,
the founder of Sikhism, wanted to create an alternative social
model—one that would put an end to the strife between Muslims
and Hindus and the inequality of the caste system, and would
improve the position of women in society.[2] He chose to put this
levelling ethos at the centre of his teaching and encouraged his
followers to sit and eat together, believing that, through the act
of sharing a meal, people from all parts of society would be able

to meet on an equal footing. Guru Nanak travelled widely preaching a philosophy of monotheism that emphasised the equality of all religions, castes, ethnicities, and nationalities. He described the Absolute as the one ultimate reality, the creator, whose name is truth, and who is infinite, timeless, formless, and genderless.

When he established the first Guru ka Langar (Guru's Kitchen) in 1521 CE, it was an act of social revolution. For centuries the caste system in India had ensured that each citizen kept to their own class and the idea of any communal activity cutting across social strata was utterly unthinkable. The act of breaking bread together as an expression of family or group cohesion arises in Islamic and Judaic pilgrim traditions, as does the principle of distributing any surplus food from a feast. But Guru Nanak's idea was fundamentally different. By welcoming people of all genders, races, statuses and faiths to sit together and eat the same food in the same way, each would be reminded of the equality of all people before God. The second Sikh guru, Guru Angad, introduced the communal kitchen or *langar* into all Sikh places, transforming the temple into something more than simply a place for Sikhs to meet for worship. It also became a place of refuge and hospitality for all people, a gurdwara. In bringing communal eating back into the temple, Sikhism was reinventing the more ancient practice of bringing faith and feasting together in one place.

Learning about the Sikh practice of breaking bread with all-comers cast a new light on events in my own history; with hindsight, I feel ashamed for failing to appreciate their meaning at the time. Our neighbours in London's East End, Kris and Rani Singh, were rich in progeny, and as each child reached a marriageable age, we would look forward to the moment when the drumming practice began, signalling that the day of celebration was approaching. Our Bow neighbourhood included people from Aarhus and Dhaka, Birmingham and Jaipur; doctors and car mechanics, artists and joiners—and when we finally heard the drums in full voice, typically quite early in the morning, windows slid up, front doors opened, and soon neighbours started to drift outside. There is a certain joy in standing on a street corner freshly minted in your pyjamas, celebrating the marriage of a young man or woman you've known since their early childhood, and while we waited for the true stars of the festivities to appear, food and drink was passed around. The Singh family fed and watered us all, Danes and Cockneys, Muslims, Christians and non-believers alike, and this same spirit marks out the Guru ka Langar at Amritsar as one of the greatest wonders of pilgrimage.

Built in a place once cherished for its tranquillity, the Harmandir Sahib or Golden Temple of Amritsar now attracts around 30 million pilgrims a year,[3] and one of the most remarkable features of this anchor point of Sikhism is the community kitchen. With the help of a largely *sewadar* or volunteer workforce, the *langar* at Amritsar serves up more than 50,000 free meals a day; during festival periods, this number rises to more than 100,000. Diners are seated on the floor in two great halls and hundreds of *sewadars* prepare and serve the food, and take care of the immense piles of washing up. The fare is vegetarian, typically comprising rice and dahl, a vegetable dish and *kheer* (rice pudding).

But what makes this feast so unique is not the dishes, the history or the scale—after all, charitable kitchens have existed all over the world for centuries, and the World Food Programme claims to distribute 15 billion rations of food each year. No, what makes this feeding of the 50,000 every day in Amritsar exceptional is something more than a transaction from rich to poor, the usual charitable construct of 'I have, and I give to you, because you don't have'—worthy though that is. Rather, the act of sitting and eating together is considered as pious as the act of preparing and serving the food. In this, our great age of inequality, imagine if just a few thousand of those 15 billion World Food Programme packages were eaten as a modest feast shared with policy-makers and food conglomerates, politicians or freedom fighters? Imagine if everyone involved in the preparation, cooking, serving and eating of those rations chose while they did so to focus their minds on sameness over difference, as is the case in the Guru ka Langar? A Sikh *yogini*, Pritpal Singh Khalsa, reports that 'When you are blessed to eat in the Guru ka Langar, you experience Cherdi Kala (the feeling of being lifted up) and Sarbhat da Bala (the loving intention of wishing the best for all people) and you realize that not only your stomach is being fed but also your soul.'[4]

Aside from the communal wonder of the Guru ka Langar, and the spiritual wonder of the pilgrimage to Amritsar, the Golden Temple itself is a huge draw, naturally enough. Begun in 1573, the original structure was a modest affair, built in brick and lime in the centre of a man-made pool and accessed by a causeway. The Temple had four entrances, one on each side, symbolising that its doors were open to the four Hindu *varna*. The marble, mirror and inlay work and the gilding, for which the building is now best known, were carried out in the nineteenth century, when the Sikhs reached the pinnacle of their power and affluence under the leadership of Maharaja Ranjit Singh. Ranjit Singh allowed talent to rise to the highest positions in his administration, irrespective of religion; orders were issued to treat citizens of all classes and occupations equally and to respect each in accordance with the doctrines of the Sikh faith. Merchants, traders, bankers and craftsmen were encouraged to come to Amritsar, and it became a centre of production, trading and distribution for a wide variety of goods including textiles, metalwork, woodwork and enamelware. Soon the Sikh Empire extended from the Khyber Pass eastwards to the edge of Tibet, and from Kashmir to Mithankot in the south. The shining jewel in the crown was the Golden Temple.

This gilded white marble temple, floating in its amber pool, married both Islamic and Hindu architectural traditions, but more than this, it was an irresistible magnet to those who came simply to see its glory. In this respect, it was a tried and tested formula, recognising the human appetite for spectacle, our desire to experience something out of this world; to be awed, and to return home with tales of what we've seen. Aside from the spiritual significance of the shrine of St Thomas Becket, Chaucer's twenty-nine pilgrims could also look forward to seeing one of the most spectacular sites in medieval Britain. The Dutch philosopher and theologian Erasmus visited the shrine in 1510, noting that 'The least valuable portion was gold; every part glistened, shone, and sparkled with rare and very large jewels, some of them exceeding the size of a goose's egg.'[5] When Becket's shrine was destroyed by Henry VIII's reforming zeal and the immense treasure of Canterbury carried off, accounts of the time record that two coffers, each requiring six or seven men to carry them, were needed to take the loot away, on twenty-six carts.[6]

Places of pilgrimage are more than simply the sum of their decorations, however, and once they are imbued with spiritual and historical significance, even grand larceny cannot truly impoverish them. Even now, stripped of its relics and worldly glitter, the sheer scale of Canterbury Cathedral impresses. If you stand within the crypt where Becket's tomb once lay and look up, you will see a floating figure of a man, hollow and outlined in iron nails, recovered from renovation work on the Cathedral. The work is by renowned British artist Antony Gormley, and while there is nothing gilded or elaborate about it, the recumbent figure is as powerful as any marble tomb or relic in connecting the onlooker to the story. It offers a perfect moment of awed contemplation for those about to set out on the long road to Rome: a path that begins just outside in the Cathedral precincts.

Before starting out on that very road one fine summer's day, as I looked up at the enormous stone flanks of this monument to

Christianity, I wondered once again at the contrast between the wealth and display of the church and the pared-down journey of the pilgrim making their way there. In that moment an image that had bothered me for many years flickered into my mind's eye.

On 1 August 1996, while travelling through Ecuador with my young son Fred, I happened upon the Jesuit Church of la Compañía de Jesús in Quito, a place both dazzling and perplexing in equal measure. Every surface appeared to be gilded, from the barrel-arched ceiling to the plasterwork of the walls and the intricately carved wooden altarpiece, beneath which lies the sarcophagus of St Mariana de Jesús de Paredes, patron saint of Ecuador. In this jewel of a church, even the floor of the aisle appeared golden as the light reflected off its highly polished surface. By comparison, the hunched figures of the women who knelt and sat in the pews were drab, dusty and poor, drawn here from the surrounding countryside where their lives on the land were undoubtedly tough. I was perplexed, because I couldn't understand why these women were not angry at the wealth of the Church compared to their own poverty, or how they could find tranquillity here amongst such sparkling inequality.

Two decades on and I have begun to understand a little more. Ornate churches like la Compañía, the mosques of Najaf and Karbala or the Golden Temple act as beacons to the faithful, and at the same time provide universal access to a material culture that is otherwise available only to the privileged few. This is a shared wealth which is free for all to marvel at, rich or poor, and while many of these places may be far from home, for the faithful pilgrim they are not out on the periphery, but at the centre of their spiritual universe. On the road to Rome, that common wealth becomes ever richer and more fabulous as one gets closer to the centre, glorious breadcrumbs of culture dotted at intervals on the path to sustain the weary soul. Travellers arriving along the popular Via Francigena enter the city via the Porta del

Popolo, literally, the Gate of the People. Emerging into a broad piazza, there is an opportunity to give thanks at Santa Maria del Popolo before continuing on. In 1600, parts of this basilica were rebuilt, and the Cerasi Chapel was created. Annibale Carracci won the commission to paint the altarpiece, which depicts the Assumption of the Virgin—the moment that Mary is carried into Heaven. But this luminescent work is eclipsed by the two Baroque masterpieces that hang on the flanks of the chapel.

Painted by the turbulent Caravaggio, these panels depict Peter and Paul, the two figures associated with the Christianisation of Rome, thereby reaffirming the city's credentials to pilgrims immediately upon arrival. More than 400 years after their installation, Caravaggio's paintings remain astonishing in their emotional and spiritual power. The first panel depicts the crucifixion of St Peter, the apostle ordained by Christ and, by tradition, the first Bishop of Rome. According to tradition, Peter—not wanting to emulate the crucifixion of Christ—asked to be crucified upside down as an act of humility, and the strong intersecting diagonals of the overall composition in Caravaggio's work suggest an inverted cross. The painting depicts the moment that the foot of the cross is being lifted, the faces of all three workmen hidden in the shadows as if in shame, while Peter's gaze is held by an inner vision.

The second panel shows the conversion of Saul on the road to Damascus. The figure of Saul (later to become St Paul) is shown lying helpless on the ground, his arms reaching up, eyes closed as he is blinded by the light of the visitation of Jesus Christ. The subject is framed against the red pool of his cloak, a reminder of his initial mission to arrest followers of Jesus and return them to Jerusalem for trial and execution. From this moment on, Saul turns away from the persecution of Christians and becomes an evangelist, travelling around the Mediterranean to convert fellow Jews and later Gentiles to his new creed. In both of the Cerasi Chapel panels, the artist draws the viewer straight into the heart of the story, reminding the pilgrim that these are the events that brought them to this very place in this very moment. *Conversion on the Way to Damascus* restates the dual themes of journey and enlightenment that appear across all the major faiths and are so central to the idea of pilgrimage; the *Crucifixion of Saint Peter* reminds the onlooker that humility and submission are central tenets of the Christian faith. The luminosity of the paintings themselves are a source of wonder for the pilgrim passing through on their way to St Peter's Basilica.

\* \* \*

For medieval European Christians contemplating a journey to Rome, Jerusalem, or Compostela, the very real risks of the road were held in balance against potential rewards in the next life. But perhaps a more immediate draw was the wonder of seeing the places where Christianity was born. More than history and geography, we need to see something tangible—something we can hold in our mind's eye and describe to others—and it is notable that the first account of European pilgrimage to Jerusalem comes within a decade of Constantine and Helena's projects to restore the city's Christian sites. Written in 333 CE by an unknown author from Bordeaux, the *Itinerarium Burdigalense* offered a useful guide to other would-be travellers for distances and stopping points along the way. By the end of the fourth century, while the theologians of the age were arguing about the spiritual merits and moral risks of pilgrimage, the flow of faithful feet was growing and would continue to do so, albeit frequently disrupted and diverted by war and conflict that continues in the twenty-first century. Like pilgrims today, those of ages past were spurred in part by the first-hand accounts of others and the glories described therein.

One such account, by the Swiss theologian Felix Fabri, proved inspirational to generations of pilgrims to the Holy Land, and through it we also we learn about the question of *curiositas*. This mercurial term, whose meaning seems to slide between lust for knowing, adventurism and simple nosiness, was considered by St Augustine to be a sin alongside pride and lust. Pilgrimage driven by an appetite for wonder was deemed impious, but by his own reckoning, Fabri's motives were pure; he was driven by the need for better understanding, in order to preach the Scriptures. With this in mind, before setting out, Fabri made a promise to his fellow monks to keep an exact record of all that he saw and experienced along the way, and he proved to be a man of his word.[7] During his lifetime, Brother Fabri's first-hand accounts of his travels were valued as teaching aids; in due course, they also came to be considered important historical records.

Before Brother Fabri set off on his first pilgrimage in 1480, he was clearly anxious about the more practical questions of what lay ahead: 'I ran hither and thither more than I need have done, to obtain advice ... [I] was frightened. I feared for my life, I dreaded the sea too, which I had never yet seen, but of which I had heard much.' He paid a visit to Prince Count Eberhard, the elder of Württemberg who had himself travelled to Jerusalem, to ask his advice. The noble Count Eberhard listened to Fabri's concerns, responding with an old medieval adage: 'There are three acts in a man's life which no one ought to advise another to do or not to do. The first is to contract matrimony, the second is to go to war, the third is to visit the Holy Sepulchre.' Not finding this hugely helpful, Fabri turned to a nun he trusted: 'Go! Quick! Quick!' she told him, 'make your journey. Stay no longer and God be with you in the way'.

Despite any lingering doubts he might have had about the dangers ahead, moral or otherwise, Fabri pressed ahead with his plan. About to take leave of his spiritual father at the friary, he recorded that this sorrowful parting filled him with regret, 'and the pilgrimage, which had appeared so sweet and virtuous now seemed wearisome, bitter, useless, empty, and sinful'. In that moment, Brother Fabri's eagerness to see Jerusalem was replaced by an almost immediate longing for Ulm, before he had even set out. For Fabri, as for many travellers, home never seemed sweeter than in the moment when he was about to leave it; but, like the bipolar migrations of the arctic tern or the gray whale, there is a gravitational pull at both ends of the human impulse for travel that draws many of us out and back, again and again.

Fabri made several further pilgrimages and, not uncommonly with such adventures, found himself in hot water from time to time. On a visit to St Catherine's Monastery at the foot of Mount Sinai, his party ran into trouble when one of them found the place so irresistibly wonderful that they broke off a piece of St Catherine's tomb by way of a souvenir. Fabri tells us that the Abbot sent a warning that, 'if we delayed to restore it, the Arabs, into whose hands he would put the matter would see that we did so without delay.' No doubts there, then. Fortunately the fragment was duly returned and the threats disappeared into the dust. At the conclusion of that eventful trip in January 1484, when Fabri returned home to the Dominican friary in Ulm, he found the door barred. The monks inside were deep in prayer and could not hear his call. As with Odysseus returning to Ithaca, only the dog recognised his presence and greeted him, tail wagging. In this moment he must have come to the realisation shared by many other wanderers: that domestic life had continued as usual in his absence.

Fabri's initial questioning of his own motives for travel has resonance today. There is a difference between pilgrimage and sightseeing, but it is often hard to separate the two precisely. The Alliance of Religions and Conservation suggested in 2014 that the annual number of pilgrims across all faiths was in excess of 215 million, based on estimated numbers of visitors at forty significant sites, plus 10 per cent to cover all other pilgrim sites around the world—although they believed the true figure to be substantially higher. Wonderment at seeing for oneself a place of great renown is common to both secular and religious travellers. At shrines such as St Peter's in Rome, pilgrims and tourists queue together to enter the iconic Basilica, and again to visit the Sistine Chapel, not only because it is a celebrated place of worship, which it undoubtedly is, but because of the great talents who created the paintings on the walls and ceilings: Ghirlandaio, Botticelli and not forgetting Michelangelo Buonarotti. This ambiguity around where devotion stops and sightseeing begins at wondrous sites makes it difficult to calculate exact pilgrim numbers, or even to pin down motives. Faith doesn't exist in a vacuum devoid of all other impulses, and equally, simple curiosity can end up leading us to a sense of awe that takes even the secular traveller by surprise.

* * *

In June 2012, while wandering down the Cowboy Trail that runs along the eastern flank of the Canadian Rockies, as I stopped to photograph the foothills and the rolling clouds above, I was overcome by a great sobbing emotion, tears dropping like rain; the landscape in that single moment was too inexplicably and unbearably beautiful. Mountains, paintings, temples: we are moved by what we see, especially when it is like nothing else we have seen before. We are drawn to seek out those experiences, and in the fourth century CE, Ptolemy I Soter harnessed this same human impulse to establish order, authority and a new kingdom.

On 11 June 323 BCE in Babylon, after a short fever, Alexander the Great passed from this life at the age of thirty-two. At the time of his death, the great warrior and empire-builder had been in the process of establishing Alexandria, a new capital city for Egypt, his latest conquest. In the ensuing power vacuum, political control of the empire was divided between a number of

governors or satraps. Alexander's childhood friend, the trusted
and loyal warrior Ptolemy, was allotted the best share, namely
Egypt.[8] Religion was central to Egyptian culture at that time, and
before his death Alexander had gone to great lengths to establish
his personal lineage from the god Amun, implying his own divine
nature. Now Ptolemy needed to find a way to unite Egyptian and
Hellenic traditions. Just as it had helped Alexandria to win the
battles that made Alexander 'Great', pilgrimage and, more precisely, an appeal to humanity's appetite for wonder would help
Ptolemy create a firm foundation for his emerging kingdom.

It is not clear whether Serapis was Ptolemy's original creation,
or whether he simply chose to promote this deity, which bor-
rowed characteristics from both pantheons. In any event, the cult
of Serapis became central to Ptolemy's project of cultural and
religious unification. Choosing the highest point of land in
Alexandria, he set about building a temple that surpassed the
imagination, designed to attract the faithful from across the
Hellenic world. Ptolemy's strategy of wonder paid off, and in due
course the Serapeum of Helios became both Alexandria's most
important sanctuary and one of the most famous pagan temples
of Antiquity.

According to the fourth-century Christian chronicler Rufinus
of Aquileia, each side of the Serapeum was approached by more
than 100 steps, light and air flowing in through the open porti-
coes with their white marble pillars. Set within this ambitious
complex of buildings was the temple itself and this was where a
truly magical spectacle was to be seen. Herein was an image of
Serapis so huge that its right hand was touching one wall, while
its left hand touched another, and the interior walls themselves
were covered by gold, silver and bronze plates. But this was not
all. Designed by 'cunning and artistry for the astonishment and
admiration of onlookers', a small window had been positioned so
that, at a certain moment, 'a sun-beam, passing straight through

that very window, would light up the mouth and lips of Serapis to give the effect, as people watched, that Serapis was apparently receiving a kiss from the sun in salutation'. And as if this were not enough, a large piece of magnetic lodestone was set into the building, large enough and powerful enough to attract an iron sun symbol, which, when put into position, would appear to rise and hang in the air. The Serapeum was truly full of wonder and, as Ptolemy must have hoped, became the centre of a cult that spread widely across the Mediterranean in the Hellenistic and Roman periods.[9]

Aside from the Serapeum, two other unique and spectacular projects served to draw the focus from Athens to Alexandria in the early Ptolemaic age. Commissioned by Ptolemy and completed by his successor in 280 BCE, the lighthouse, or Pharos, was estimated to be 100 metres high and topped by a giant statue of Zeus. The Pharos of Alexandria was a beacon that burned day and night, its light magnified by mirrors signalling to ships far out at sea that here was place to trade; here was a city like no other. But Alexandria's most alluring siren of all was the Great Library. Ptolemy established an academy and a museum, which lured the best brains in the Hellenic world to the capital with the promise of academic freedom and a salary paid directly from the royal treasury.[10]

At the heart of this intellectual community was the greatest collection of books anywhere in the world. The Great Library of Alexandria numbered half a million papyrus rolls, many of which were acquired through theft from libraries in Athens, representing the sum of human knowledge in every subject. The wonder of this collection drew, among others, Euclid, Archimedes and the astronomer Aristarchus of Samos. On the death of Ptolemy I Soter, his son Ptolemy II hosted the first *Ptolemaia*—a trans-Hellenic festival that briefly rivalled the Olympiad. Within a century, Alexandria had become the largest city on Earth.

Library, lighthouse, temple: the city had succeeded through that special alchemy of trade, knowledge and worship that has, so many times through history, succeeded in translating ambition, curiosity and faith into political power.

\* \* \*

Like the Serapeum of Helios, the Shaolin Flying Monks Theatre in Henan, China, is designed to harness our appetite for awe, to attract pilgrims and other visitors to a place at the heart of Chinese national identity. The place is named as both the Shaolin Flying Monks Theatre and the Shaolin Flying Monks Temple, effectively eliding the two concepts of miraculous faith and broader spectacle into one. This gives a clue to the intense interface between religious traditions and secular interests in the modern age. Pilgrims spend money, but so do tourists, and perhaps the latter are more plentiful. Why not attract both? How many of the 5 million annual visitors to the Sistine Chapel are pilgrims, or even Christians, and does it matter? Was Chaucer's Wife of Bath, a widow who spent her days on endless pilgrimages to holy sites, so different from those widows and widowers who today cruise through the religious and cultural sites of the Middle East, Europe and the Americas? In this difficult question of where pilgrimage ends and tourism begins, surely what matters is the motive and experience of the individual visitor, rather than the commercial interests that may stand to benefit from their visit.

Designed by the Latvian architect Austris Mailitis, the Shaolin Flying Monks Theatre/Temple serves our desire to experience something exceptional, outside of our everyday experience—a desire that has proved over millennia to be one of the most powerful forces in attracting pilgrims. Here in this steel and stone structure, which references the surrounding forests and mountains, Buddhist monks appear to achieve levitation, although without pretence to magic or meditation: through the use of wind-tunnel technology. Aside from the stage and operational spaces common to theatres anywhere, there is a large engine room and, like the hidden lodestone in the Serapeum, this is the key to the spectacle. During performances, the vertical wind tunnel sends monks up, allowing them to achieve what no amount of meditation or physical training ever could. Describing his building, Mailitis says, 'The concept is to tell the history of Zen and Kung-Fu through artistic performances and [the] architectural image of the building itself.'[11]

Located below the Wuru Peak of Mount Song, the Shaolin Monastery has been a centre of Zen Buddhism since the fifth century CE, and this region more broadly has been a centre for Daoism (or Taoism) since at least the third century BCE. At one time, Mount Song was considered to be the centre of Heaven and Earth, and worship here was used by emperors as a way of signalling their power. The monastery was built in 496 CE by Emperor Xiaowen for an Indian Buddhist monk and teacher, Batuo; under his leadership, Shaolin grew into a major centre for scholarship and meditation. At around the same time, the Indian monk Bodhidharma arrived in China and travelled around the north, before finally settling down in Shaolin. Myths abound concerning the life of Bodhidharma, including one story that, before he entered the Shaolin monastery, he lived in a nearby cave, where he faced the wall in silence for nine years. In other accounts, he is said to have found the monks to be in poor physical shape, and kung-fu manuals published later describe him as a martial arts master who laid the foundations for Shaolin kung-fu.

Somewhere in the midst of these legends began the reality of Shaolin as a centre for meditation and the seemingly gravity-defying art of kung-fu. Now no longer unfit, the monk-warriors and temple featured in many episodes of Chinese history earned an important place in national identity. Inevitably over the centuries, the fortune of the monastery rose and fell many times, but since the late twentieth century, when the Cultural Revolution came to an end, things have started to look up once more. At the same time as the Chinese regime began to introduce economic reforms, it decided it was also time to introduce greater freedom of religious practice. In October 1978, the central government instructed that 'policies outlined in the constitution, which offer protection for religious freedom' should be implemented; and that a small number of monasteries and churches should be opened so that people 'can openly practice religion'. Religious reform continued to roll out, and by the 1980s the government was actively supporting the renovation of selected mosques, churches, monasteries and temples.[12]

In line with the fresh embrace of marketisation, it became clear that renowned Buddhist and Daoist monasteries had great potential as tourist attractions that could boost local economies. This might seem like the cynical act of a society in which religion had been suppressed for decades, but the same economic logic has been applied in Europe in the twenty-first century: routes like the Via Francigena have been revived, and new ones such as St Cuthbert's Way in England have been created in line with an EU initiative to use sacred paths as a means of stimulating tourism in rural areas. Pilgrimage is good for business, and wonder is a critical ingredient, whether it comes from the beauty of the natural landscape, as can be found along those routes, or from a spectacular destination building, as is the case in Cologne, Canterbury or Compostela.

Shaolin was an obvious candidate for renovation and in 1982 its popularity suddenly took off, largely thanks to a martial arts film distributed across mainland China. Unlike earlier cinematic kung-fu dramas, this one was filmed in the historic Shaolin Temple itself and starred a national kung-fu champion, Jet Li.[13]

Helpfully entitled *The Shaolin Temple*, the picture told the story of thirteen Shaolin monks who had assisted the Tang emperor in battle in the seventh century. The film proved to be fabulously popular, breaking all box-office records, and soon visitors from around China started to travel to Mount Song, amongst them many young people hoping to learn kung-fu. This cultural revival had got a little out of hand, and the government initially became anxious, issuing broadcasts to the effect that 'the Shaolin Temple is not as it appears in the movie'.

The year the film came out, the Shaolin Temple received 820,000 visitors; four years later, that number had risen to 1.96 million. Taking advantage of this public appetite, film-makers in both mainland China and Hong Kong created a whole new genre of cinema based on Shaolin kung-fu with titles like *Kids from Shaolin* and *Once Upon a Time in China*. There was no going back: the kung-fu craze had truly taken off, and the government looked for ways to harness the high. Martial arts boarding schools began to open up across Dengfeng county (there are now fifty of them, teaching around 70,000 students a year), and live performance became an important part of the external marketing effort. The Shaolin Warrior Monks Troupe was formed to promote both Zen Buddhism and Shaolin kung-fu, at home and abroad; the Warrior Monks were invited to Buckingham Palace and the Kremlin, to meet leaders in Africa and Latin America, and to the UN Headquarters in New York. By 2013 the Troupe had performed Shaolin kung-fu in more than eighty countries across the world. Back in Dengfeng, thousands of pilgrims and tourists continue to arrive every day, drawn by the appeal of Zen Buddhism and kung-fu, and, more recently, by the spectacle of the floating monks.

Does it matter that many of these tourists and pilgrims are motivated by *curiositas*, the natural human desire to see something legendary? Perhaps not. Sometimes seeing is believing and without our sense of wonder we would have no Golden Temple in Amritsar, nor the equally wondrous Guru ka Langar; no Imam Hussein Mosque in Karbala, nor the joy of the Arbaeen pilgrimage; no Great Library of Alexandria; no religious reform in Mount Song; no St Peter's Basilica nor the Sistine chapel—the genius of Ghirlandaio and his young apprentice Michelangelo would never have seen the light of day. As pilgrims, we strike out, to find the edge or to place ourselves in the centre, so that we can see and experience it for ourselves. Then, like Brother Fabri and millions of others before and since, we come home and say: I was there, I saw it, I was part of it.

5

# SOLACE

*'By the rivers of Babylon, we sat and wept when we remembered Zion'*

Psalm 137[1]

In the summer of 1956, the writer Jack Kerouac retreated to a remote fire lookout post, high on Desolation Peak in the Cascade Mountains of Washington State. While his literary output to date had been prolific, much of it still remained unpublished, and he was struggling both financially and psychologically. First drafted in 1951 on a single continuous scroll of paper, his manuscript for *On the Road* had been with Viking Press for many months—concerns about defamation and public decency had led to seemingly endless delays. It was not clear that these problems would ever be resolved and in February 1956, by then deeply anxious, Kerouac wrote to his agent Sterling Lord to reiterate his frustration:

Dear Sterling,

Haven't heard from Cowley yet. I feel something's wrong somewhere. Will you please mail him a copy of VISIONS OF GERARD at once, special delivery and registered, with please-forward tag, to make sure he gets it, so that he'll HAVE to write back and acknowledge something. Do that, send Cowley the Gerard ms. and make sure he gets it, and let me know you've done this to relieve my mind on this end... [Hoping] to hear from you very soon, Impatiently & down-cast—Jack Kerouac

The postscript is even more despondent:

p.s. I just keep turning out manuscripts like a machine
   and they just keep flying away into the void...
      what other writer can keep this up and not go crazy
         like I'm about to do?

      It's been going on such a long time
      and it doesn't seem like
      accidental neglect anymore.
      I'm about ready to quit.[2]

Looking for a way to break free of his demons, Kerouac had volunteered to be a summer fire-spotter, and in mid-June the call came to take up his post. Along with the other seasonal hires, Kerouac received a week's training, bought $45 worth of groceries on credit and set off, travelling first by truck, then by boat across lakes and down rivers, and finally on horseback up to the isolated lookout. Here he was to spend sixty-three days living in a one-room hut, 24 kilometres from the nearest road, surrounded only by mountains, forest and sky; his only contact with the world via a two-way radio to the area ranger, who later complained that Kerouac often turned it off in order to write. It was night when Kerouac first arrived on Desolation Peak and the interior of the hut was filthy. Outside the landscape was shrouded with fog and he began to wonder whether he could tolerate the stay here; and, if not, how he could possibly get down from the mountain.[3] Alone in the middle of the night, he awoke suddenly, his hair standing on end, to see 'a huge black monster standing in my window.' It was Mount Hozomeen. The fog had begun to clear, and he could already see the bigger picture.

Kerouac was raised Catholic, but—in common with many other Beat writers including the self-described Jewish-Buddhist Allen Ginsberg—he dabbled with eastern religious practices. In taking off to the Cascades, Kerouac was consciously following the Daoist tradition of pilgrimage to sacred mountain peaks. He kept a detailed notebook during his retreat, which provided the material for several works including *The Dharma Bums* and *Desolation Angels*. In the latter, the narrator Jack Duluoz hopes that, when he gets to Desolation Peak and is left wholly alone, he will come face to face with God, or Tathagata (Buddha), and 'find out once and for all what is the meaning of all this existence and suffering and going to and fro in vain'.

Alone on the mountain, Kerouac faced the Daoist paradox of desiring relief from desire and through his writing we feel the torture of his soul, his obsession with embracing the void and a sense of nothingness. Instead, he came 'face to face with myself, no liquor, no drugs, no chance of faking it'. Waking in the middle of one starlit night, he stared out at the Rockies and 'Hozomeen, Hozomeen, most beautiful mountain I ever seen', and every time he thought of the void he thought of this immense immutable creation.[4] Almost inevitably, his despair got worse before it could get better, and as the days and hours dragged on, he considered jumping off the mountain to put an end to it all—but he 'had no guts for such a leap'. Finally Kerouac recognised he must wait. After many days and nights of tears and pacing back and forth outside his small hut, staring at Hozomeen, it came to him that 'The void is not disturbed by any kind of ups and downs'.[5] It just is, and everything is temporary, even the mountain itself. Kerouac told himself, 'Hold still, man, regain your love of life and go down from this mountain and simply be-be-be...'

Even those of us not driven mad by drink and drugs can understand Kerouac's pursuit of peace of mind, and whether we are seeking a salve for disappointment, anxiety or grief, pilgrimage can offer a way to step outside of that everyday suffering in our normal existence. By being on the road, we are everywhere and nowhere. We are not at home, but neither are we anywhere else; we simply are. For the seventeenth-century Japanese poet, Buddhist monk and eternal wanderer Matsuo Bashō, 'each day is a journey, the journey itself home'. Bashō predates Kerouac by almost three centuries and he too was a writer looking for something on the road that cannot be found elsewhere—not least the sense of being truly alive that comes from recognising the impermanence of everything; the mountains, by their immutability, bringing the past into the present. 'Has spring come, or has the year gone?' Bashō asks.[6] Everything changes and nothing changes, and this sense of being connected to the hearts of the ancients, Bashō writes, is 'one virtue of the pilgrimage, one joy of being alive.'[7] It helps us forget the aches of our journey, even if it brings with it tears.

\* \* \*

Pilgrimage can prove a cathartic response to a heart broken by love or longing, as I found out at first hand when, as a young art student, my sapling spirit was in danger of being crushed by the merciless ivy of unrequited love. As the prospect of a summer of painful introspection stretched ahead, the road beckoned, with its timeless promise of living for the day—no past, no future, just the moment. I determined to hitchhike to Afghanistan to see the mighty Buddhas carved into the sandstone cliffs of the Bamiyan Valley. These colossal statues, 58 and 38 metres tall respectively, were once amongst the great wonders of the world,[8] and although it may seem odd in hindsight, in 1977 the desire to travel overland to see them was an aspiration shared by many young people. Wonder, liberation and perhaps even enlightenment were wrapped up in their journey; but for me it was also about solace.

Although the journey was more usually made by bus, youth and prudence have never been comfortable bedfellows. With a small canvas backpack and my equally foolish friend Angie, I set off from London. The journey most certainly helped me forget my aches and my tears, not least when we found ourselves in a dark lay-by in Bulgaria, with a Turkish truck driver wielding what looked like a pirate's cutlass and beckoning us out of his truck with a smile. We truly and viscerally feared for our lives and stayed paralysed in the cab. He disappeared briefly, and we stared out into the black void of the open door. Now what? Run or pray? The driver reappeared with a large slice of watermelon skewered on the end of the scimitar. Seems he didn't want to kill us after all; he just wanted to share his supper.

The strange incident of the cutlass in the night-time was one of many during those months on the road. We ran from snarling spike-collared shepherd dogs who chased us through a field of sunflowers in Anatolia, and later we in turn chased opportunist thieves who had stolen our jeans, hung out to dry during the interminable wait at the border crossing with Iran. This is pilgrimage. It reminds you of your mortality and makes you feel alive. And, as you recognise that you are indeed alive, it makes you grateful to be so; a perfect salve for any aching heart.

We never made it to Afghanistan, turning back once we reached Tehran, where rumours of what awaited women travellers made the blood curdle in our veins. In all, our journey meandered through eleven countries and, by the time we returned home, we had travelled thousands of miles with virtually no money. Like medieval mendicant friars, or Hindu *sadhus*, we had relied throughout on the kindness of strangers for food and somewhere to sleep, and that special pilgrimage cocktail of freedom, gratitude, adrenaline and fresh air had proved a great cure for heartache. Stepping off the cross-Channel ferry in Dover months later, I knelt down and kissed the ground, glad to be alive, and ready to live.

By March 2001, the chance to see the Bamiyan Buddhas had disappeared forever. They had been blown out of existence on the orders of an iconoclastic Taliban mullah, and all that remained were the two empty voids of rock in which they had once stood. At the time of their destruction, these immense figures had drawn Buddhist pilgrims since at least the sixth century CE, and had stood peacefully in an Islamic land for more than 1,000 years. People across the world still feel their loss. Built by the Buddhist community in Bamiyan to capitalise on the valley's position along the silk route between India and China, over time the statues' original spiritual significance had become overlaid by folk legend. One story tells how they were modelled by the survivors of Noah's Ark, a homage to God formed from clay still wet from the Flood.

In another version reported by the nineteenth-century English spy Edward Stirling,[i] the larger figure was that of the great warrior Salsal, whose people both dreaded and admired him in equal measure. Salsal saved them from defenders of Islam who sought to take over the land, but, undeterred, the retreating leaders took counsel from the Prophet. He promptly sent his son-in-law Ali to resolve the problem. As soon as Ali encountered Salsal, he saw that he was clad in chain mail belonging to Hazrat-i-Daoud (the Prophet David), on which each link was engraved with pious words from the holy book. Attack seemed impossible. How to kill Salsal without committing a crime against the Word? As is often the case with decisive legendary battles, the answer came in a dream. A spirit appeared to Ali, ordering him to fashion an arrow from tamarisk wood and then shoot it into the eye of his

---

[i] Stirling was one of many East India Company employees who travelled incognito across India, Persia and Afghanistan in the 19th century gathering information for the British Crown; see Chapter 6.

adversary. Ali followed the instructions, and the arrow met its mark. Salsal fled, but all was not lost for him or his people: Ali offered a deal. 'Accept the word of God and your eye will be restored.' And so it came to pass. Islam had arrived.[9]

In another version of the myth, two lovers separated by their families—Salsal, prince of Bamiyan, and Shamana, a princess from another kingdom—have somehow turned to stone in order to live together for eternity. This ancient and enduring theme of the grief of separation also appears in an eighteenth-century CE account of a Hajj pilgrimage by the widowed Persian aristocrat known only as 'the Wife of Mirza Khalil'. This widow turned to pilgrimage as a route to solace and healing, and set off alone from Isfahan to Damascus in the hope of joining an Ottoman convoy travelling to Mecca. She later recounted her journey through an epic 1,200-line poem. *The Song of Travel* or *Ahang-e Safar* opens with a lament in which the widow likens herself to Majnun, the ancient Persian folk hero who is driven mad by longing for his beloved Layla:

When the devious hand of fate
Bled my heart by the loss of my beloved
I was unable to sleep comfortably in bed
I had no choice but to travel
I could not sleep at night, nor rest in daytime
Until I decided to set off for pilgrimage to Ka'ba
I tightened my belt and stretched my arms
And set foot in that direction with determination
No friend or relative joined me on this visit
Like Majnun, I set off into the desert
Who needs to be aided by a friend?
Indeed God is the only friend of the lonely
I freed my heart of all fears
And took this journey as a good omen
Riding on the couch, I broke the spell of the desert
Like a bird I flew off from the branches of sorrow

Towards the House of the Unrivalled Lord
I journeyed, alone by myself, through the plains.[10]

Stopping first at the grave of her husband some 24 miles north of Isfahan, the Wife of Mirza Khalil continued onwards to Qom and to one of the most important Shia shrines, which is dedicated to the sister of Imam Reza, a descendant of the Prophet Muhammad. Today Qom attracts around 20 million pilgrims each year and is an important centre for Shia scholarship, but it is thought that Qom was a destination for pilgrims many centuries before either the Sassanid or the Islamic Empires; in that distant time, it was associated with a Zoroastrian divinity and river goddess, Anahita, who has the cult-title of Banu or 'Lady'. Anahita has the power both to bring fertility and abundance and to wreak vengeance and destruction; she is both a divinity and a personification of the mythical Sarasvati river that looms so large in Indian pilgrim traditions.[ii]

Once she arrived in Damascus, the widow joined the safety of the Ottoman convoy. But, from her account in *The Song of Travel*, we learn that there were many small prompts along the way that pricked her grief afresh, not least the simple reminders of home. The Wife of Mirza Khalil tells how, in that 'piece of Paradise' Aleppo, the people 'were kinder than one's sister, even than a mother' and that 'its similarity to Isfahan brought tears to my eyes as I remembered my own country and my children and relatives. I sighed and moaned and cried: O world! Where are you taking me to?' For the Wife of Mirza Khalil, the pilgrimage to Mecca was spurred in part by her religious duty as a Muslim, but her decision to travel at this exact moment in her life puts her motives in the same category as Jack Kerouac and many other pilgrims before or since: to face the abyss and to find a way to live.

---

[ii] See Chapter 9 for more on the Sarasvati River.

# SOLACE

On the road to Rome with my friend Constance in 2016, I met another Majnun, a man driven mad through grief and loss who had been travelling the pilgrim routes of Europe for nearly two years without respite. Erik was a Norwegian of indeterminate age, his face browned by the sun and creased as if dug from a peat bog. The thing that distinguished him from a train-hopping vagrant was that he had chosen a life on the road as a salve for his broken heart. He carried with him everything he might need, including a small stove and a bivouac bag for sleeping outdoors. His tall frame was slightly stooped from the relentless weight of his immense rucksack; but more than this, his whole body leaned forward when he moved, echoing the forward thrust seen amongst hill walkers, relentlessly striving onwards and upwards. As is ever so on the pilgrim trail, over the course of a few days we converged many times at convents and hostels along the Via Francigena, and one evening over supper Erik showed me a fistful of pilgrim 'passports', thickly inked with the stamps of churches and hostels, bearing witness to his 15,000-kilometre journey through Europe.

Once a distinguished professor living a settled work and family life, Erik's entire world had disintegrated in the course of a single year. First his only child, a daughter, went off to university in France. A short while later his wife moved out. The winter that followed was especially harsh and, with the snow still deep on the ground, both of Erik's elderly parents closed their eyes for the last time. All alone, Erik looked for consolation in the bottom of a glass. He did not find it, no matter how determinedly he drank. He found it hard to get out of bed in the morning and his students began to complain that he was constantly late, turning up unprepared and unkempt. Before too long his employers let him go. There was now nothing to keep him in Stavanger and, when the first shoots of spring appeared, Erik sold his car, locked up his home and strode out in search of solace. When we met Erik he was on the way to Rome, but his plan was to continue on from there to Jerusalem and onwards, ever onwards. I often think of him, this eternal wanderer, and wonder whether he finally found peace on the road that had become his home.

Erik was not the only sore soul we met along the Via Francigena; there were many others treading that dusty track. While we tended to our blisters in a cold convent dormitory in Acquapendente, Maria, a young Chilean woman with dark hair and even darker eyes, shared her story. As a small child she had been adopted by a wealthy Italian family and had grown up in Milan. Struggling to find her way after graduating from university, Maria had decided to find out who she really was and, with the help of her adoptive parents, had contacted her birth mother and travelled to Chile to meet her. What she discovered there confounded her. Out of her five young children, the mother had chosen only Maria, then aged two, to place for adoption. Looking at the creased family photograph Maria pulled from her notebook, it was clear that the smiling figure in the centre, then still in her twenties, had given up the most beautiful of her brood. It is just possible to imagine that this poor creature had made the ultimate sacrifice in the hope of securing a better future for her little daughter; but whatever her motive, the emotional cost had proved very high for Maria. The pain of rejection by the one person who might have held her close was too much to bear. For her the road to Rome was salted with tears and it was clear that many more would fall before she ever arrived at its gates.

For all her emotional fragility, Maria had immense personal courage. Like the Wife of Mirza Khalil, she had set out alone. While a solo pilgrimage through modern Italy may not be quite as dangerous as traversing eighteenth-century Iran and Syria, it carried a measure of risk. That evening, someone at the hostel had their pocket picked in the market square, an event that soured the general mood, and the next morning Constance and

I rose even earlier than usual when it was barely light. We stepped out into the cobbled street, pulling the heavy wooden door shut behind us. On the eponymous Via Roma that led out of town, we passed a sign boasting 'Brigands' Way'; without a further glance, we strode on into the embrace of the misty dawn.

* * *

Acquapendente was not the only place where travellers might be vulnerable to thieves, of course. Pilgrim routes across Europe and the Middle East have long been targets for bandits keen to get their hands on the purses of those who by necessity carried their wealth about their persons and as a consequence, many travelled as part of heavily protected convoys. For the Church authorities, perhaps the greatest concern was for the moral safety of women. In the Middle Ages, social norms demanded that women be closely supervised in the interests of public decency. Today, the lives of many women around the world remain just as constrained, and they cannot travel without the permission of a male relative. (A group of highly skilled Kuwaiti petroleum engineers once described to me the near impossibility of having a career in an international industry, given the need for a male chaperone.) But, as is the case now, many medieval women found ways around such constraints.

Amongst their number was Margery Kempe, the fifteenth-century mystic from King's Lynn, Norfolk, who left very detailed accounts of her travels to the Holy Land, Rome, Assisi and Compostela. Kempe dictated her story to a scribe; in common with even relatively wealthy women of the time, it appears that she did not have enough literacy to write the account for herself. In *The Book of Margery Kempe*, she refers to herself throughout in the third person as 'this creature', and a very sorry and troubled creature she seems to have been.

Her story opens with a description of a pregnancy characterised by sickness, followed by the traumatic birth of her first child. Margery was twenty years old at the time and, thinking she was not long for this world, sent for her confessor. Something was weighing heavy on her mind, but we never learn what was bothering her so profoundly: before she could complete her confession, the priest began to reprove her, and she lost the chance to unburden herself. This incomplete confession contributed to months of mental anguish that included disturbing visions of, 'as she thought, devils opening their mouths all inflamed with burning waves of fire, as if they would have swallowed her in, sometimes ramping at her, sometimes threatening her, pulling her and hauling her, night and day.' Kempe describes the raging storm of her demons and the attempts at self-harm that included biting her own hand 'so violently, that the mark was seen all her life after'.

After the storm, the calm, and the visitation of 'Our Merciful Lord Jesus Christ', who addressed her with the words 'Daughter, why hast thou forsaken Me, and I forsook never thee?', Kempe made a recovery of sorts and set herself up in business as a brewer. This enterprise failed, as did the one that followed, and the spiritual hallucinations continued. Margery Kempe went on to have a further thirteen children, finally negotiating with her husband to remain chaste within the marriage. From what Kempe herself tells us, the husband certainly seemed less committed to this course of action than his wife. In one episode, Margery recounts how, on a Midsummer Eve in very hot weather, as she was coming from York with her husband, a bottle of beer in her hand, and he with a cake tucked inside his shirt against his chest, he asked his wife to consider the following question. 'Margery, if there came a man with a sword who would strike off my head unless I would make love with you as I used to do before, tell me on your conscience—for you say you will not lie—whether you would allow my head to be cut off, or else allow me to make love with you again, as I did one time?' With great sorrow Margery replies that she would rather see him killed 'than that we should turn back to our uncleanness'.

Oh dear. This was not quite the answer Mr Kempe was looking for and, unsurprisingly, he was not willing to accept it. It was a warm Friday afternoon. They had cake, they had beer. They had opportunity. Margery prayed for guidance and, perhaps fortunately for them both, was commanded to give her husband what he wanted. Finally the two struck a deal, her inner spiritual guide acting as notary to the contract: Margery would lie with her husband one final time, eat and drink with him as they once did, and in addition would pay off all his debts. (He was clearly a keen negotiator.) In return, he agreed to release his wife to go on a pilgrimage with a clear conscience. This passionate 40-year-old religious visionary was thus relieved from her household duties (including, presumably, care for those children yet to leave home) and free to focus on her spiritual needs. Except for one small problem: Kempe received a visitation in which the Lord said to her, 'Daughter, you are with child'. It is not clear from her account whether the pregnancy arose from her midsummer amour with her husband, or through some subsequent event, but the voice of the Lord assured her, 'Daughter, don't be afraid, I shall arrange for it to be looked after'. Although we never learn the details, we are led to understand that, like the mother of our young Chilean friend Maria, Margery gave up the child in some way.

Finally, in 1413, Margery set sail from Great Yarmouth on the first leg of her journey to Jerusalem. Through her *Book*, we learn of the many visitations she received along the way, and the seemingly incessant wailing and tears that marked her piety. Sometimes she wept with contrition for her own sins, and at other times, for the sins of others. She wept with compassion at the memory of Christ's suffering, and on Sundays she wept through communion, sobbing so violently that 'many people marvelled and wondered at the grace that God worked in his creature.' Perhaps unsurprisingly, the noise of this constant keening seems to have put off Margery's fellow travellers, who, she tells us, were always trying to encourage her to be merry and, more importantly, to be quiet. At one point, in order not to be abandoned by her party, Kempe is forced to wear a 'white canvas, in the manner of a sacken apron, so that she should be held a fool and the people should not make much of her or hold her in repute'. This attempt by the pilgrim party to distance themselves from Kempe by highlighting her 'otherness' had unintended consequences. The wearing of the white sack seems to have made her look more authentically visionary and, as she notes, 'notwithstanding all their malice, she was held in more worship than they were, wherever they went.'

Margery Kempe's desire for pilgrimage was as complex as she was herself: a deeply spiritual woman, yet commercially enterprising; chaste, yet accidentally pregnant; proud of wearing great finery (as she tells us herself), but equally proud of the hairshirt she wore underneath. By the time she set out for Jerusalem she was in desperate need of respite from her own life. She had endured a disastrous marriage, borne fourteen children, set up and wrapped up two failed businesses, and barely survived several episodes of acute mental illness. In the years which followed, her many travels to shrines in Europe and the Holy Land, albeit marked by much weeping along the way, seem to have brought some solace to Margery. The determination with which she set about recording her account of life on the road, despite the handicap of illiteracy, is an enduring testament to this woman who embraced her misery and found a way to live despite it. When the fifteenth-century manuscript of her book resurfaced in 1934 after years of languishing in a private collection, it was heralded as the earliest surviving autobiographical writing in English. In this regard Kempe was every bit as radical as Kerouac. These two troubled souls who lived five centuries apart both bared their torments through writing; but, more than this, both found solace through the act of pilgrimage.

* * *

Kerouac's meditation on the mountain culminates in the counterpoint between his own weakness and the strength of the natural world around him: 'my God look at Hozomeen, is he worried or tearful? Does he bend before storms or snarl when the sun shines or sigh in the late day drowse?' This same theme of cosmic power versus personal frailty reappears in the hopes of women pilgrims some 10,000 miles further down the same fold in the Earth's crust; the fold that forms the spine of America, North and South. Not far from the city of Cochabamba lies Quillacollo, one of Bolivia's most important pilgrimage sites. Here, the high point of the year is the *fiesta* which takes place over three days in mid-August, when tens of thousands of pilgrims come from across the country to take part in a festival to honour the Virgin of Urkupiña. Like many such events, this coincides with more ancient rites related to the agricultural cycle of planting and harvest, and blends old and new beliefs—in this case, marking the Ascension of the Virgin Mary and expressing reverence for Pachamama, the powerful cosmological time–space force sometimes known as Mother Earth.

According to Catholic tradition, soon after the arrival of the Spanish Conquistadors in the sixteenth century CE, the Virgin Mary appeared to an Aymara shepherd girl who was tending her sheep on a hill near Quillacollo. The Virgin told the girl to gather stones from the hillside and take them home. By the time she came down, the stones had turned to silver, and the girl's family were poor no longer. When asked of the whereabouts of the Virgin, the shepherd girl responded in Quechua, her native language: '*Urqupiña.*' She is in the hill. This Virgin of Urkupiña embodies both the gentle compassion of the Virgin Mary and the unpredictable Pachamama, whose power over the forces of earth, water, sun and moon is equally capable of bringing good fortune or bad luck.

Pilgrimage to the Virgin of Urkupiña's shrine brings a very particular solace to thousands of Bolivian women. A 2007 survey revealed that seven out of every ten of them are subject to physical violence, most of it at the hands of their male partners. Unlike the relatively wealthy Margery Kempe, who abandoned her unhappy marriage with no regard for her personal reputation, these women are trapped by the double bind of economic necessity and social convention. According to Dutch social scientist Sanne Derks, women pilgrims draw on the spiritual powers of the Virgin, who is 'not only venerated for her capacity to endure suffering, but also as a powerful goddess of vengeance.'[11]

Many beseech her to change the behaviour of their husbands, to stop the violence or to avenge their suffering. Derks's study at the Urkupiña shrine includes the account of a female pilgrim who sees the hand of the Virgin in her husband's unfortunate fate: 'I have begged Urkupiña for years to intervene in my marriage. My husband was a tailor, and now he is becoming blind. I think it is Mary's punishment for being such a bad husband all those years.' Whatever we might think of this vengefulness, pilgrimage seems to bring comfort and strength to these women whose world is shaped by violence.

In the manner of Ancient Greece's Delphi and Dodona, requests at the Urkupiña shrine are made via an intermediary, here known as a *yatiri* or 'one who knows'.[12] Rituals vary but can include the burning of miniature fake money or incense and orations to the Virgin, and, in reference to the original legend, typically involve the mining and blessing of local rocks. The symbolic power of rocks in the legend of Quillacollo is not unique, nor is their role in pilgrimage. The Stoning of the Devil or *ramy al-jamarat* is part of the annual Hajj ritual. Muslim pilgrims throw pebbles at three walls (formerly pillars) called *jamarat*, in the city of Mina just east of Mecca. It is a symbolic re-enactment of the story of Abraham, who stoned three pillars while wrestling with the temptation to disobey God and preserve his son Ishmael. Catholics who climb Croagh Patrick in Ireland often carry a stone that they leave on a cairn to mark their passage; along the foreshore of Lindisfarne Island, deliberate piles of pebbles, large and small, stand to await the tide.

There are scores of other possible examples. Most recently, in the gardens of the Yad Vashem Holocaust Remembrance Centre in Jerusalem, I encountered a line of small stones picked up from the path and arranged by visitors. It raised the question yet again of why stone or rock is so ubiquitous in pilgrimage. Perhaps, as with Kerouac's contemplation of Mount Hozomeen, a stone in its immutability helps us embrace the inconsequential and temporary nature of our own travails, against the infinite and enduring universe. There is some comfort in that: by placing the pebble on the cairn, we can at least say, 'Here is my mark, I passed this way once'. Equally, the act of carrying a pebble and then leaving it behind at the end of a pilgrimage can mark the moment of letting go of your problems, releasing the sorrow that drove your journey in the first place.

Much of the original Via Francigena route through Tuscany and Lazio is now gleaming highway, and those travelling on foot, including myself and Constance, are often sent meandering through the countryside along a network of bridleways and footpaths. At times, however, the Via rejoins its ancient course and here it is possible to glimpse, through the rough scree of the rural tracks, the original granite sets of roads built many hundreds of years earlier. Ascending the steep path to the medieval hill fort of Radicofani, the sight of these Roman cobbles beneath the dust prompts the relief that comes from truly accepting that, while much remains the same, everything is temporary: time rolls on.

For some, the feeling that all is meaningless sends them into deeper darkness, but for others it promises a great sense of relief.

When we set out for Rome, Constance and I were not, like Kerouac, hoping to find God, or the meaning of life; nor were we driven by the grief of heartaches long since passed. We simply wanted to go on a pilgrimage and to understand what that might mean. Almost everything about the journey was unforeseen—we had no itinerary, just a path and a destination—but the greatest surprise, for me at least, was the solace that came from facing my own insignificance. After days of walking, of letting the mind do its work without questioning, of looking up at the sky and down at my feet, this was a moment of recognition; a sliver of light. Rock endures, and through its essential nature expresses the infinite. Rupert Brooke captures this in his poem 'Dust', imagining an endless future in which

> We'll ride the air, and shine, and flit,
> Around the places where we died,
>
> And dance as dust before the sun,
> And light of foot, and unconfined,
> Hurry from road to road, and run
> About the errands of the wind.
>
> And every mote, on earth or air,
> Will speed and gleam, down later days,
> And like a secret pilgrim fare
> By eager and invisible ways,
>
> Nor ever rest, nor ever lie
> Till, beyond thinking, out of view,
> One mote of all the dust that's I
> Shall meet one atom that was you.[13]

6

## REDEMPTION

'*I travelled among unknown men*
*In lands beyond the sea;*
*Nor, England! did I know till then*
*What love I bore to thee.*'

William Wordsworth[1]

On 12 July 1174, crowds of onlookers gathered as the King of England, barefoot and dressed in sackcloth, made his way from St Dunstan's Church through Canterbury, to the crypt of St Thomas Becket. Here he would be whipped by the bishops, abbots and eighty monks present as he lay prostrate and naked by the Martyr's tomb. Henry II had long been held responsible for the murder of Becket, the Archbishop of Canterbury hacked to death as he knelt in prayer in the Cathedral. Almost immediately after the deed was done, ripples of revulsion and devotion spiralled out across Christendom and, within weeks of the murder, miracles of healing were reported. Almost four years later, vials of the Martyr's blood were still proving popular amongst pilgrims who continued to arrive in their thousands; some travelling on foot from across England, others braving the Channel in small boats.

In the immediate aftermath of the crime, Henry had protested his innocence, but the controversy refused to disappear. Rather than resolving the power struggle between Crown and Mitre in Henry's favour, the martyrdom of Thomas Becket further amplified the influence of the Church. Fearing the ultimate sanction of excommunication by the Pope, this public act of penance was the king's final desperate bid for political survival. To make matters worse, his eldest son, Henry the 'Young King', had risen up against him, along with young Henry's brothers Richard and Geoffrey and their mother, Eleanor of Aquitaine. The Young King had promised his neighbouring allies land and revenues; thus suitably motivated, they begin to attack his father's kingdom from all sides. In this Great Revolt, William the Lion, King of the Scots, stood to get Northumberland—but it was not to be. The day after Henry II's pilgrimage of penance in Canterbury, word reached him that William had been defeated and captured. Some took it as a sign of divine intervention, and the tide began to turn once again in King Henry's favour.

On 7 July 1220, fifty years after his death, Becket's remains were moved to a specially built shrine within the Cathedral. The act of moving the martyr's bones to the Trinity Chapel was marked by a huge public celebration, which had been two years in the planning. The Church authorities made a proclamation throughout Europe, adding by way of incentive that hay and provender were to be provided along all the routes to Canterbury on the day of the festivities, and that wine was to be distributed gratis from barrels placed at each of the four entrances to the city. It was a masterful act of promotion for the Church, and 7 July was to become a widely celebrated feast day for decades to come. As importantly, the initial festival not only ensured the popularity of Becket's shrine but provoked an outpouring of generosity from the rich and powerful across Europe, who gave jewels and valuable reliquaries and signed up to pay annual fees to the Cathedral.

Here then was the prize of penance: redemption and a new beginning. Public penance was a common act in medieval Europe; it demonstrated the acceptance of guilt and, equally importantly, submission to the ecclesiastical authorities.[2] The dramatic device of making a pilgrimage in bare feet, sackcloth and ashes, as Henry had done, was all part of the performance. (Expressing contrition via the privacy of the confessional box would come much later.)[3] What began as a personal matter between the individual and their priest, or indeed their God, ultimately became institutionalised. By the thirteenth century, pilgrimage was readily meted out as a penalty to those who had transgressed against the rules. It was a form of ritual exile which often involved head-shaving and the wearing of yellow or red crosses sewn onto garments to enhance the shame of the penitent and alert others to the heretics in their midst. One great advantage of this form of punishment was that it removed offenders from society, without the cost of maintaining them in prison. Sometimes the sentence included being sent to multiple shrines, some local, others distant, such as Canterbury, Compostela or Rome, with a schedule set for completion of the deed. Pilgrims were often required to bring back official documents as evidence that they had gone the full distance, and this tradition continues today in the shape of the paper passports issued by the fraternities supporting pilgrims on the Via Francigena, the Camino de Santiago and other overland routes.

In May 2017, after returning from my pilgrimage to Rome with Constance, my stamped passport and Testimonium from Rome neatly filed, I settled back into my study at home, Marsh Acres. The journey had been inspiring, uplifting, illuminating even; but I was still grappling with some of the questions that had been there at the very start of this quest. Why are humans so drawn to this practice of setting out for a place of special significance? Where does the balance of meaning lie between the journey and the destination? Why do certain places have such potency? Why do we need physical objects or locations to spark spiritual feeling?

I picked up a piece of bleached animal bone from the window ledge and held it up for scrutiny. As it had done many times before, this object magically transported me to the moment when I found it in the dusty desert of the Central Kalahari Game Reserve. My study is littered with such objects—a small jar of frankincense resin from Damascus, the tiny steel silhouette of a horse by the Israeli artist Zadok Ben-David, given to me when we worked together years ago. All these objects have the power to evoke a moment, a person or an emotion, and Marsh Acres itself is a testament to the potency of place, that indefinable quality that led the ancients to travel to Dodona and Delphi, Mecca and Jerusalem.

Once the home of the German poet and translator Michael Hamburger, this house gave me a strange feeling when I first entered it of belonging there, a real and tangible sense at the exact moment of crossing the threshold. We didn't realise it then, but Marsh Acres features in *The Rings of Saturn*, a literary work by Hamburger's fellow countryman W.G. Sebald, and this same powerful atmosphere of familiarity had struck Sebald many decades before when he wrote, 'on my first visit to Michael's house I instantly felt as if I lived or had once lived there, in every respect precisely as he does ... as if the spectacles cases, letters and writing materials ... had once been my spectacles cases, my letters and my writing materials.'[4] Ostensibly about a long walk in the country, *The Rings of Saturn*, which is neither a novel nor a travelogue, is a journey into the human condition, a pilgrimage of sorts—and perhaps a quest for redemption.

# REDEMPTION

The Hamburgers, along with their friends the Freuds, had left Germany in 1933 at the dawn of the Third Reich and, over time, strands of both families had migrated to the Suffolk coast. The house was marked by their common history and by Michael's wider connection to a German diaspora: when we first came to view Marsh Acres, a faded void above the hearth framed the place where a sketch by Lucian Freud had once hung; next to it, an etching of a flounder by Günter Grass. There were 40,000 books stacked on shelves, window sills and every other horizontal surface, and letters and notes for poems escaped from the open filing cabinet in the library. More than this, the fabric of the house itself had remained essentially unchanged for almost a century. 'We liked it the way it was when we bought it,' said Michael's widow, Anne Beresford. 'Besides, Michael couldn't tolerate disturbances of any kind.' Even the gardener had to come in the afternoon while Michael was napping and, taking care not to crack any branches, attempt to cut back in total silence the trees and shrubs that wrapped the house in a perpetual gloom.

Diligently pointing out every drawback (including the perilous electrical wiring), Anne warned us, 'You will get pilgrims, and they can be a nuisance.' These visitors came not just because of Michael's reputation as a poet, or indeed her own, but very largely because of *The Rings of Saturn*. In Sebald's account of his walk across East Anglia, which includes his visit to Marsh Acres, the German Gentile Sebald merges his own identity with that of the Jewish Hamburger as he attempts to make sense of events in Europe in the twentieth century. There is a dreamlike quality to Sebald's prose and the narrative somehow floats across the landscape, touching down from time to time in physical locations, such as Dunwich or Orford—vignettes that are nominally related to the geography through which he travels.

When I discussed the book with Anne, she pointed out the liberties Sebald had taken in his encounter with Michael at

Marsh Acres. She noted his account of stopping at the village shop, which had in fact been closed for decades, to buy a can of Cherry Coke, which he drained 'at a draught like a cup of hemlock', and of Michael making a pot of tea for a visitor—something, she said, he had never done in his life. Of their parting, Sebald writes,

> As Anne was talking, we had walked out together into the garden, where night had already fallen. We waited for the taxi beside the Hölderlin pump, and by the faint light that fell from the living-room window into the well I saw, with a shudder that went to the roots of my hair, a beetle rowing across the surface of the water, from one dark shore to the other.

Despite being set in a landscape noted for its big open skies and clear, cool coastal light, Sebald's pilgrimage is very dark indeed, and an epigraph to the first edition gives us a clue to what lies ahead.[5] Quoting Joseph Conrad's description of those who witnessed the horrors of the Belgian slave trade in the Congo, it reads, 'One must, above all, pardon those unhappy souls who have chosen to make the pilgrimage on foot, who trade along the riverbank and see without understanding the horror of the conflict, the joy of the victors, nor the profound despair of the defeated.'[6]

The power of the prose that follows carries us from one sensation to the next, whether melancholy or wonder, remorse or disgust; and, by this means, we are drawn into Sebald's journey. Together we stumble forward over the rock-strewn topography in search of an answer to the central question of the book: how could the highly evolved civilisation of Western Europe, with its post-Enlightenment principles and great technological prowess, at the same time provide the conditions for systematic extermination of the greater part of European Jewry? In 1933, when the Freud and Hamburger families left Germany, the persecution had already begun; by the end of the war the Germans and their collaborators had murdered 6 million Jews and many millions of others.

More than the fictionalised account of tea-making and imagined hemlock draughts, Anne was discomfited in part by Sebald's assumption of cultural equivalence between himself and Michael, but it is exactly through this device of creating a wider inhumanity that Sebald searches for redemption. In *The Rings of Saturn* we encounter many gross acts of barbarism, including the working to death of thousands of women in Germany's slave labour system; the slavery of men who toiled to build the Congo railway; and the casual sadism of everyday life, as illustrated by the deliberate mutilation of live herrings by the inspector of Rouen Fish Market. Through these and other digressions in his pilgrim tale, Sebald invites the reader to consider the cruelty and neglect, the folly and excess of human nature, and to share culpability.

Hamburger was a great admirer of Sebald; unconcerned by his fusing the documentary with the imagined, Michael considered that 'it is the transformation of everything he touches that makes "Max" Sebald a magical and fascinating writer.'[7] In many respects Hamburger remained an alien throughout his life: an ardent communist[i] in rural England, a German writing in English, a Jew who had never set foot in a synagogue.[8] But despite his retreat into the bookish chaos of Marsh Acres, he remained connected to the literary world, not least through his orchard. He cherished rare apple varieties and friends often arrived with the gift of a sapling, or sometimes just a few seeds. Through the window of my study at Marsh Acres, I can see my favourite apple tree, which—despite its advancing age—gives an abundant crop each autumn. It was grown from a Devonshire Quarrenden, picked in Ted Hughes's orchard, and each spring the pale pink blossom

---

[i] When we moved into Marsh Acres, the cat's basket had been left behind, the name 'Trotsky Hamburger' stuck on the front.

comes alive with bees. On the return from Rome, with pilgrimage still in the front of my mind, the mesmeric thrum of the bees transported me to the West Country, and in through the window of a remote farmhouse on the edge of Exmoor.

\* \* \*

Here, in an armchair, the poet Samuel Taylor Coleridge once drifted in an opium-induced reverie, his head bent forward over an open book. Behind the flicker of his eyelids, his mind glided through the first imaginings of one of his most enduring poems, *Kubla Khan*. It begins:

> In Xanadu did Kubla Khan
> A stately pleasure-dome decree:
> Where Alph, the sacred river, ran
> Through caverns measureless to man
> Down to a sunless sea.

The volume open on Coleridge's insensible lap at this moment was *Purchas his Pilgrimage*, and herein was the retelling of Marco Polo's encounter with Kublai Khan, the Mongol leader whose magnificent excess was legendary.[9] It was almost twenty years before *Kubla Khan* appeared in print, but Coleridge's other great work conceived at this time was published almost immediately. It tells of crime, remorse and the quest for redemption. At the time of his opium dream, Coleridge was living in Nether Stowey in Somerset. In July of 1798, he was joined by his friends William and Dorothy Wordsworth and all three embarked on a walking tour along the coast, from Alfoxden to Lynton, a distance of around 33 miles. The two men conceived the idea of co-writing a poem to defray the expenses of the trip and began work on the project as they walked. Wordsworth reported that

> Much of the greatest part of the story was Mr Coleridge's invention:
> but certain parts I suggested; for example, some crime was to be

committed which should bring upon the Old Navigator, as Coleridge afterwards delighted to call him, the spectral persecution, as a consequence of his crime and his own wanderings.

However, it soon became apparent that the two Romantics' differences in approach to writing would make the exercise impossible. Wordsworth immediately stepped back from 'an undertaking upon which I could only have been a clog', leaving Coleridge to press on with the poem alone.[10]

In *The Rime of the Ancient Mariner*, the eponymous narrator tells of the events that led him to slay the albatross, and the terrible consequences of this crime against nature. Without the bird to guide it, the ship drifts in the windless seas; one by one the crew die of thirst. The curse of the Ancient Mariner is that he does not die, but is condemned to wander eternally, endlessly recounting his tale, in order to gain relief from his guilt. The Mariner first makes his appearance at a wedding, as guests enter the church:

Forthwith this frame of mine was wrenched
With a woeful agony,
Which forced me to begin my tale;
And then it left me free.

We have all encountered an Ancient Mariner at some point, whether on the pilgrim trail or elsewhere: a stranger who must tell their story at every turn, in the hope of getting some relief from suffering they have caused or which they must endure. At the wedding breakfast of two friends, I encountered such a Mariner. Soon after the guests sat down to eat, and before the speeches had begun, the man to my right, a stranger, embarked unbidden upon a tragic and moving lament. One bright winter's morning, with hard frost still on the ground, his wife had taken their two dogs out walking. Choosing a footpath that ran alongside the nearby riverbank, she had somehow lost her balance and fallen into the freezing current. Despite being a strong swimmer, she had perished instantly, automatic reflexes causing immediate inhalation on contact with the water. The husband had been abroad at the time, and his absence from the scene, his helplessness to save his beloved wife, only added to his grief. As I listened to the widower's tale, my tears began to well, not only because of the events he described, but because it was clear that, like Coleridge's Mariner, this man was condemned to recount the story to everyone he met, in some compulsive hope of purging his 'woeful agony'.

\* \* \*

The notion of achieving catharsis or redemption through wandering or pilgrimage is an ancient one, but it carries with it a dark shadow. The very word vagabond, which we associate with bandit and brigand, derives from the Latin *vagus:* the wanderer or fugitive. When Coleridge placed his Ancient Mariner at that most intimate of community gatherings, a wedding, he was aiming deep into our fear of the outsider—a stranger who by their very presence may threaten what we value most. One such example is the spectre of the Wandering Jew, condemned to roam the earth until the second coming of Christ. This figure appeared in European folklore sometime in the Middle Ages and there were supposed sightings of him as late as the sixteenth century.[ii] By the time the *Ancient Mariner* was written in the late eighteenth century, the myth was enjoying a revival: Coleridge himself had already begun work on *The Wanderings of Cain*, a poem he was never to finish, and within a few years, Shelley had penned *The Wandering Jew* (1810), about a figure forced to roam

---

[ii] Despite the anti-Semitic overtones of the medieval legend, it is possible that it has earlier roots in the Norse figure of Odin.

'until the dead // Hear the last trump and leave the tomb'. We will always treat the wanderer, the 'other', with suspicion, even when, like the Mariner, they are calling for compassion. This moral conundrum is played out today in our response to the refugee crisis in Europe, as we despair over the fate of migrants drowning in the Mediterranean, while at the same time bolting our doors firmly against them.

Setting out one Sunday to walk the pilgrim path from Canterbury to Dover, my thoughts soon turned to those families who were waiting across the Channel in the shanty town of tents outside Calais, many of whom had carried their young children over great distances in search of a safe haven. My compassion was very real in the moment, but such empathy is both abstract and cost-free, and carried no measure of redemption. Others have taken more direct action, and the tradition of pilgrimage across the chalk Downs of southern England has played a part. In 2015, human rights activists Anna Pincus and David Herd mobilised asylum seekers, ex-detainees and volunteers to walk the Old Pilgrims' Way in the south of England. Their aim was to highlight the plight of refugees being held indefinitely in Kent's detention centres. Reimagining Chaucer's *Canterbury Tales*, the group stopped each night in barns and church halls, where they held readings of stories about what it means to be a refugee in Europe. At the time of writing, this project, Refugee Tales, has become an annual event, with some of the greatest storytellers of our age lending their unique talents in support of those who are yet to taste freedom.[11]

My own opportunity for action of sorts came when I was invited, along with my Catholic friend Miriam, to teach at a summer school run by a charity in Northern Lebanon.[12] Upon arriving in the country, we first travelled to the Maronite Monastery of Qozhaya, which hangs off the steep sides of the Qadisha Valley. It is remote and difficult to get there, but worthwhile for the tranquillity that awaits. The monks here have retreated from the strife of this very troubled land, spending their days in prayer and cultivating the fruit and vegetables on which they depend. Here and there, small hermitages are cut into the rock itself for those who seek complete isolation.

Miriam and I spent a few days in quiet contemplation walking amongst the peach and apple orchards. Coming out of Vespers one evening, we met an elderly woman keen to share her story. Despite her evident ill health, she had come far to give thanks for a prayer answered: her son and his wife had been delivered of a child after many barren years. There were other pilgrims here too, including a young man who had arrived on foot along the Lebanon Mountain Trail, which passes this way. He was a lost soul, searching for something more meaningful than working as a waiter in the UAE or Beirut. Later that month, our journey took us further north, to Bkarzla and to the communal house where we would live for the next few weeks. There Miriam and I met three young Syrian refugees who had endured acute hardship and danger in their flight from Damascus. Detained by security forces on the border between Syria and Turkey, they had been held in a camp high in the mountains with nothing to eat and nowhere to sleep, at one point burning what few belongings they had in the hope of keeping warm. They had watched children younger than themselves perish through cold and hunger, and their story brought home what Sebald had tried to convey in *The Rings of Saturn*: that cruelty and injustice are part of our shared human story, and we are all in need of redemption, pilgrims or not.

In the twelfth century, two mendicant Christian orders arose out of this sense of shared responsibility. The Dominicans (founded by Dominic de Guzman) and the Franciscans (founded by Francis of Assisi) were seen by many as socially subversive at the time, not just because of their rejection of material wealth, but also because of their consequent inability to pay taxes. The son of a wealthy silk merchant, as a young man Francis of Assisi lived the high life typical of any spoilt scion, but as he grew into manhood, the stark inequalities between rich and poor gave his sweet pleasures a bitter taste. He made a pilgrimage to Rome, joining the poor begging at St Peter's Basilica; later, while praying in the semi-derelict chapel of San Damiano near Assisi, he had a vision of Christ that led him to offer his father's money to repair the chapel. Perhaps unsurprisingly, Francis's father was outraged, and when he finally got his hands on his son, he locked him up in a small storeroom. The filial dispute eventually concluded when Francis renounced his father and his inheritance before the Bishop of Assisi, stripping himself naked as a symbol of this renunciation. A friend provided him with the robe, girdle and staff of a pilgrim and Francis went forth into the Umbrian countryside, preaching peace and penance.

Francis soon attracted eleven followers, and he asked these 'friars' to adhere to one simple rule: to live a life of austerity, with no possessions, and to beg for food while preaching. They travelled to Rome to ask permission from Pope Innocent III to create the Franciscan Order. Despite some opposition to the principle of a mendicant order, Francis won the approval of the Pope and this marked the beginning of what was soon to become one of the fastest growing religious orders of the age. After years of toil and adherence to the vows of poverty, Francis received the ultimate sign of his purgation: during a forty-day fast on the mountain La Verna, the stigmata—the five wounds of Christ on the Cross—appeared on his body. This was to herald Francis's end, and after much suffering, he was brought back to a hut next to the tiny Chapel of Porziuncola and it is here that St Francis died in 1226. After his death, it was claimed that pilgrims to the chapel would receive the benefit of a plenary indulgence, the reduction of the time spent in purgatory for sins during life. The

'Pardon of Assisi' proved to be a popular draw, paradoxically resulting in great influence and wealth for a shrine which marked a life devoted to penance and poverty.

The idea of finding salvation by living the life of an ascetic appears in many faiths, but the figure of the indigent holy man, answering to none but his God, seems to attract suspicion and hostility almost wherever and whenever it occurs. This is as true of the *sadhus* of India today as it was in the early days of the Franciscan order. Written more than a century after the death of St Francis, Chaucer's 'Summoner's Prologue' conveys a view prevalent in his time that, despite their apparent poverty and life of penance, friars were amongst the worst scoundrels of the age, essentially using the pretence of collecting alms to enrich themselves while avoiding the need for work:

> You will permit me to begin my tale
> How familiar this friar is with hell!
> And, Lord knows, that's little cause for wonder;
> Friars and fiends are not so far asunder.

The Summoner continues with some rather graphic language about a friar arriving in Hell who looks around and, seeing no others, presumes himself to be the only one of his kind. The guiding angel quickly disabuses him, and lifts up Satan's tail to reveal 'The place where all the friars have their nest'.

Chaucer was writing in the late fourteenth century, a time when travel was very constrained and most people's lives were heavily scrutinised by the Church; it is therefore hardly surprising that there was deep-seated antipathy towards those who were free to roam. Added to this, by the time of Henry VIII's Dissolution of the Monasteries in the 1530s, the population of monks in England, for example, had proliferated to the extent that they were in effect an independent class, answerable to the heads of their orders or houses rather than directly to the bishops. Even less accountable to higher authority were the mendicant orders, who—with the licence to evangelise the masses and to beg while doing so—walked the land largely unsupervised. This was not only a matter of jealousy, but also of prejudice: the fact that pilgrimage was often given as the punishment for moral crimes cast a shadow of suspicion on any religious wanderer. Many were the friar's robes concealing an indolent who had chosen a life of begging over one of toil, or a free spirit who had chosen discomfort over responsibility to others. But many other mendicant friars were true penitents, the ultimate embodiment of the commitment to redemption through their asceticism.

* * *

Mendicant friars were not the only wanderers on the pilgrim trail who were not always quite what they claimed to be: the pilgrim's mantle offered a perfect cover for political infiltration into foreign lands. In the late nineteenth century, Russia and Britain were locked in the political and diplomatic struggle to control Afghanistan and surrounding territories that became known as the Great Game. Both empires sent spies (like Edward Stirling from Chapter five) to carry out surveys and seek out the mineral wealth concealed within the rocky folds of the Himalayas. The mountains and deserts of these lands were hostile and often inaccessible, but perhaps the most difficult place to penetrate was Tibet. The players of the Great Game wanted to know what lay within this hidden valley, but Tibet remained closed to Europeans throughout the century, the Lhasan authorities believing that foreign interests in the region represented a threat to the Buddhist faith and to the Buddhist state itself. Despite many attempts by both Russian and British surveyors, very few managed to reach Lhasa's inner sanctum. But there was a strong will to succeed, and it was only a matter of time before the way would present itself.

The restrictions on foreigners visiting Tibet extended to some Buddhist pilgrims of Asian origin, but not all, and the British sent several surveyor spies, typically disguised as pilgrims from India. Russia, too, was looking for a way in. Within its empire there were two ethnic groups that might prove a source for effective spies: the Buryats from Siberia and the Kalmyks from the north-western shores of the Caspian Sea. Each of these Mongol communities adhered to Tibetan Buddhism and pilgrims from both groups had successfully completed the arduous round trip to Lhasa. But their personal and spiritual travelogues were of little value to the Russian authorities. Then, in 1898, Gombozhab Tsybikov, a Buryat student at the University of St Petersburg, sent one of his professors a manuscript he thought might interest him. It was a lama's account of a journey through Nepal and Tibet. The professor promptly responded by suggesting that Tsybikov attempt such a journey himself, as soon as he had completed his studies.

Tsybikov's father had long held the ambition that one of his sons would devote himself to secular knowledge, another to religious knowledge; but, following a series of misfortunes, now only one son remained. The opportunity to travel as a pilgrim-scholar enabled Tsybikov to fulfil his father's dream. The timing proved almost perfect. Dorzhiev, a Buryat emissary of the Dalai Lama, had just travelled to St Petersburg to ask for help in repelling the steady encroachments of the British, bringing a fresh rapport between Russia and Tibet. Within months Tsybikov was formally commissioned by the Imperial Russian Geographical Society to undertake the expedition, and he started out for his Siberian homeland of Buryatia to look for a suitable travelling companion. This proved fruitless and Tsybikov pressed on to Urga (now Ulaanbaatar). It was from here that he set out in earnest in November 1899, with four hired camels and a party of Mongol grain traders.

While Tsybikov's primary motive was to gather intelligence, he nevertheless described himself as a devout pilgrim and behaved as such, taking care not to draw the attention of local inhabitants. Where possible, he stayed in Buddhist monasteries, recording in detail the customs of the monks. One such monastery, in the Kangyap-tan (Snowy Plain), was known as Labrang Tashi Kyil (Swirl of Blessings). Here the most venerated object of worship was an enormous gilded copper statue of the Maitreya, the Buddha of the Future World, who Lamaist Buddhists believe will be 80 feet tall. But it was the culture of extreme discipline here that proved most startling to the Buryat spy. Every morning the monks came together in an assembly where they faced scrutiny over their actions and where any transgressions were dealt with immediately with the cane. As is so often the case with licensed flogging, it was considered a sign of great fortitude not to cry with pain or to ask for mercy. Attendance at the assembly was not compulsory, but it seems that monks came along in order to receive their daily ration of butter.[iii] Those whose transgressions demanded permanent exile from the community were flogged in the marketplace, before being dragged by their legs out of town.

At certain times of the year, some monks retreated to the roofs of their houses, there to recite the texts they had learnt by heart; meanwhile, the kitchen staff 'poured' the tea for the next day. This ritual of repeatedly lifting and pouring the mixture of tea, butter and milk in and out of the cauldron was said to improve its flavour, but more than this, it was a form of devotion in which the mantra '*Om mani padme hum*' was chanted over and over. The phrase's exact meaning is contested, but one literal translation attributed to the fifth Dalai Lama is 'O, you who have the jewel

---

[iii] This 'butter and cane' system has its equivalent in the British navy's rule of discipline, 'rum and the lash'. Flogging was not officially suspended in the Royal Navy until 1871, as MPs argued over how discipline might be enforced without the sharp sting of the whip.

and the lotus'. In the Chenrezig yogic tradition, each of the six syllables represents a 'perfection': generosity, ethics, patience, diligence, renunciation and wisdom. All of these self-improving qualities were embodied in this ritual of remixing.

On his arrival in Lhasa, Tsybikov observed another elaborate ritual in which much butter and many delicacies were added to a large cauldron of tea. In Tibetan society, the official Nechung Oracle plays an important role, providing insight and guidance to the Dalai Lama. Tsybikov described how, in this ceremony, and in the presence of many priests and monks, the oracle fired a single arrow towards the east. The oracle then called down the wrathful *chokyon* deities and, in a special rite ordered by the Tibetan government, the cauldron was emptied into a pit—a punishment for the Buddhist deities' negligence in the Boxer Uprising against the enemies of the Chinese emperor. The deities were then expected to exact their revenge against those same enemies in retribution for the loss of the delicious tea, thus protecting Tibet. The ritual pouring out of the tea was divine penance for past defeat; redemption might come if the *chokyons* saw to it that the next war was won.

A few weeks later, Tsybikov finally got his opportunity to venerate the Dalai Lama. We learn that he paid in advance a sum of eight *liangs* of silver and, on the day, climbed the main sets of stairs in the Potala Palace, which led to a bare unfurnished room. Here he waited for hours with other pilgrims until his turn came. Among their number was a married couple who had travelled from the remote Mongol saltmarshes of Tsaidam. Not part of a caravan, they had been readily attacked by bandits; their horses and all their belongings had been stolen, and they themselves had been left to die, covered in wounds. It seems that they had not volunteered to make the perilous trek to Lhasa, but rather had been obliged to do so as an act of penance. The husband had seduced his neighbour's wife and, like the European penitent pilgrims, the arduous and expensive journey was his punishment. (His wife, it would seem, was being doubly injured both by and for her husband's infidelity.)

Eventually, Tsybikov and the other patient pilgrims were asked to line up in single file, and,

> After about ten minutes, during which the interpreter again repeated the rules of the coming ceremony, we were led into the hall, which turned out to be a large room ... A tall throne was placed directly opposite the door and facing towards it. On this the Dalai Lama sat in the eastern manner wrapped in the yellow cloak called the *gyanshi* ... His head was covered with a pointed yellow hat of the *Tsongkhapa* type.

On either side of the throne stood a retinue of four or five people, including two imposing bodyguards. As soon as they entered the room, Tsybikov and the other pilgrims were chivvied along, being physically hustled if they dawdled too long. After they got close to the Dalai Lama, they hastily performed three prostrations and then, holding symbolic offerings in their outstretched hands, approached the throne. The Lama reached out to touch them, as if accepting these offerings, which were then whisked away.

The Dalai Lama was then 'handed a cord made of a band of some silk material; he tied a knot and, after breathing on it', placed it on Tsybikov's neck; the knotted cord was a talisman to protect its wearer from misfortunes. There followed some ritualistic tea-drinking and a brief enquiry (via an interpreter) into the pilgrims' journey before they were hustled out. 'With whips in their hands the two immense bodyguards shoved us out and shouted, in the presence of the Dalai Lama, "Get out quickly!" We understandably ran out in some confusion and went home. The whole ceremony had not lasted even ten minutes.' Reading Tsybikov's account over a century later, it doesn't feel as if this was a wholly satisfactory encounter; true pilgrim or Tsarist spy, our narrator was a devout Buddhist when all was said and done, and he seems to have been shocked by this peremptory exchange. He had come expecting something truly spiritually uplifting, and instead the redemption on offer seemed nothing more than a starkly transactional experience.

Tsybikov may not have found any absolution or catharsis at the Potala Palace, but his journey to Tibet and back lasted almost three years. He had crossed steppe and mountain to get there, and along the way had been abandoned by porters and robbed by traders. At the end he ran out of funds, but remained stoic, saying that this was entirely common and to be expected, as local superstition considered it bad luck to leave Tibet with money. By enduring this strange pilgrimage, Tsybikov had at least made good on his commitment to provide unique intelligence to the Russian state, whilst also fulfilling his father's desire for a son who was a scholar of religious knowledge—a redemption of sorts.[iv] Tsybikov's trip was deemed a great success, partly due to the fact that the cultural and scholarly bounty he brought back for his sponsors at the Imperial Russian Geographical Society was immense.[v]

As well as his personal journals and photographic negatives, Tsybikov supplied 333 Tibetan books, which were reprinted to commission from original wood blocks held by local monasteries; others had been bought from the market, where they were 'laid out on the ground' like any other goods for sale. As Tsybikov began to prepare for the journey home, the books were expertly

---

[iv] For more on pilgrimage as a means of redeeming debts of obligation or fulfilling promises, see Chapter 8.

[v] Tsybikov was the first to photograph the Forbidden City, although Ovshe Norzunov's pictures were published first. The books he brought back, donated to the Asiatic Museum in St Petersburg, are now in the Institute of Oriental Manuscripts.

wrapped in cloth and then sewn into raw hides, which in turn were smeared with flour and pig's blood; all this to protect them from their inevitable immersion into the rivers on the route ahead. Within these bundles lay the writings of lama scholars, on topics such as astrology and medicine, reaching back almost a millennium. This was surely one of the greatest cultural hauls in the history of espionage.

The ritual spilling of the deities' tea failed to protect Tibet. Within two years of Tsybikov's return to Russia, the Dalai Lama was forced to flee Tibet, taking refuge in Urga.[13] Believing that the British had the right to protect their trade interests, Lord Curzon, Viceroy of India, directed British forces to march on Lhasa. They were faced by 2,000 Tibetan soldiers who walked forward as a single mass into the face of their machine gunfire. It was a massacre. A month later in September 1904, a trade agreement was signed giving the British unique and exclusive trading rights with Tibet. Meanwhile, Buryatia, Tsybikov's homeland, had become the subject of competing Russian and Japanese ambitions and, within decades, the Soviet policy of forced collectivisation of agriculture was to lead to an uprising. As was the case for many ethnic-minority groups, Stalinist purges in the late 1930s resulted in the death of tens of thousands of Buryats. By 1976, only 300 Buryat Buddhist lamas remained, down from 16,000 in Tsybikov's era. These events illustrate Sebald's point in *The Rings of Saturn* that we don't need to look far to see that we are all in need of redemption, either as individuals or as part of wider humanity.

In Autumn 1998, the year *The Rings of Saturn* appeared on my bookcase, I was travelling regularly to Moscow for work. One evening I shared some fresh pine nuts with Alexei, an engineer who had just returned from Buryatia. There, with the scent of the forest stealing out of the paper bag that passed back and forth between us, Alexei told me of one of the great environmental crimes of our age, one that no barefoot pilgrimage or declaration of piety can redeem: the catastrophic degradation of Lake Baikal, the world's largest freshwater lake by volume, whose once pure waters have been polluted through human folly and greed. It is a tragedy of our collective making and, as Sebald suggests throughout his book, we must own up to our crimes.

The 40,000 books and letters that once lay in Michael Hamburger's library are now gone, variously redistributed to archives around the world; and few are left to recount the events that prompted the Hamburgers and the Freuds to make their exodus to England in the mid-twentieth century. Amongst those who lived to tell the tale was my mother-in-law, Bep. As an adolescent, Bep endured the Luftwaffe's blitz on Rotterdam, and soon after watched as Jewish friends and neighbours were taken away following house-to-house searches by the occupying forces. Her family and others in her neighbourhood faced famine and peremptory punishment for breaking the evening curfew. She told of a young boy shot dead in the street for going out in search of bread; his parents were forced to leave his body out for days as a warning to others. Making her own brave exodus at the first opportunity, Bep travelled to the UK and finally settled in the quiet landscape described by Sebald in *The Rings of Saturn*. But peace of mind proved elusive and, like the Ancient Mariner, from time to time the deep longing for catharsis drove Bep to recount the scenes she had witnessed as a young girl.

Almost immediately after World War II ended, a new kind of pilgrimage site emerged from the wreckage of violence and suffering—one that offered the possibility of redemption, not just for the individual pilgrim, but for us all. Yad Vashem, the World Holocaust Remembrance Centre in Jerusalem, is the exemplar of such monuments. Through its carefully conceived architecture, and its presentation of first-hand accounts and objects from the time, Yad Vashem leads visitors along a path that brings us face to face with both the gross calumny and, conversely, the extraordinary courage of our fellow creatures. Dedicated to preserving the memory of the dead and honouring Jews who fought against their Nazi oppressors, as well as commemorating those Gentiles who aided Jews in need, the centre reveals to us the essential duality of good and evil that marks much of human history. For those in search of meaning, of redemption, of hope, a journey to Yad Vashem holds such a possibility.

7

# HOPE

*'In Kyoto*
*Hearing the cuckoo*
*I long for Kyoto'*

Matsuo Bashō[1]

In July 2016, I travelled with my husband Tony to Lindisfarne, a small island off the north-east coast of Britain. As we waited for the ebbing tide to reveal the causeway that would allow us to cross from the mainland, lapwings and oystercatchers arrived to take advantage of the muddy feeding grounds and a mackerel sky swam overhead. This peaceful place is popular with bird-watchers, but we were here to visit the opening scene of a pilgrim tale: a story about St Cuthbert, who in life brought hope to the poor and ailing, and whose death is thought to have inspired the magnificent Lindisfarne Gospels, perhaps the greatest of all medieval manuscripts.[i]

---

[i] The exquisitely illuminated Gospels, written in Latin on the very finest vellum, were likely commissioned in preparation for Cuthbert's elevation

Christianity had arrived at these shores with the Romans in the first century CE, but by the seventh century Anglo-Saxon paganism was thriving in many parts of the country. When the young Northumbrian King Oswald came to the throne in 634 CE, he was determined to reintroduce Christianity to his people. Under Oswald's patronage, the monk Aidan (later St Aidan) was sent from the Celtic community on the small Scottish island of Iona to establish a priory in his kingdom.[ii] Little Lindisfarne would do perfectly: quiet and with enough land and fishing to be self-sufficient. Within thirty years, Lindisfarne Priory had become an important anchor point for Christianity in Britain. But things were far from settled on this peaceful isle. In 664 CE, following an eclipse of the sun, plague had broken out across parts of Britain and Ireland. The land was immersed in a dark wave of death, and the people were turning back to 'the false remedies of idolatry'.[2] Lindisfarne was essential to the Christian mission in Northumbria, but the Synod of Whitby that year had agreed that, from then on, all would follow the practices of the Church of Rome. Lindisfarne's leadership and many of its monks returned to Celtic Iona and a new Bishop, Eata, was appointed. As is so often the case, he called on someone he knew and trusted to help him.

Aside from familiarity, Cuthbert had two particular skills that recommended him for the job. First among these was his persuasive evangelism, going where no other preacher was willing to go. The eighth-century chronicler the Venerable Bede tells us, 'He was wont chiefly to resort to those places, and preach in such

---

to sainthood. Their 518 elaborately decorated pages carry the gospels of Matthew, Mark, Luke and John.

[ii] The Iona religious community was founded by the Irish monk Columba in 563. Like Asoka the Great (see below), Columba had turned away from a life of violent conflict towards peace and spirituality.

1. The Omphalos of Delphi, marking the sacred site's connection to the world's origins in Greek mythology.

2. The amphitheatre at Delphi, which has hosted crowds gathering for special events since ancient times.

3. Monks at Singapore's Buddha Tooth Relic Temple prepare for Chunyun, or Chinese New Year, when many millions return to their ancestral villages or family homes.

4. In silent prayer at Jerusalem's Church of the Holy Sepulchre, a place shared and safeguarded by many religious peoples.

5. The Umayyad Mosque in Damascus, where the stone courtyard has been worn smooth by the feet of the faithful.

6. Worshippers in Cologne Cathedral on Christmas Day.

7. The Imam Hussein Mosque in Karbala, Iraq: a gleaming wonder attracting over 20 million pilgrims every year.

8. The Golden Temple of Amritsar, once the shining jewel in the crown of the Sikh Empire.

9. Caravaggio's powerful *Crucifixion of Saint Peter* (1601), in Santa Maria del Popolo, the first church encountered by pilgrims entering Rome from the north.

10. Stone cairns on the shores of Lindisfarne Island, Northumberland, marking the meditations of pilgrims and walkers.

11. Walking out of Acquapendente into the serene embrace of the early morning.

12. Hermitage chapel at Lebanon's Qozhaya Monastery. A humble and contemplative life offers a route to redemption for Maronite hermits.

13. Reminders of journeys past in my study at Marsh Acres, itself heavy with history and new beginnings.

14. Lindisfarne Castle is now the only significant landmark on Holy Island, but it serves as an icon for this place which has drawn pilgrims for almost 1400 years.

15. Helen and Avi's *sukkah* in Jerusalem, a space for shared appreciation of family, friendship and faith.

16. The Orientalist explorer Richard Burton's London tomb, in the shape of a
Bedouin tent. Burton sought escape and adventure in Arabia, disguised as a
Muslim.

17. The sacred River Ganga at Varanasi, the holy city where dying Hindus come for their final liberation.

18. My travel companion Constance on the Via Francigena, enjoying the freedom of the road.

19. Walden Pond, Massachusetts, where Thoreau retreated in search of meaning amid natural beauty and stillness.

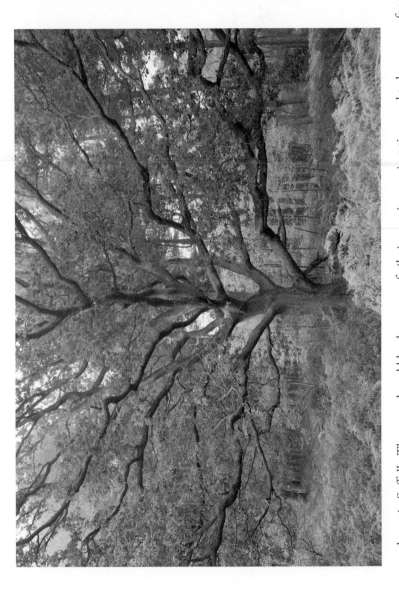

20. An oak tree near home in Suffolk. The natural world has been part of pilgrimage since ancient times and today concern for the environment is spurring new pilgrim practices.

villages, as being seated high up amid craggy uncouth mountains, were frightful to others to behold, and whose poverty and
barbarity rendered them inaccessible to other teachers'. In addition to his skills as an orator, by the time he arrived at
Lindisfarne, Cuthbert had already gained a reputation for miracles and healing. He had apparently been inspired to take up the
religious life as a teenager when, on the night St Aidan died, he
saw a light descend from the night sky and rise again, as if lifting
a human soul to heaven. According to another report, Cuthbert
was cured of a swelling in his knee after having been visited by
an angel on horseback. Bede suggests this would not seem so
incredible if we were to read the history of the Maccabees, 'in
which angels are said to have come on horseback to the assistance
of Judas Maccabeus, and to defend God's own temple.'[3]

Such reports helped build Cuthbert's reputation and standing,
but life at the heart of this wealthy and busy monastery seems
not to have suited him, and after a while he retreated to a hermitage on the nearby Inner Farne Island. Here he lived in search
of solitude and contemplation, ultimately dying in this small
remote place in 687 CE. Already a popular figure during his lifetime, after his death Cuthbert's body was taken back to
Lindisfarne, where pilgrims came to pray at his tomb. In this age
of miracles, the incorruptibility of the flesh after death was a sign
of saintliness, and eleven years after his death, as Bede tells us,
'Divine Providence put it into the minds of the brethren to take
up his bones'. When his tomb was opened, Cuthbert's remains
were found by the monks to be in perfect condition 'as if he were
still alive, and the joints of the limbs pliable, like one asleep
rather than dead'. The garments in which Cuthbert reposed in
his tomb were removed, and locks of his hair were cut, both
these artefacts having value as saintly relics.

This discovery of Cuthbert's body intact, a decade after his
demise, duly confirmed his status as a saint and brought ever
more pilgrims to the tomb, many in the hope that a miracle

might save their fortunes in some way. Amongst their number was a young monk whose eyelid was disfigured by a tumour, growing daily and threatening the loss of the eye. Physical remedies were applied but failed. Some of Cuthbert's stolen hair was applied to the ailment by another brother and, within hours of touching his eye, the eyelid became 'as sound as if there never had been any disfigurement or tumour on it.' Cuthbert's tomb was an enormously valuable asset to the monastery: it brought pilgrims, who in turn brought gifts, and while donations might have been distributed to help the poor, as Bede indicates, Cuthbert's remains were nevertheless a crucial cog in the spiritual and economic engine of the Church in Northumbria.

So far, so good, but in June 793 CE, this quiet island was visited by a storm the likes of which it had never seen. The year hadn't got off to a great start: the *Anglo-Saxon Chronicle* reports that there were 'dreadful forewarnings come over the land of Northumbria, and woefully terrified the people: these were amazing sheets of lightning and whirlwinds, and fiery dragons were seen flying in the sky.'[4] A great famine followed and then, heaping trouble upon trouble, the Vikings arrived.

The same shallow mudflats that draw wading birds to the shores of Lindisfarne also make an ideal landing place for long-boats. In his *History of the Church of Durham*, the twelfth-century monk Simeon tells the story:

> On the seventh of the ides of June, they reached the church of Lindisfarne, and there they miserably ravaged and pillaged everything; they trod the holy things under their polluted feet, they dug down the altars, and plundered all the treasures of the church. Some of the brethren they slew, some they carried off with them in chains, the greater number they stripped naked, insulted, and cast out of doors, and some they drowned in the sea.

The Vikings didn't get their hands on Cuthbert's carved oak coffin or the Lindisfarne Gospels, but in 875 CE, facing the prospect of yet more Scandinavian visitors, the monks of Lindisfarne fled, taking the treasures with them. Cuthbert's cult thrived and miracles attributed to him continued; Alfred the Great himself was inspired in his struggle against the Danes by a dream of St Cuthbert.

After years of wandering the north-east of England, the guardians of St Cuthbert's mortal remains settled in Durham, and he was laid to rest once more—at least for a while. A great cathedral was built in his honour, and Durham now became the pre-eminent locus of medieval pilgrimage in England. It would remain so for more than a century, until the martyrdom of Thomas Becket in Canterbury in 1170. The Bishop of Durham became almost as powerful as the King of England himself, and in time presented yet one more reason for Reformation. In 1538 Henry VIII succeeded where the Viking invaders of Lindisfarne had failed. Cuthbert's ornate tomb was destroyed, and his coffin opened once more. Found by the monks to be uncorrupted still, he was reburied behind the high altar of the cathedral.

Since then, the simple gravestone inscribed *Cuthbertus* has been worn smooth by the knees of pilgrims, and still they come; drawn by this miraculous figure who once offered so much hope to the poor and the infirm. The Lindisfarne treasures associated with him had survived against the odds, and both saint and manuscript continue to inspire hope in believers today. In 1966 a new pilgrim path, St Cuthbert's Way, was created to mark Cuthbert's original seventh-century journey from Scotland to Lindisfarne. In the summer of 2013, the Lindisfarne Gospels attracted nearly 100,000 visitors when they were displayed in Durham's Palace Green Library.

The monks of Lindisfarne were successful in converting the people of Northumberland, by persuading them that Christianity offered something that raised life above the inevitable; harness-ing their hope for something better in an era when most were not only poor, but powerless to change their lot. Bede reports how St Aidan set an example by living a life of abstinence and how, 'whatsoever gifts of money he received from the rich, he either distributed ... for the use of the poor, or bestowed in ransoming such as had been wrongfully sold for slaves.' This is social reform at its most fundamental: leading by example, buying slaves out of bondage, redistributing wealth to those in need. But as I roamed under the scudding skies and along the wind-blown dunes of Lindisfarne, I couldn't help but think that the natural beauty of this golden place contributed something to its appeal to monks and peasants alike.

Lindisfarne and later Durham were part of a movement that revolutionised religion in Britain, one that saw over the following centuries a growth of the Church until it exceeded the power and wealth of the monarchies that had once helped it take root. In the end it was not Viking invaders but the whole excessive edifice of ornate shrines and the relentlessly accretive monasteries that proved to be the undoing of the Catholic Church in England and elsewhere in Europe. After the English Reformation of the sixteenth century had seen many shrines destroyed and the monasteries disbanded, what remained amongst the glitter and the dust was the enduring poverty of working people, and the fundamental human need to have hope that things might, could, would get better.

\* \* \*

Across the Channel in France things were little different, and the Protestant Reformation there was not enough to lift people out of poverty and despair with their lot. Hubris and inequality form the tinder of any revolution, and eighteenth-century France had both in abundance, but it is when hope departs that the flint is finally struck. A rapacious Church and Crown had been a fact of life for aeons, but successive poor harvests meant that the French people were now not only powerless but starving. On 14 July 1789, an angry mob stormed a state prison, the Bastille, and the sparks flew. By the middle of the nineteenth century, many of the liberties of this first French Revolution had been wiped away, and commoners were gathering tinder for the second. In June 1848 the people of Paris rose in protest, and by December—with support from the peasantry—Napoleon's nephew had been elected the first president of France, now in its Second Republic. This newly dawned democracy was to be short-lived, and in 1852 the Second Empire was declared, following a coup d'état staged by the same leader, now self-appointed as Napoleon III, Emperor of the French.

Although liberties and rights were far from settled as a result of the French revolutionary period, these events catalysed a shift in social attitudes, and the notion that common people had lives that mattered became an inescapable, if inconvenient, truth. This shift was reflected in the art and literature of the time, with the lives of ordinary people increasingly replacing heroic or historical themes as the subject matter. In Gustave Courbet's 1854 painting *The Meeting*, the artist portrays himself as an itinerant pilgrim, free from the cares of bourgeois life, all the while dependent on his wealthy patron Alfred Bruyas, who also appears in the work. In England, Charles Dickens threw the spotlight on social injustice through hugely popular stories including those of *Oliver Twist* (1839) and *Little Dorrit* (1857), children whose lives were blighted by an uncaring society.

In the same period, the Church in France had suffered a loss of power following the introduction of the Napoleonic Code, while Pope Pius IX had been hounded out of Rome by Italian revolutionaries and had lost power over the Papal States covering much of the Italian peninsula. Then, as now, the Vatican was the Pope's only remaining territory. In this perfect storm there must have been anxiety amongst Church leaders that religion was losing not only its authority, but its appeal to the masses, many of whom continued to endure grinding poverty despite the new promises of '*liberté, égalité, fraternité*'. In this regard, the visions of Bernadette of Lourdes in 1858 came not a moment too soon, bringing hope both to the people of France and to the Church itself.

On 11 February 1858, Bernadette Soubirous, a diminutive and undernourished teenage girl, went out with her sister Toinette and their friend Jeanne to look for old bones and firewood, to burn or perhaps to sell for food. Bernadette lived in extreme poverty with her parents and siblings in a dank room that had once served as a prison cell in the town. The winter air was cold that day, but staying inside the damp cell must have been even less appealing. A mile or so from the town of Lourdes was Massabielle, a steep rocky hill whose wooded slopes offered the possibility of firewood. At its base was a cave or grotto. Here, at some time in the distant past, a child had proclaimed that a chapel would one day be built; as the three girls were passing, it is quite possible that they carried with them some sense that this was a spiritual or mystical place.

Poor, illiterate, ignorant and on the brink of starvation, on this icy day Bernadette beheld a vision and fell to her knees in wonder. In a niche in the rock above the grotto, she saw the figure of a young girl dressed like the Virgin Mary. Three days after this first vision, the sisters and a group of around twenty similarly poor country girls returned to the grotto to see what might be seen. A second vision followed, and although none but Bernadette witnessed the apparition, she became frozen in her position of adulation and had to be carried home. The apparition was now telling her to return every day for the next fortnight. Day by day, the crowd that followed Bernadette to the grotto got bigger and bigger as the story spread to nearby villages.

Each time, as she knelt in front of the niche, Bernadette became entranced, her body perfectly still, her gaze directed upwards. Soon they were coming in their thousands, men, women and children; people of all classes and ages. They were hoping to see something miraculous and they were not disappointed. One day, as Bernadette was leaving the grotto, a father stepped forward with his weakling daughter, Eugénie, who amongst other ailments suffered from some eye complaint. Her father begged the young visionary for help, and as Bernadette threw her arms around the girl, the effect on Eugénie was electrifying. The crowd witnessed the flush to her cheeks and the sudden light in her eyes and the cry went out: 'Miracle! The girl was blind and now she sees.'

Hope springs eternal, and soon the waters that sprang from this rocky place were attributed with curative powers: a barren couple bore a child, a sick child recovered to live another day, and so on and so on. After initial scepticism from the Church, Bernadette's visions were accepted as authentic, and as word of the healing power of the waters spread, pilgrim numbers grew. Many were hoping for relief from their sickness and, by 1875, around fifty *malades* arrived in a group.[5] Soon, helping the sick became a part of the pilgrimage itself.

In a compelling account of his experience as a *brancardier* (helper) at Lourdes, John Eade describes how the sick and disabled, who more usually sit on the margins of society, occupy centre stage during the pilgrimage, and are treated with reverence by the body of volunteers there to support them.[6] One such volunteer is Christopher, a helper with the Handicapped Children's Pilgrimage Trust. This Catholic charity owns a former hotel at Bartrès, 4 kilometres outside of Lourdes, and each year the Trust takes groups of disabled children and adults from England to stay at this specially created pilgrim hostel. There are usually two groups staying here at any one time: a typical group would be forty people, twenty of them disabled and the other half able-bodied helpers. Each group, made up of parishioners drawn from one local area in England, is accompanied by a priest and a nurse. Christopher has been making the trip annually for two decades. I asked him why he went, and why the pilgrims themselves return year after year.

'Like many of the things one does,' he says, 'it starts with someone asking you to. I was invited to go once long ago by a friend and have been going almost every year since. The round trip is a week, Friday to Friday, and it's a holiday for the disabled. It's exciting to go to France for a week. Their full-time carers stay behind at home, so they get a break too. Some sixty-seven miraculous cures at Lourdes have been accredited by the Vatican, but today science is the master of everything, and none of our pilgrims is expecting to be cured. The cost of travel is supported by bursaries and affordability is not a barrier to anyone who wants to come along. Two-thirds of the group have been before and there is a wonderful moment of reunion when we meet each year at the gate at Stansted Airport at the start of the trip. There is a lot of camaraderie, and laughter and joy are a big feature of the pilgrimage. The logistics are made easier by the fact we travel with a specialist charter airline, which takes our group and other Lourdes pilgrims. This means that flight crew are unflustered by the high number of wheelchair users and other disabled adults, which makes boarding a complicated process.'

For Christopher, 'Coming together as a group can be a transcendent experience and this dynamic is one thing that keeps me coming back each year: another is taking on the role of a helper and all that entails, working under the direction of our group leader and nurse. I relish being a follower for a change and have no leadership role at all on the pilgrimage, unlike in my professional life. The adults in our care are very experienced at having others attend to their personal needs and I continue to learn from the dignity and good humour with which they endure their travails. More than this, they teach us by example what it means to give yourself up to others.' He is reluctant to discuss the personal spiritual dimension of his experience at Lourdes, but when he eventually does open up, his whole being comes alive. He describes the intensity and frequency of his spiritual experiences throughout the week, choosing as an example how it feels to join other pilgrims in singing *Ave Maria* as they walk in the candlelit procession late in the summer night.

As Christopher points out, most of the 7 million or so pilgrims who visit Lourdes each year are not expecting any kind of miracle. But, in this interconnected community of sick and disabled people and helpers, there is a more universal kind of hope: the hope that, through pilgrimage, we might experience a better version of ourselves. Perhaps this is what draws many pilgrims to return year after year, not just to Lourdes, but to many other sites. Such journeys offer the rare opportunity to look both inward at our 'self' and outward at the great unseen forces that guide the universe, reminding us that while we are wholly insignificant in the greater scheme of things, what we feel and think and do really matters.

\* \* \*

For Christopher and others, pilgrim journeys provide a context in which to embrace their spiritual selves, but the hope of many is tinged with desperation. Pilgrimage shrines have been described as pre-eminent centres for dealings between human beings and the divine, a marketplace in which hope is the currency.[7] Writing about folkloric religious practices in Finland in the early twentieth century, Laura Stark considers that primitive societies using reciprocity and barter as a means of securing the things they need take the exact same approach when interacting with their gods and spirits. In other words, 'I make this offering or sacrifice to you in return for something I seek, whether this be health or fertility, for myself, my family, my animals or crops.'[8]

This transactional view of humanity's spiritual practices may seem rather cynical and simplistic, but isn't it natural that we should want to appeal to higher powers to help us, and equally natural that we should offer something in return? In such exchanges between the material and the spiritual world, the effort expended in undertaking a pilgrimage is a tangible expression of the sacrifice offered in return for a hoped-for adjustment to our fate. Indeed, what could we offer of greater value than time and effort? In Winchester Cathedral, England, a small hole was built into the fabric of the building, directly under the shrine of the ninth-century St Swithin. This encouraged pilgrims to crawl on their knees below the saint, to get as near as possible to his healing powers and to demonstrate their submission to the will of God. On Station Island in the centre of Ireland's Lough Derg, County Donegal, pilgrims fast for three days and go twenty-four hours without sleep, walking barefoot around the isle as they pray, suffering openly and willingly in exchange for the chance of healing or redemption.

Caroline has been making annual pilgrimages to Lourdes since her schooldays, and for the past five years has led a group to St Winefride's Well in Holywell, north-east Wales. It is said that here, in 660 CE, Caradoc, the son of a local prince, severed the head of young Winefride after she spurned his advances, and a spring rose from the ground at the spot where her head fell. She was later restored to life by her uncle St Beuno, and people have been coming here since the seventh century in the hope of similarly miraculous cures. Aside from the poor and the sick, many British monarchs have visited the Well: Richard I came in 1189 to pray for the success of his Crusade, and in 1686 James II and Queen Mary Beatrice came here, to pray for an heir after many barren years. Shortly after this visit, Mary became pregnant with a son, James.[iii]

---

[iii] The Jesuits then in charge of the Well made a somewhat unusual gift to the King: the shift his great-grandmother Mary Queen of Scots had been wearing when she was beheaded.

All in all, Caroline has made dozens of pilgrim journeys to Catholic shrines, and jokes that that she is a platinum card holder; but her intent, like her faith, is serious. While indulgences are no longer bought and sold, for observant Catholics the concept of being able to demonstrate penitence through action remains, and Caroline's true hope is that, through such acts, she will acquire 'indulgences' and reduce the punishment of her sins after death.[iv] While Caroline's actions may be particular to her faith, her hopes and fears for the unknown and unknowable future are not: the desire to influence our fate in eternity for the better through personal actions in this life can be found in one of the most ancient pilgrim traditions of the Hellenic world.

\* \* \*

Thought to date back to the late Bronze Age around 3,600 years ago, by the fifth century BCE the Eleusinian Mysteries had become the most important and widely attended cult activity in the Greek-speaking world. Like many other pagan practices, these rites prevailed until the late 300s CE, when the Roman Emperor Theodosius systematically dismantled pre-Christian sanctuaries and shrines across the Mediterranean, sweeping out the old cults to make way for the new. At the heart of the Mysteries was the promise of a better afterlife. Those who were accepted into the cult went through an initial purification before being admitted into successively more secret rituals that would result in them being 'loved by god and living with the gods', rather than condemned to the darkness below.[9] While much of

---

[iv] This powerful idea was mobilised by the Catholic church in the 11th century, when Pope Urban II called upon Christians across Europe to embark on the First Crusade to liberate the Church of the Holy Sepulchre from Seljuk Turks. Despite the promise of remission of sins, this was no pilgrimage, but an act of war.

the Eleusinian Mysteries remains just that, we do know that the public rites included a pilgrimage along the Sacred Way that ran the 11 miles or so between Eleusis and Athens.

Outlined in the *Hymn to Demeter*, the myth behind the Eleusinian cult describes how Hades opened up a chasm in the earth, through which he abducted Persephone, the daughter of Demeter, goddess of fertility, and Zeus, god of thunder. Along with Persephone, a litter of piglets also fell into the hole. Poor Demeter was stricken with grief for the loss of her daughter, but she didn't give up. She scoured the earth, looking everywhere, and finally, exhausted, arrived in Eleusis. Here King Keleos and his family showed her great kindness. One of the king's servants, Iambe, gave Demeter a stool covered in fleece, inviting her to sit, to eat and drink. After some hesitation, Demeter asked for *kykeon*, barley water flavoured with herbs. (The rites of the Mysteries featured both *kykeon* and the piglets, who were sacrificed by pilgrims preparing for initiation.)

Despite the hospitality, Demeter was inconsolable and, trenchant in her determination to recover her daughter from Hades, she withdrew her gift of fertility, hiding the seed under the earth so that it couldn't grow. Demeter's loss of Persephone now became a shared problem with the other gods: no fertility means no food, and without food the mortals will die; with no mortals, the gods are largely out of business. Zeus intervened. He persuaded Hades to release Persephone, which Hades agreed to, but while in the Underworld, she had eaten the seeds of the pomegranate, thereby triggering a clause that said anyone who had partaken of food in the Underworld could no longer return to the land of the living. A deal was struck: Persephone was allowed to live above ground for most of the year, as long as she returned to Hades for four months each winter, during which time Demeter's seed would remain hidden under the earth, only reappearing in the spring. Meanwhile, during her stay with King

Keleos, Demeter suckled the King's sickly son, Triptolemus, who not only recovered his health, but immediately sprang forth as a fully grown adult. Demeter taught Triptolemus the art of agriculture, and he in turn introduced farming to the Greeks.

While the rites around the entry level to the cult (the Lesser Mysteries) took place in spring, the Eleusinian pilgrimage associated with the more advanced Greater Mysteries typically took place at the end of the agricultural year, on the threshold of winter. Perhaps this was the moment when the Eleusinian hope of securing a better afterlife was at its most potent. Celebrating the natural cycle of life and death and the fecundity of the earth is also a celebration of inevitable rebirth, marking the fallow period by looking ahead to the return of new life. The rites of homage to Demeter were spread out over eight days and across two locations about 14 miles apart. Sacred objects were transferred from Eleusis to Athens, where purification rituals took place, and the festival culminated in a processional pilgrimage back to Eleusis. Both fasting and feasting were involved, and on the last day of the festival, libations were made in honour of the dead, followed by great celebrations of music and dancing. The cycle of initiation into the cult of the Eleusinian Mysteries appears to have been complex and protracted, requiring many, successively more secretive stages of admission. What kept initiates coming back was the promise of a more congenial afterlife as a full member of the cult. The *Hymn to Demeter* concludes: 'Happy is he among men on earth who has seen these mysteries, but whoever is uninitiated ... will have no share in these good things once they die, down below in the dank realms of mist.'[10]

While the Eleusinian Mysteries centred on the human fears and hopes regarding the unknown world we enter after death, the cult of Asklepios focussed firmly on improving life in the land of the living. In 1990, I travelled to Greece with my two young children, Fred and Clare. We had been reading the Greek myths together and it seemed a good moment to go and see some of the places that feature in the stories. On this pilgrimage of sorts, our first stop was Mycenae, the scene of Agamemnon's bloody homecoming from Troy. The legendary Lion Gate had been restored here, but the site was largely rubble, and it was too much of a stretch to imagine this as a once-powerful kingdom. We caught the bus to Epidavros and this proved far more promising. Climbing up the steps of the steeply terraced amphitheatre, we witnessed a Greek tour guide strike a match to demonstrate its perfect acoustics. The tiny sound was carried from the stage to the back of the vast auditorium, clear as a bell. Clearer, in fact.

The amphitheatre at Epidavros was built in the fourth century BCE to entertain pilgrims who came to be healed. The quest for a cure was a central driver of pilgrimage activity in Ancient Greece, and at the heart of this was Asklepios, the god of healing and son of Apollo.[v] At one time sanctuaries dedicated to him, known as *asklepieia*, could be found in towns and cities across the Hellenic world, and the most important of these was at Epidavros. Founded sometime in the sixth century BCE, the *asklepieion* here remained in use as a healing centre until Theodosius closed it down as part of his wider purge. Pilgrims came here to be cured of anything from infertility to worms and would make votive offerings of terracotta body parts, indicating the location of their malaise. The rituals of the cure involved both induced dreams and the use of non-venomous snakes. These roamed freely in the *abaton* or dormitory building at Epidavros, providing the opportunity for a snake to bite a patient on the affected part while he or she slept.[11]

---

[v] Both shared the epithet *Paean* (the Healer), a reference to a healing deity who can be traced back to the much earlier Mycenaean culture and is referenced in Homer's *Iliad*.

Around a century after the creation of the sanctuary at Epidavros, another was founded on the island of Kos in the southern Aegean. Although there is no evidence that medicine was practised within the *asklepieion* itself, Kos became notable for its association with a local physician, Hippocrates, whose name lives on through the eponymous oath, historically taken by those entering the profession. Asklepios had five daughters, two of whom are worthy of note in this respect: Hygieia, goddess of health and cleanliness; and Panacea, goddess of universal remedy. Along with Apollo, these pagan deities were mentioned in the opening passage of the Hippocratic Oath (being dropped in the later Christianised version): 'I swear by Apollo the Healer, by Asklepios, by Hygieia, by Panacea, and by all the gods and goddesses, making them witnesses, that I will carry out, according to my ability and judgement, this oath and this indenture.' The healing cult of Asklepios endured for almost a millennium, and the Rod of Asklepios, a symbol depicting a snake wound around a rod or staff, remains in use today, featuring at the centre of the World Health Organization logo.

The miracle of healing that drew pilgrims to Epidavros, Kos and elsewhere gives us a clue to one of the factors that still drives pilgrimage today: namely, the impulse to look beyond the boundaries of our immediate community, in the hope of resolving some of the most fundamental questions that shape our existence. If you have a particularly challenging issue, such as sailing into battle or trying to improve fertility, there is an obvious value in appealing to forces more powerful than those available via the shrines or rites, priests or priestesses within your own community. Attributing a premium to distant shrines is not simply about the importance of the 'ask'; rather, expertise and influence seem somehow more authoritative when harder to access.

We know that pilgrims travelled great distances to Delphi and to Siwa to ask for guidance, and this trust in the remote is something we see today—not just through pilgrimages to notable healing shrines such as Lourdes or Mashhad in Iran, but also more obliquely in our secular faith in foreign hospitals to cure those whose local medics have failed to heal them. A retired schoolteacher of my acquaintance remortgaged his house to send his wife to the US for cancer treatment, and at the end of it he had neither a wife nor a home. There are scores of such stories to be gleaned from the hand-drawn posters and collection tins in corner shops around the UK in which a local family is raising funds to send a loved one abroad for a cure. When we are desperate, and searching for even the faintest glimmer of hope, we are willing to place our trust in forces beyond our familiar boundaries and take a leap into the unknown. We don't necessarily need to know the exact rationale for doing what we do; sometimes it is simply enough to believe.

* * *

In 601 CE, Pope Gregory the Great wrote to the monk Mellitus, who was setting off for Britain to help St Augustine convert the natives. The new religion, he advised, should be layered gradually over the old and, 'since they have a custom of sacrificing many oxen to demons, let some other solemnity be substituted in its place, such as a day of Dedication, or the Festivals of the Holy Martyrs whose relics are enshrined there.'[12] While many in the early Church condemned as pagan the fixation with these inanimate objects, part of the value of saintly relics was in opening up new locations for pilgrimage, enabling more people to participate in this activity, which was central to the spread of Christianity. At a time when most people lived out their whole lives within a few miles of their place of birth, and most travel was on foot or by cart to local markets and annual fairs, the prospect of encountering a spiritually powerful object must have been an enticing proposition.

In the era of Gregory the Great, or even during the lifetime of St Bernadette over 1,000 years later, the life and death of people in rural communities was subject to the highly unpredictable forces of the natural world: crops might fail, or fishermen be lost at sea; or the migrating shoals of sardines and herrings might simply fail to arrive.[vi] Risk management was attempted through rites and rituals designed to assuage bad spirits or win over favourable ones; inanimate but potent objects vested with spiritual significance played an important role in these attempts to influence the trajectory of fate for the better. It is hardly surprising, then, that the relics of the Apostles or other iconic figures were thought to be imbued with special powers to heal or to connect directly with God, and that people's hope was strong enough for them to travel in order to see or touch them. This was not only the case in Christian Europe, but was a feature of human society common to cultures across time and space.

It was 11 March 545 BCE, or 13 May the following year, or perhaps many years later.[vii] We do not know the date precisely, but something took place in Kushinagar, India that would ripple out from that day to this. A humble blacksmith, Cunda, had brought an offering of food to a great teacher and sage—it would prove to be the sage's last meal. Sensing that the end was near, the sage sent word to poor Cunda not to feel distressed that his food had despatched Siddhartha Gautama from this world.

On the night of his passing, the Buddha—or Tathagata, as he is also known—instructed his chief attendant Ananda on the

---

[vi] Norman Lewis's *Voices of the Old Sea* paints a moving picture of a 20th-century Spanish fishing community on the brink of starvation after the annual sardine shoals fail to arrive.

[vii] Exact dates of the Buddha's life and enlightenment are contested. Western scholars date his death as 483 BCE while Chinese sources use 368 BCE.

spiritual value of pilgrimage. He declared that any enlightened person or ruler should be buried under a mound or *stupa*, adding that people would gain joy from 'worshipping journeys to such places.'[13] With respect to his own being, he cited four places of significance:

> Here the Tathagata was born ... Here the Tathagata awakened to the unexcelled right self-awakening ... Here the Tathagata set rolling the unexcelled wheel of Dhamma ... Here the Tathagata was totally unbound in the remainderless property of Unbinding. ... And anyone who dies while making a pilgrimage to these memorials with a bright, confident mind will—on the break-up of the body, after death—reappear in a good destination, the heavenly world.[14]

On his death, Buddha's body was cremated, and his ashes and other material relics distributed amongst eight rulers. Eight *stupas* were constructed to hold the relics, and festivals created at each place. This solution, however democratic, constrained pilgrimage to the north of India and, as Buddhism spread, demand arose for *stupas* and relics that could be accessed by those living further afield. Eventually, providence intervened. In around 260 BCE, the ruler Asoka, whose empire extended across most of the Indian subcontinent, waged a terrible war against the Kalinga people of northern India. Sometime after this conflict, which claimed an estimated 200,000 lives, Asoka encountered a young Buddhist monk. Struck by the tranquillity of his bearing, he invited the monk to the palace.

Once inside, Asoka invited him to take a seat. Believing that even the most junior monk should take precedence over the most senior of laymen, and seeing no more senior monk present, the novice sat down upon the king's throne. Asoka's reputation was fearsome: he had reputedly killed ninety-nine of his half-brothers. Courtiers held their breath. Surely, vengeance was coming? But no; Asoka did not punish the novice for his presumption. Rather he listened while the young monk preached to him on the need for diligence, and this fearsome warrior became converted to Buddhism. After his conversion Asoka publicly repudiated violence and pledged to rule by *dhamma* or righteousness. He sent religious missions out across his empire and, as legend has it, created 84,000 *stupas*, each containing an object or fragment associated with the life of the Buddha or one of his saintly followers.

While that number is considered unreliable, there is little doubt that Asoka made a significant contribution to the spread of Buddhism, not least through the creation of such reliquaries and the religious houses associated with them—a further demonstration, if one were needed, that physical objects or locations create a focal point that can bring stories to life. Like the journey to Greece with my children, going to the scene of events or even seeing objects that were present at those events translates into a special kind of connectivity. But we are more than simple observers on such occasions; when we visit these sites, we bring with us our hopes for what we might learn, feel or gain. In this sense, pilgrims—whether processing from Eleusis to Athens or walking to Lindisfarne—are really journeying into themselves, with the expectation of an improved self at the end of it.

This argument holds if you are visiting historic sites, but if faith is your motive, and your god is omnipresent, then why go on pilgrimage at all? Won't your prayers at home be enough to act out your hope of divine intervention in your plight? The Lourdes volunteer Christopher and my Sufi friend Musa each helpfully explain in their own terms. 'There is no value in you going to Lourdes as an onlooker,' Christopher tells me. 'All you will see is the paraphernalia of tourism: the bottles of holy water, the Virgin Mary fridge magnets, the tour buses that can be found in Paris and London and Berlin: this is akin to sightseeing rather than pilgrimage. Rather, come with our community; be part of something. Only then will you understand.'

'We don't go to Mecca to admire the home,' Musa explained. 'We go to admire the home owner; to connect with God within ourselves.' I pressed him further: mmm, but if God is within you and within everything, as you suggest, then why go at all? Why not just stay exactly where you are? 'Because,' he replied, 'context is important. By moving from the kitchen to the garden, or here, out into St James's Square, we change the nature of our conversation. And so it is with pilgrimage. When we go to a place of significance, whether it be Mecca or Rome, or any other such place, we carry our hopes and our intention into a very particular context. It is this, rather than the physical activity of going, that defines it. And there is no faking it. God sees what is in your heart.'

8

# GRATITUDE

*'I only went out for a walk and finally concluded to stay out till sundown, for going out, I found, was really going in.'*

John Muir[1]

In August 1973 I was hitchhiking around Ireland with my friend John. The going was very slow: there was little traffic and the cars passing by were typically too small to fit both us and our big rucksacks. After several days of inching up together from Rosslare in the south, we decided to try our luck separately. Almost immediately, I got a lift from a passing truck, and three hours later the driver dropped me in a suburban street in Sligo, right outside the home of John's aunt. It was late at night and, though rather surprised at this young teenage girl showing up, the family welcomed me in. After a cup of tea and a chat, I was put to bed in a room where three young children were fast asleep. This seemed oddly trusting at the time, but with hindsight I see that I was barely out of childhood myself.

I slept like a log floating down the Zambezi, but the following morning there was no sign of John. By lunchtime we were all in a state of high anxiety, and when he finally arrived, the aunt suggested we make a short visit to the Holy Well at Tobernalt, to give thanks for his safe delivery. It was the weekend and there were many families here, clambering up the stone steps and along wooded paths close to the fresh flowing water. Some had come simply to enjoy the day, others to give thanks or to ask something for themselves or for loved ones: coins were tossed into the waters or small strips of cloth tied to a tree as a token of these wishes. This folk practice of tree-tied wishing is widespread and sometimes these acts are accompanied by a ritual of walking thrice 'sun-wise' around the tree or the well in question. In Scotland these rags are known as 'clooties' and the wells where they are hung known as 'clootie wells'. At Avebury's stone circle in Wiltshire, in the lea of the Ridgeway, stands an immense oak tree festooned with coloured streamers. Not far from Stonehenge, the Ridgeway path and the equally ancient Avebury ritual site both date back around 5,000 years, and one can only wonder how long travellers have been tying their wishes to trees here as they pass by.

Back in Ireland, the supplicants I encountered at Tobernalt were almost certainly all Catholics, but local people had been coming to this waterfall for thousands of years, bringing with them their heartfelt desires, fears and feelings of relief. Heraclitus' refrain that 'you never step into the same river twice' describes the fluidity that seems to imbue bodies of water with magical properties. Water the purifier, water the healer, and water the boundary—the medium that allows communication from this world into another. The Styx or the Ganga: how will you cross to the eternal realm when your time comes? But, setting all that aside, clean, fresh water truly is magical: it is the life force without which no living thing can survive for long. Starting from this fundamental truth, there remains room for belief in the unseen and the unknown shaping our destinies.

# GRATITUDE

The Boyne and the Shannon, both major Irish rivers, are closely identified with goddesses (Bóann and Sionann respectively) who were once thought to be part of the water's flow. Tobernalt is only one of hundreds if not thousands of holy wells and rivers in Ireland to which people came in pre-Christian times, making offerings to naiads (female water spirits) for the purposes of healing, divination or thanksgiving. When Christianity arrived on these shores, the new traditions were simply layered over the old, the nymphs replaced by saints. Christian churches were sometimes constructed next to long-established holy wells; the fonts of infant baptism and other sacred water receptacles were eventually relocated inside the building. Unlike John and his aunt, I am neither Irish nor Catholic, and this was my first encounter with a local shrine; but there are many thousands both in Ireland and elsewhere, inviting a type of ritual journey that begins and ends during the course of a single day. The pilgrim may be stepping out of their daily routine to find peace or to give thanks, but in Ireland at least, many sites are especially popular on those days of the Christian calendar that overlap with the seasonal festivals of the agricultural year.

Notable in this respect is Croagh Patrick, a mountain rising 2,500 feet up from Clew Bay on the west coast of Ireland in County Mayo. Writing in his *Irish Sketch Book*, William Makepeace Thackeray (author of *Vanity Fair* and a few other good books besides) describes how, upon his arrival at the Croagh,

> the road ... was covered with people, who were flocking in hundreds from Westport market, in cars and carts, on horseback single and double, and on foot.

> And presently ... I caught sight not only of a fine view, but of the most beautiful view I ever saw in the world.

From the summit of Croagh Patrick, one can see the whole of the surrounding landscape, and out to the string of small islands threaded amongst the crashing waves of the Atlantic. The Bay and the mountain together, as Thackeray told it, are 'dressed up in gold and purple and crimson, with the whole cloudy west in a flame. Wonderful, wonderful!'

Tradition holds that, in 441 CE, during his mission to convert the Irish to Christianity, St Patrick fasted on this summit for forty days and nights, and it is from here that he is said to have banished snakes from Ireland, casting them into the sea below. This triumph over the demon, the dragon, the serpent on the sacred mountain, recalls Apollo's own battle with the Python at the centre of the earth in Delphi, only a few thousand miles and years separating the two events. By the ninth century, this mountain, known locally as 'the Reek', had become a major destination for Christian pilgrims, and today around 100,000 people make the ascent annually. The highlight of the year is Reek Sunday: the last Sunday in July, when up to 40,000 climb the rocky slopes.[2] Even at this time of year, before the first russet leaf has fallen, the mountain can be cloaked in cold mists coming off the Atlantic; but, despite the weather, many will choose to make the climb barefoot, scrambling over scree and stones to reach the top.

It is a long walk, around 23 miles, and for the Christians soldiering up the mountain, this pilgrimage is seen as earning plenary indulgences, the automatic forgiveness of sins. Many will carry a stone in their pocket to place on the summit's cairn, and Catholic pilgrims stop at three 'penance' stations along the route to the summit, each a Neolithic cairn. As the pilgrims recite their prayers, they walk around the cairn, circling it off from the surrounding landscape; making it separate, more sacred. As with the tree-tied rags of Tobernalt, these practices and their purpose are derived from much earlier sacred rites, which mixed gratitude with humility, fear and hope. Known previously as *Cruachan Aigle*, Croagh Patrick has been a focus of ritual for over 5,000 years. Bronze Age cairns have been found, as well as Neolithic art on a rocky outcrop today known as St Patrick's Chair; this, along with standing stones nearby, provides much evidence to anchor the ceremonial importance of this landscape in very ancient times. Mira Johnson, who has studied the Croagh Patrick pilgrimage in detail, has found that various rituals associated with climbing the Reek today are rooted in the footprint of our Stone Age ancestors.[3]

For primitive pastoralists, there were only two seasons of the year, and the transition points from one to the other were marked by important festivals: Imbolc on 1 February heralded the end of winter, and Samhain on 1 November the end of the grazing season.[4] On Samhain, the Gaels would express hopes of surviving the dark days ahead; on Imbolc, they would give thanks that they had indeed made it through the dark days just passed. With the advent of agriculture, two further festivals were added: Beltane on 1 May, which marked the start of summer, and Lughnasadh on 1 August, which marked the beginning of the harvest season. The harvest festival takes its name from the deity Lugh, who—in common with many Greek or Hindu gods—has an array of fine attributes: a king, a warrior, a brave youth skilled in swordsmanship and other arts, a symbol of war and peace. He is variously a sky god, a sun god, a storm god and, most importantly, a member of the Tuath Dé Danann, the tribe of the gods in pre-Christian Ireland. In some versions of the legend, Lughnasadh is a celebration of Lugh's triumph over the spirits of the Underworld, who might otherwise have wrested the bounty of the harvest for themselves.

Lugh's feast day was once celebrated right across Ireland and typically involved the ritual of walking to the top of a hill or peak. Here the year's first sheaf of corn was buried, as a symbol of the harvest's success and Lugh's triumph over the demons of blight. By moving this Celtic harvest festival from 1 August to the last

Sunday in July, the early promoters of Christianity once again managed to embrace the old pagan traditions, while simultaneously redirecting them towards the patterns of the new faith.

\* \* \*

While people now come from far and wide to take part in the Reek Sunday climb, at its core that journey remains one completed in a day, between sunrise and sunset. This same phenomenon of localised pilgrimage can be seen across many parts of the world, and Japan is no exception. In the eighteenth and nineteenth centuries, the Shinto shrines at Ise—Japan's pre-eminent shrine complex—typically attracted around 200,000 pilgrims a year, but 1705, 1771 and 1830 saw spontaneous mass pilgrimages, where numbers rose into the millions. The 1830s in Japan would be marked by successive poor harvests, with thousands dying of starvation in the Great Tenpo Famine, but the decade's first year gave no clue to what lay ahead: 1830 had been a good year for farmers, and so for the enterprising *onshi* (priests) who were responsible for the Ise shrines. The abundant harvest had reaped a bumper crop of grateful pilgrims: with some encouragement from the *onshi*, and perhaps because of rumours that protective amulets were falling from the sky, an estimated 4.5 million people had made their way to Ise to give thanks.[5]

Shintoism, or *Kami-no-Michi*, is the Way of the Gods, and each shrine is dedicated to a specific deity or *kami*. At Ise, the *kami* of devotion is the sun goddess Amaterasu-omikami. This cult is closely tied to the Japanese nation, with the first Japanese emperor, Jimmu (d. 585 BCE), considered to be the great-grandson of Amaterasu. Historically, imperial virgins held the role of priestess here, and an adapted version of that tradition continues today: in 2017 the 48-year-old daughter of Emperor Akihito, Sayako Kuroda, assumed the post of supreme priestess at Ise, replacing the 86-year-old Atsuko Ikeda, elder sister of the

Emperor. The supreme priestess attends the shrine for festive events including Kanname-sai, held annually in October, at which offerings are made in thanks for the harvest. As with the myth of Persephone and Demeter, this festival celebrates a tradition according to which the loss of a nature deity disrupted the seasons, and her return has ensured their natural resumption for the rest of time.

One version of the myth of Amaterasu tells of the constant harassment of her brother-husband Tsukuyomi, following which the sun goddess retired to a cave and the world was plunged into darkness. Night reigned and the voices of the *kami* filled the air like summer flies; myriad evils arose. Hundreds of *kami* gathered on the bank of the Peaceful River of Heaven to devise a plan. Collecting rocks from the upper reaches of the river, and iron from the Iron Mountain of Heaven, they then called upon Ishikori-dome no Mikoto (the *kami* of mirrors) to make a mirror, as well as the *kami* Tama-no-ya to thread 500 strands of shining beads. They dug up the sacred sakaki tree with 500 branches, and onto it they hung both beads and mirror, letting white and blue cloths trail from the tree's lower branches. Then the *kami* set up a wild rumpus, thundering and laughing and dancing, until—driven mad by curiosity—Amaterasu opened the door of her Heavenly Rock Cave. 'Why are you celebrating?' she asked. The *kami* replied that they were rejoicing because there was a *kami* greater than the sun goddess, holding up the mirror to show her. Amaterasu stepped forward to take a closer look—it was a trap. A rope was quickly drawn behind her and she was unable to retreat back into the cave. Thus light returned to the Land of the Rising Sun.

The first shrine was built at Ise in the third century CE by Princess Yamatohime, charged with a place to enshrine the mirror of the myth. The *Naiku* (inner shrine) holds the mirror, sword and jewels, while the *Geku* (outer shrine) is the home of the agriculture goddess Toyouke-omikami. Comparable to the practice of Christian baptism, Japanese babies are taken to Shinto shrines such as Ise, where participants make an offering of the evergreen sakaki tree and are offered a sip of sacred wine in return, marking a promise made between the worshipper and the *kami*. Since 690 CE, both shrines have been rebuilt every twenty years, thereby passing on the traditional skills of shrine-building from one generation to the next. Shintoism shares with other faiths ritual traditions involving water, trees and rocks, particularly rituals around thanksgiving for the continued blessings of nature.

This Japanese reverence for nature goes beyond the annual cycle of sowing and harvesting, critical though that remains. The country's 430 or so inhabited islands lie in an area of high seismic activity, and the risk and uncertainty that this implies perhaps helps to explain why Shintoism's animist appeal prevails, even in today's highly industrialised era. On 11 March 2011, in the middle of a Friday afternoon, the Tohoku earthquake struck out of the blue waters of the Pacific. Its force was so great that Japan's main island of Honshu was jolted eastward by 2.4 metres, and—as the shockwaves of the consequent tsunami rippled south—the Sulzberger Ice Shelf in Antarctica calved a new generation of icebergs. Closer to home, Japan's Fukushima nuclear plant was inundated with seawater, knocking out the plant's emergency generators and threatening catastrophe on an epic scale. Most of the workers ran home to check on their families, but a few extraordinarily brave men remained at the plant to do what they could. In so doing, they saved the lives of millions; but over the coming weeks and months, the death toll from the quake rose above 18,500.

Tohoku was especially significant because of its sheer magnitude (9.0–9.1 on the Richter Scale) and because of the consequences of the Fukushima disaster, but it was by no means unique. In 1923 some 143,000 people were killed in the Great

Kanto earthquake, and at the time of writing Japan has experienced fourteen minor earthquakes in the eight years since Tohoku struck. But, despite sophisticated instrumental records and first-hand observations collected over decades (including from Japan), the scientific community failed to anticipate Tohoku. Nature was all-powerful on that day in 2011, more powerful than human ingenuity, it seemed. Perhaps the *kami* would be of more help?

Japanese mythology tells of the Namazu, a giant catfish who lives beneath the mud and from time to time leaps up and thrashes about, causing violent tremors of the earth. In the lead-up to an earthquake, as stresses begin to build up in the earth's crust, highly mobile electronic charge-carriers can flow out of the bedrock and up to the surface, spreading rapidly over great distances and causing physical and chemical effects, including vibrations and changes in atmospheric pressure. For the many creatures with the receptors to pick up these changes, this is tantamount to an alarm going off. Sadly, humans are not among them, but catfish apparently are: they are known to rise from the mud to the surface before an earthquake strikes. It is hardly surprising then that the Namazu features on the logo of Japan's Earthquake Early Warning system. Takemikazuchi, otherwise known as Kashima-no-kami, is the supremely strong god of thunder often depicted as pinning down the giant catfish, and at the Kashima shrine visitors can see the stone with which he does so. (Only a small part of the rock protrudes above the ground, and although a Samurai once spent seven days looking for its root, it has never been uncovered.) Over the first few days of each year, this shrine to the god of thunder attracts hundreds of thousands of pilgrims, who bring both offerings and wishes for the year ahead. When it comes to earthquakes, it doesn't hurt to take precautionary measures, not least by expressing gratitude to Takemikazuchi for his continuing protection.

Perhaps the most popular pilgrim shrine in Japan is the one at Ise devoted to Amaterasu, which attracts around 9 million visitors a year. In this country of 80–100,000 shrines and a booming pilgrimage industry, it's perhaps surprising that opinion polls report the Japanese have little appetite for organised religion, and few identify themselves as Shintoist.[6] Yet all these shrines, and the priests who attend them, are funded by individual and community donations, a testament to the ongoing popularity of Shintoism. This at first appears to be an inherent contradiction: that Shinto is a ritual practice and yet not necessarily considered by practitioners to be a distinct religion; just as, in the world of *Kami-no-Michi*, there is no clear differentiation between the triumvirate of *kami*, human beings and nature.

The poet Dylan Thomas was one of many who recognised this interconnectivity, reminding us that 'the force that through the green fuse drives the flower' also drives all else, and that 'the force that drives the water through the rocks' also drives our 'red blood'. These elements—vegetation, water and rock—are the base materials of life on our planet and feature in some of the very oldest known pilgrimage sites. But what of the highly evolved society of present-day Japan? On the surface, the continuing practice of making offerings to the *kami* might seem paradoxical, but modern technology affords little protection against the natural forces that can wipe out thousands in a single tremor. Giving thanks for being spared these disasters still offers the best alternative.

* * *

On 14 July 2018, I set out to walk from Canterbury to Dover along the first stage of the Via Francigena. The whole enterprise would take less than a day, but in the course of those few hours in the height of summer, I would fully inhabit my own existence; striving, fearing, losing my way, finding it again; feeling pity, remorse, shame, disgust; experiencing the kindness of strangers along the way and, once again, that sense of mystery about the impulse that had led me to embark on this journey in the first place. In the heat of the day, I had to ask for water at a remote farmhouse, and later was spontaneously offered a ride on a vintage diesel engine by a railway enthusiast, who recounted the story of a son dying young and his search for solace through the renovation of the old train—another Mariner like those we saw in Chapter Five.

As the afternoon wore on, I encountered two women intending to walk the entire length of the Via Francigena in stages, to mark their fiftieth birthdays. Quizzing them on why they had chosen this particular act, they didn't have a ready reply, each looking to the other for an answer. 'Somehow,' said one of them, 'it had just seemed the right thing to do.' Further discussion revealed that the pair had chosen pilgrimage as a way of celebrating their lifelong friendship, and wasn't it well known that such matters were best done by stepping outside the everyday cares of domestic life? I had met them on day one of their enterprise, and I have often wondered since whether they carried through on their intention to cover the 1,200 miles or so to Rome. My own brief and solitary journey lacked their camaraderie and ambition, but I knew that by evening I would be back in London, sitting down to dinner with my family, relieved and grateful to be home. In this sense my own purpose in setting out was clear: by parting from home, I longed to feel its magnetic pull; to revive my appreciation of something easy to take for granted.

Leaving the women behind, I continued on my way. At a certain point, the land ahead rose up. Across a stile, the path narrowed to a barren strip through a field of ripening wheat; the corn-gold crop was thigh-high on either side, the sky empty blue, the chalk Downs rolling away to the horizon. The path was both in and of the landscape; the walker both on and of the path—we crossed the field together. Though seemingly an act of going out, this long walk of mine was a meditative retreat through the wide fields and the silent, sleeping villages of Kent, and towards the end of the afternoon, as I broached the outskirts of Dover with their tattoo parlours and betting shops, there was still time and space for quiet contemplation. For pilgrimages that take days or weeks, this outside/inside journey can lead the way to revealing or simply reviving the fundamental core of what does or doesn't matter to the individual concerned. Stripping away everyday comforts or pleasures and living plainly can help focus the mind; while carrying all your personal needs in a backpack as you walk may seem heavy at times, it provides relief from the burden of material life. When we deliberately remove ourselves from the mundane, we can truly appreciate what we have.

This idea of setting aside the comforts of daily life as a means of prompting gratitude is in part what lies behind Sukkot, the Jewish pilgrimage festival that follows Passover and Shavuot. While visiting Jerusalem during Sukkot in 2009, I was warmly welcomed into the home of Helen and Avi. The family of friends in London, we had only met via email before I stepped across their threshold late one Saturday evening. (Hosting a perfect stranger in your home is not part of the culture of London, but this was not London.)

The next morning, as Avi prepared the *sukkah*—the temporary palm-roofed structure in which we would eat our meals over the days ahead—Helen explained what the festival meant to them and other Jews:

> Eating and sleeping in the *sukkah* is a reminder of our forty years in the wilderness after we were freed from slavery, a time when we survived on the *manna* from Heaven that was gathered up each day; except, that is, for the morning of the Sabbath, when enough was gathered to last for two days.

# GRATITUDE

Aside from the historical significance of the festival, Avi told me that it is an also an opportunity to reflect on your good fortune and to share it with friends and family:

> Sitting in a temporary hut with fabric walls and a roof of wood and foliage raises questions about the nature of our normal existence in buildings of concrete. Our homes seem so solid and permanent, but are they really? We host many guests in the *sukkah*, as we do at home during the rest of the year, but sitting together in a *sukkah* feels different. We are in a temporary box, more fragile than our normal surroundings, separated by a thin fabric wall from the outside world. The feeling of transience is in the air.

At the synagogue that evening, the congregants bade me welcome, and it was clear why Avi and Helen had chosen to build their lives in this community which placed so much value on friendship and family. Later that evening, once the dinner dishes had been cleared away, the table was pushed aside to make space for the inflatable mattress where their son and young grandchildren would spend the night. This great adventure for the children marked the beginnings of a lifelong practice of expressing gratitude for their daily way of life, through a temporary return to more simple ways.

In other pilgrim traditions, humility and simplicity of living is expressed through special clothes that mark out the pilgrim from the regular traveller. *Kanvarias*, devotees of the Hindu god Shiva, must wear saffron robes and travel barefoot to collect the holy waters of the River Ganga. For Muslims, the Hajj begins when they enter the state of *ihram*. Women cover their heads and bodies, leaving their face and hands unconcealed; men change into simple, unstitched white cloth. On the Shikoku Henro, the circuit of eighty-eight shrines on the Japanese island of Shikoku, pilgrims traditionally wear a *hakui*, a white shirt symbolic of a shroud, signifying both their death to everyday life whilst on the pilgrimage and their readiness to face whatever fate awaits them.

Pilgrims also wear a *kasa*, a large straw hat inscribed with a Buddhist poem that is commonly engraved on coffins. The pilgrim staff is an aid to walking, but also represents both a tombstone and Kobo Daishi, the legendary spiritual leader who is said to accompany all pilgrims on the Shikoku *henro* trail. All items are inscribed with the words *dogyo ninin* (two people, one practice), with the implication that the pilgrim is never alone, but walking with the miraculous figure of Kobo Daishi.

Known as Kukai during his lifetime (774–835 CE), this Buddhist monk introduced the esoteric Shingon Buddhist tradition to Japan from China. He travelled the country, studying, teaching and retreating to the mountains to perform austerities associated with this form of Buddhism. Many of these involve *suigyo*, or purification in waterfalls, which in Japanese cosmology are associated with either the fiercely protective Shingon deity Fudo, or Suijin, the Shinto water god. During the ritual one should become one with the water, letting it flow over the whole person, imbibing it—echoing Shintoism's god–nature–human unity. Sometime after his death, the Emperors bestowed Kukai with the posthumous title of Kobo Daishi (Great Teacher Who Spread the Law of Buddhism). When the priests opened his tomb in order to place the imperial scroll within, his knee was found to be still warm; this was taken as evidence that he had not died, but was meditating.[7] Today Kobo Daishi remains in eternal meditation in his mausoleum at Koyasan, as he awaits the coming of the Maitreya, the Buddha of the Future. Thanks to his travels across Japan during his lifetime, performing miracles and spreading good luck, many pilgrim routes are attributed to this priestly roamer, including the Shikoku Henro around the island where he was born. The simple humility of the white-robed Shikoku pilgrim, enacting the journey of life while acknowledging the inevitability of death, has the same duality as the Eleusinian Mysteries or the rites of Lughnasadh: signifying both that we are humble and grateful to be alive, and that life itself is a miracle, a gift.

* * *

On a London summer's evening in June 2017, in the midst of an informal gathering at her family home, Ina shared with me her extraordinary tale of death deferred, and the pilgrimage she made to fulfil a promise pledged by others on her behalf: 'I was travelling through Croatia with my husband. We were on one of those roads that climbs up away from the coast, twisting and turning and hugging the mountainside until it joined the main highway. I was about six months pregnant, and while we hadn't planned to have a baby so soon, I was very happy. I called my aunt in Vancouver and told her we were enjoying a great trip. It was about 11 o'clock at night in Croatia and probably around lunchtime in Vancouver.'

Shortly after Ina's call to her aunt, her grandmother rang the same aunt saying she'd had a vision in which the baby was dead and that Ina was in mortal danger. The aunt was reassuring: 'I've just spoken to her on the phone, please stop worrying, she's fine.' But Ina wasn't fine. About twenty minutes after hanging up the phone, Ina and her husband had been involved in a catastrophic road accident.

'You know this gap in the central reservation they have to allow emergency vehicles to pass through?' Ina said to me. 'Well, a pick-up truck decided to do a U-turn through the gap. Of course, because it was an illegal manoeuvre he had his lights off, and we didn't see him. Our car ran straight into the back of the truck and we ended up hundreds of metres away, upside down off the side of the road. The seat belt that was meant to protect me did most of the damage. The baby died instantly as my uterus ruptured. My diaphragm ruptured, my spleen ruptured, I broke my vertebrae in three places. The baby ended up in my lung cavity with the result that only about 10 per cent of my lung capacity remained.'

The surgeons worked for ten hours to save Ina's life. It was just a small local hospital in a Croatian town, but they were used to treating really terrible injuries because of the recent Yugoslav Wars, and the staff were very skilled. 'One of them wanted to give me a hysterectomy as part of the triage to minimise internal bleeding. But the obstetric surgeon present said that if I lived I would want the chance to be a mother. So, he repaired the uterus. They didn't really believe I would survive the night, but the surgeon thought it worth doing—just in case. Perhaps because of the war, they embraced hope more readily.'

By the time Ina came out of surgery, her parents were sitting by her bed. Miraculously, even though she had several broken vertebrae, her spinal cord remained intact and she was helicoptered back to the UK. She was in a coma at first, and then in an induced coma for almost four weeks while surgery continued; she was rolled and moved, cut and stitched many times over this period. All is not peaceful inside the comatose mind, and during those four weeks Ina struggled against the terrifying morphine dreams that haunt her still. Meanwhile, 'My grandmother prayed for me, promising that if I survived I would make a pilgrimage to the shrine of Imam Reza in Mashhad, in Eastern Iran, and that if I had a son, I would call him Reza.'

Over the months that followed, Ina had many more operations, and she remained in a body brace for two years, but eventually she was well enough to travel and set out for Mashhad with her mother, Sabine. This was an act of enormous courage for them both. During the Revolution of 1979, Sabine, her husband and their children had been forced to flee Iran, leaving everything behind—their home, their friends, their work. Canada had been their refuge for a while, and then London. Going back to Iran meant risking arrest and the painful prospect of revisiting a lost existence, but the grandmother's promise had been made to be honoured. Ina and Sabine arrived in Tehran late at night but couldn't take the chance of checking into a hotel. They spent the night dozing in the airport lounge and early the next morning caught an onward flight to Mashhad.

'It was an amazing experience,' she told me. 'There were so many people around the burial chamber. Like swimming against the tide to get back to the shore, we had to be firm, determined and steady, and had to take care not to get exhausted and risk being swept back out by the current. Finally, we were there and we held onto the railings of the tomb and gave thanks.' The shrine in which this great whirlpool of pilgrims swirled contains the mausoleum of Ali ibn Musa al-Rida, or Imam Reza, the eighth Shia imam. He was believed to have been poisoned in 818 CE and this act was responsible for the naming of Mashhad, which in Arabic means 'holy tomb' and is related to the word for 'martyr'. The city grew in importance in the early thirteenth century and, over the years that followed, many new buildings were added to the holy precinct, including another mosque, several madrasas, a library and a museum. The mosque complex at Mashhad now claims to be the largest in the world by area, and each year attracts an estimated 12 million Shia pilgrims from Iran and beyond, with those completing the pilgrimage earning the honorific title of Mashtee.

On their way back through Tehran, Ina and Sabine couldn't resist calling by the old neighbourhood where they had lived before the Revolution. Ina told me how they encountered two young girls aged about six or seven, linking their fingers loosely as they bowled along together, happy and laughing, throwing back their heads, not a care in the world. 'Seeing them transported me back to my own childhood and reconnected me to my 6-year-old self. It was in this brief moment that I suddenly acknowledged what had happened during my coma; that at the very moment when I found myself poised between life and death, I had chosen to live, to turn back and fight for survival.' Ina described how her pilgrimage was an act of both humility and gratitude: a recognition that she had survived, that her family and friends had prayed for her and promised on her behalf that if she lived, she would undertake this journey. 'It was a profound event in my life,' she said. 'I have three children now. My eldest son is called Reza.'

While Sabine and her family had to flee Iran, there are others who have sought refuge there, and among them are the many Hazara Afghans who have chosen to settle in Mashhad.[8] The Hazara are an ethnic group with mixed ancestry who speak Hazaragi, a variant of Persian; most are Shia Muslims, a religious minority in Afghanistan. Once persecuted by the Taliban at home, they comprise nearly half of all documented Afghans in Iran. Many left their country as a consequence of the Soviet invasion in 1979, and this coincided with the Islamic Revolution in Iran, which saw an open-door policy to Shia Muslims wishing to settle there. Some Hazara who initially came on pilgrimage to the shrine of Imam Reza chose not to return to a homeland where they faced discrimination and violence. In common with other marginalised groups around the world, life is often far from easy for the Hazara in Iran, but it appears that women in particular are grateful for their new home. One 60-year-old Hazara widow, interviewed as part of a 2007 study of the Hazara in Mashhad, described the advantages of remaining in Iran: 'Here [people] know us and we have been here for twenty-one years. No place is better than here; we are neighbours with Imam Reza.'

Such proximity to the shrine is believed to enhance both one's life chances in the present, and one's chances of salvation in the afterlife. Where hope lives, there is a sense of the future. More practically than this, living close to the shrine of Imam Reza appears to help with the healing of the spirit for those whose lives have been scarred by war. Islamic medicine underlines the connection between calm heart, calm breath, calm mind. The act of prayer is believed to be particularly effective, and these pilgrim-refugees' closeness to the shrine, combined with their thanksgiving and other religious practices, is thought to be hugely beneficial to their emotional recovery.

Indeed, gratitude seems to be a powerful agent for healing. It is a big topic in medical research, and several studies have found that a sense of gratitude can be of enormous value to patients recovering from traumatic illness or injury. One team of scientists from Poland and the US conducted a study into the role in the healing process of both predisposition to and expressions of gratitude. In the course of their research, the team worked with women suffering from breast cancer. All participants were assessed in advance for their dispositional differences and then divided evenly between two groups. One group was asked to actively report on why they felt grateful each day, while those in the other group were simply monitored on their state of mind and ability to cope with their condition. Those who were asked daily to list reasons to be thankful demonstrated better psychological well-being, and were able to find ways of coping with the fact of their illness.

Is Ina grateful that she survived? Undoubtedly, but could it also be the case that she recovered so completely because she was able to express her gratitude through pilgrimage? Very possibly. Giving thanks, it seems, is good for us. In recognising what we have, we spur the green shoot of hope in the unknown future: spring, autumn, and spring again.

9

# LIBERATION

'*The mountains are calling and I must go*'

John Muir[1]

In April 2017, after one last check, I closed my small rucksack, adjusted my bootlaces, switched off the lights and headed out of the door. By the time I had walked a score of yards, the bag already felt too heavy; but the airport train was due to leave in six minutes and I was committed. When the flight landed in Florence that evening, everything seemed lighter, and by the time I strode out from Siena the next morning with my old friend Constance, the sky a clear, cloudless blue, I felt almost weightless. Where did this sense of liberation come from? I have fulfilling work and a loving family, and I live in a functioning democracy—in every respect I am already free.

Setting out on this leg of the Via Francigena, the ancient route between Canterbury and Rome, Constance and I had laid aside the comforts and obligations of modern urban existence (she in Paris, me in London) to follow in the footsteps of the innumerable others down the ages who have traded the assurance of home for liberty, on the road to a sacred site. We had uploaded a helpful route app to our smartphones, but still preferred to be guided by the intermittent brown signposts depicting a medieval pilgrim: staff in hand, bundle over one shoulder. These signs acted as a reminder that we were on a journey of discovery, not just a hike through the glorious Tuscan landscape. The stereotypical figure on the route markers hails from an era when freedom was a rare privilege, and most ordinary people were villeins or serfs, the legal property of feudal lords. In the Middle Ages, with the exception of journeymen (specialist craftsmen) who had licence to roam, few could leave the confines of their village or town without permission. Added to this physical constraint, it was obligatory to make confession at least once a year to the local parish priest, and the threat of eternal damnation was a compelling inducement to bare all. This scrutiny of people's private lives by the Church authorities might have served to maintain a level of social order, but it was also open to abuse.

In his *Canterbury Tales*, the most despised of Chaucer's pilgrims is the Summoner, an official whose task was to bring those suspected of moral crimes to be judged by an ecclesiastical court. Paid a percentage of the fines imposed, summoners were often highly corrupt, seeking out sexual misdemeanours, imagined or real, and were not always beyond extorting money from the innocent through the threat of prosecution and public shame. Chaucer's Friar tells of how an archdeacon had 'a summoner ready to his hand':

> There was no craftier rascal in England;
> For he'd a secret set-up; private spies
> Told him of things that he could put to use,
> And he'd let off a whoremonger or two
> If they could lead to half a dozen more.
>
> ... That thief, the summoner (the friar went on)
> Had pimps ever ready at his beck and call,
> Like lures to fetch a hawk; and they'd tell all.

Confiding his trade secrets to a fiendish bailiff he meets along the road, the Summoner boasts how he will extort money from an innocent 'old girl who would rather cut her throat/Almost, than yield a penny of her goods.' By the end of the Tale, the extortionist gets his comeuppance and is carried off to Hell by the devil, who, by tradition, exacts his own toll from the wicked. But in the real-life Middle Ages, pilgrimage offered ordinary citizens a rare freedom from authority; for many, the considerable risks and discomforts of the open road were a price worth paying.

\* \* \*

Beyond the physical and the moral, there are other kinds of freedom: the space to think fresh thoughts; freedom from the comforts that bind us with coddling kindness; freedom from the inner 'governor' that keeps us safely within life's speed limits. In short, we can trade certainty and security for the chance to reconnect with the free spirit that lurks within, and millions of pilgrims do just that each year. Almost every June, around the time of the summer solstice, over 130,000 people begin to converge on a cattle farm in Somerset, England. In the days and weeks before they arrive, contractors work around the clock, building stages, installing sound systems and securing the boundaries of the 900-acre site that will host Glastonbury Festival. Almost 21 million people watch the televised highlights, but for those who actually take part, the conveniences of normal life are set aside in pursuit of a transcendent communal experience with music and dance at its heart. For teenagers leaving the jurisdiction of parents and joining their peers in unseen acts of revelry, being at Glastonbury is a mark of liberation; for older festival-goers, it's a sign that a free spirit lives on, despite the kids, the mortgage or the grey hair.

First held in 1970, Glastonbury has gained an almost mythical status: to be there, to be part of it, is an end in itself. There is no pilgrim passport to prove you made it, but 'selfies' in muddy boots (it almost always rains) serve just as well. In common with other major pilgrim gatherings, there is an air here of belonging to a much wider community: the festival's headline acts take a reduced fee; proceeds from ticket sales go to support good causes; and carefully chosen politicians are invited to address the crowd directly. This nod to collective goodwill echoes the Panhellenic festivals of old such as Olympia, where foreign dignitaries were invited to attend irrespective of any ongoing wars between the host and guest states. Glastonbury Festival may only have been around for a few decades, but the idea has been around for thousands of years. Worthy Farm is not technically in Glastonbury, but it's not too far; when the farmer Michael Eavis created the festival, he chose to take advantage of a place name already freighted with centuries of magic, romance and religion, at one time second only to Canterbury as a centre for pilgrimage in England.

Built on a high point of the Somerset levels, Glastonbury was once surrounded by the marshes and waters of an inland sea. Almost 2,000 years ago, Joseph of Arimathea is said to have landed by boat upon this Isle of Avalon. This is the same Joseph (there are many in the Bible) who asked permission of Pilate to take Jesus' body from the Cross once he was dead. With help from Nicodemus, Christ's body was then wrapped in linen and spices and placed in a man-made cave or tomb in Joseph's garden. Joseph is thought to have been a wealthy trader, and as such, it is conceivable that he travelled from the Levant to Britain, then a remote outpost of the Roman Empire. As legend tells, when he planted his staff into the ground, there sprung forth a tree of thorns. The direct descendant of the Glastonbury Thorn can be seen today and still magically blooms twice a year at Easter and at Christmas, when a sprig of blossom is sent to the British monarch for their festive table.

# LIBERATION

Some traditions suppose that Joseph brought with him to Glastonbury the Holy Grail, a vessel used variously at the Last Supper and to catch the drops of blood shed by Jesus on the Cross. Another tradition suggests that in earlier years Joseph brought with him the young Christ. In his poem 'And did those feet in ancient time', later set as the hymn 'Jerusalem', William Blake asks,

And did those feet in ancient time,
Walk upon Englands mountains green:
And was the holy Lamb of God
On Englands pleasant pastures seen!

While Blake's question must remain unanswered, we know with certainty that a church was built at Glastonbury as early as 712 CE. The bold (but erroneous) claim that this was the oldest church in Christendom marked it as a special destination for pilgrims, and in the tenth century an abbey was established here by St Dunstan (later Archbishop of Canterbury). When the Normans conquered England in 1066, they helped develop the site, and by the time it was recorded in the Domesday Book in 1086, Glastonbury Abbey had become the richest and most powerful monastery in England, thanks in part to the association with Joseph of Arimathea, a status that attracted pilgrims and their money. The scale of the site can still be seen today, and it is truly impressive, but in the twelfth century a devastating fire destroyed much of the immense church at its heart.

Following the blaze, the monks set about rebuilding but before long ran out of money. Critically the Lady Chapel, the big attraction for pilgrims, remained exposed to the elements and the Abbot now turned to the King for funds. However, as the Crown had been pursuing some expensive wars in Europe, the royal coffers rang hollow. What to do? Henry II knew at first hand the political value of being helpful in such matters—his crown having narrowly survived the murder of Thomas Becket—

and instead of money he reputedly offered the Abbot information that was worth its weight in gold. In his travels through Wales, the King had learnt on good authority (from a Welsh bard) that the legendary King Arthur was buried between two pyramids in the Abbey's churchyard. With no other prospect of solving the cash-roof-pilgrim problem, the Abbot grasped this slender straw of opportunity and ordered the monks to start digging. Sure enough, as the bard had predicted, Arthur's remains were discovered entombed in a hollowed oak 5 metres below ground, beneath a stone which, so it is told, read, '*Hic iacet sepultus inclitus rex Arturius in insula Avalonia*'—Here lies interred the famous King Arthur on the Isle of Avalon.

The legend of King Arthur and his Queen Guinevere had recently been enjoying a popular revival,[2] and the late-twelfth-century discovery of Arthur's remains brought tens of thousands of pilgrims to Glastonbury. Their generous offerings enabled the monks to complete the building work and Glastonbury's status as the richest and most powerful abbey in England was restored, for the time being at least. Much later, Glastonbury's wealth and influence made it an inevitable target for Henry VIII's Reformation, the King ordering for the Abbey to be plundered and burnt down. As a final nail in the coffin, the last Abbot, Richard Whyting, was hung, drawn and quartered here on the orders of Henry's 'enforcer' Thomas Cromwell. But life is long, especially when it comes to sacred sites, and aside from the summer festival crowd, each year thousands of pilgrims from many faiths visit this deeply spiritual place. 'The Pilgrim Reception in Glastonbury' rejoices in 'unity through diversity' and serves all who come.

Many of them come to climb the mysterious Glastonbury Tor: a cone-shaped hill that overlooks the small town, notable for a system of terraces leading up to the summit. Thought to date from Neolithic times, the purpose of the terracing remains unclear, but some believe it is a three-dimensional labyrinth, which was used for ritual purpose. Others see the terraces as notches in the slope of the Tor corresponding to the trajectory of the sunrise on the winter solstice some 5,000 years ago. One might easily view Glastonbury's enduring appeal through the dark glass of cynicism: successive religious, political and economic interests using legend and brand identity to attract funds from pilgrims and, more latterly, festival-goers intent on letting their hair down. But setting all this aside, Glastonbury shares with other enduring pilgrim destinations that elusive sense that 'the veil between heaven and earth is more transparent here.' The desire to feel liberated would seem to be in high demand even amongst those who enjoy life in a liberal democracy.

\* \* \*

This idea that there are places where Heaven is closer to Earth is shared by many faiths, including Hinduism, and the association between festival and liberation is nowhere greater than at that greatest of all pilgrim gatherings, the Kumbh Mela. Rotating across four sites over a complex twelve-year astrological cycle, the Mela attracts tens of millions of Hindus who come to wash away their bad karma in the hope of attaining liberation from the cycle of birth, death and rebirth. The sites (Hardwar, Ujjain, Nashik and Prayagraj) are all close to rivers and it was at these four places that the elixir of life, *amrita*, was spilt by the demigods after a battle with demons. Two opposing forces—the demons and the demigods—had assembled on the shores of the Milk Ocean, which exists in a certain region of the cosmos. They agreed to work together to churn the ocean, to produce the nectar of immortality. Using the serpent king Vasuki as a rope for churning, and with the demons at the head and the demigods at the tail, they churned for 1,000 years, until a pot of nectar was eventually produced.

The original proposition was that they would share this elixir, but trust between the two parties was weak, and a battle ensued.

The demigods stole the pot, or *kumbh*, and the demons gave chase. Drops of the precious substance were spilt along the way, conferring magical properties on the places where they fell.[i] Today, there is a chance of achieving salvation through the act of pilgrimage to one of these places, the greatest of which is Prayagraj (formerly Allahabad). Also known as the *Tirtharaja*, the King of Sacred Places, Prayagraj sits at the Triveni Sangam, the confluence point where the waters of the Ganga and Yamuna Rivers flowing down from the Himalaya converge with each other, and with the mystical Sarasvati River, which has no earthly form. It is thought that here, at the time of the *mela*, a bridge or *tirtha* opens up between this world and the next, giving the Hindu devout the hope of being freed from *samsara*, the endless cycle of reincarnation. Upon cremation, the remains of the deceased ascend into the atmosphere, returning to Earth with the monsoon rains, where they enter the life of plants, animals and ultimately humans, at which point, entering the semen of men, a soul once again begins the cycle of new life.

Religious ascetics known as *sadhus* (men) and *sadhviya* (women) seek to achieve *moksha*: liberation from these earthly bonds, and becoming one with *brahman*—the absolute reality or indefinable state of supreme existence that is the universe. To this end, they give up their worldly goods and adhere to Vedic practices, including yoga, which date back many thousands of years. On the most auspicious day of the Kumbh Mela, the *sadhus* are first to enter the river as dawn breaks. By doing so at the auspicious time of the festival, they are purified by the waters of the Triveni Sangam. The *sadhus*, often naked or semi-naked, their bodies daubed in ash and their faces painted according to their particular devotional practices, are a great feature of the event, often holding court and

---

[i] The word *kumbh* refers not only to the pot of nectar but also to the zodiac sign of Aquarius, the water-carrier in Western astrology.

offering wisdom, blessing or comfort to the faithful, who make small offerings of food or money in return.

Like Glastonbury, Prayagraj has had many incarnations during the long course of history. Originally Prayag, it was renamed Ilahabad in 1575, later anglicised to Allahabad, and only recently officially changed to Prayagraj. The first known witness account of a *mela* there comes to us through a Chinese Buddhist monk, Xuanzang. Born in c. 602 CE in the east of China, in what is now Henan province, Xuanzang made an epic, seventeen-year trip to India to learn about Buddhism. At the time of his journey, foreign travel was forbidden by the Chinese rulers, and Xuanzang—also known as the Prince of Pilgrims—had to persuade many along the way to help him overcome the obstacles that lay in his path, not least the arid deserts and mountain ranges along the Silk Road of Central Asia.

In his work *Great Tang Records on the Western Regions*, Xuanzang records his observations of a 'great event at the confluence of two rivers, where an estimated 250,000 pilgrims ritually washed away their sins'.[3] Xuanzang witnessed the festival in 644 CE—by Indian standards, recent history. The spiritual traditions of the Ganga are truly ancient and hark back to many thousands of years earlier. The sacred river's foundation myth tells how a sage ordered it to be brought down from the heavens to purify his souls and those of his ancestors. Enraged by this command, the mighty Ganga decided to bring forth her great force to destroy the earth. In the hope of saving the world from this terrible fate, Lord Shiva was called upon to restrain her impact by receiving Ganga into his matted locks. Thanks to Shiva's action, Ganga took a thousand years to descend, her power ultimately dispersed through the many streams that thread down from the mountains and out towards the sea.

But what of the Sarasvati, the river that has no earthly form? Given that the Ganga exists as both a real and a sacred river, there is no reason to assume that the mythical Sarasvati might not also once have been a real, life-giving force. The river's identification has been the quest of many scholars, and it has variously been identified as the Ghaggar-Hakra River in northern India and Pakistan, the Helmand River in Afghanistan, and the Milky Way. All three rivers of the Triveni Sangam are mentioned in the *Rigveda*, a liturgical text of indeterminate antiquity but thought to date back to c. 1500–600 BCE, as well as in the *Mahabharata*, an epic poem thought to have its origins in the eighth or ninth century BCE. The *Rigveda* describes the Sarasvati as flowing out to the Arabian Sea, while the *Mahabharata* describes it as flowing into the sands.

Starting with these two clues, a group of geologists, palaeontologists and oceanographers from universities in India and the US came up with a hypothesis: the Great Rann of Kutch (GRK) was formerly a gulf in the Arabian Sea, but became silted up and filled in over the course of time. Could this have been the end of the Sarasvati's journey from the mountains to the sea?[4] They examined archaeological evidence of Bronze Age settlements in and around the GRK and embarked on a programme of exploratory drilling, cutting through layers of sediment representing many hundreds of thousands of years. The cores they brought up suggested to the team that a 'large Himalayan or Sub-Himalayan Sarasvati-like river may have discharged into the Arabian Sea until around 10,000 BCE'. This finding did not conclusively prove the prior existence of the Sarasvati, but it does illustrate the merit of taking the long view when trying to understand why some places exert such a profound pull for pilgrims.

In India as elsewhere, rivers are life-giving forces, but it's hard to overstate the spiritual significance of the Ganga in particular. The *Mahabharata* spells out its value to pilgrims: 'by holding that sacred stream, touching it and bathing in its waters one rescues one's ancestors to the seventh generation, one's descendants to the seventh generation.' It's a powerful idea—the river as a source of liberation and salvation not just for the individual, but for the generations before and after—and this sense of the eternal recurs as a motif in the writings of one of the most notable liberators of the twentieth century, Jawaharlal Nehru. In a letter to his daughter Indira, Nehru writes of his feelings towards the landscape he can see from his prison cell, where 'for two thousand years or more, innumerable pilgrim souls have marched through these valleys and mountains to Badrinath and Kedarnath and Gangotri, from where the baby Ganga emerges.' As the letter continues, he declares his love of India's rivers—how he longed to explore them not only literally but also metaphorically, 'to trace them from the dawn of history, to watch the processions of men and women, of cultures and civilisations, going down the broad streams of these rivers.'[5]

Nehru's feelings for the landscape of his homeland offer a glimpse of why certain places maintain their hold in the spiritual imagination, in some cases across millennia. The poetry of his writing owes much to the *Mahabharata* itself, which iterates all of India's rivers in a long melodic flow: 'the enormous Ganga, Sindhu or Indus, Sarasvati, Godvari, Narmada, the great river Bahuda, Shatadru, Chandra-bhaga, the mighty river Jamuna, Drishadvati, Vipasha, Vipapa, Sthula-valuka, the river Vetravati, the river Krishna-vena, Iravati, Vitasta, Payoshni, Devika, Veda-smitra...'[6] This Sanskrit epic then provides the clue to what draws pilgrims to the Triveni Sangam in their tens of millions: not just the confluence of the three rivers, but the confluence of the past, the present and the unseen future.

Nehru's family belonged to a community of Pandit Kashmiri Brahmans who had moved to Allahabad as a consequence of the Indian Uprising of 1857 and, through the generations, remained fiercely committed to the cause of independence from British rule. Wanting his son to get a broader view of the world, Nehru's father appointed a tutor who introduced the young Jawaharlal to the teachings of Theosophy, a spiritual movement that became closely associated with India's independence movement. Nehru recounts the effect this had on him in his autobiography, describing a dream that began in adolescence and recurred throughout his life in which he experienced astral flying: his soul floating free above the mountains and plains, covering vast distances and seeing the panorama of India spread out below. Nehru's vision of a country equally free was to land him in prison many times—he spent 3,529 days in prison in total, equivalent to almost ten years of his life—but ultimately, he and others prevailed. In 1947, Nehru was appointed as the first prime minister of a newly independent India.

Notwithstanding his later frustration with the effect of religious taboos and superstition on India's ability to modernise, the Ganga remained spiritually significant for Nehru, and he asked that, on his death, a portion of his ashes be cast into the Triveni Sangam:

> I have discarded much of past tradition and custom and am anxious that India should rid herself of all shackles that bind and constrain her and divide her people, and suppress vast numbers of them, and prevent the free development of the body and the spirit; though I seek all this, yet I do not wish to cut myself off from the past completely. I am proud of that great inheritance that has been, and is ours, and I am conscious that I too, like all of us, am a link in that unbroken chain which goes back to the dawn of history in the immemorial past of India. That chain I would not break, for I treasure it and seek inspiration from it.[7]

Nehru was the third generation of his family to fight for self-rule, but this 'great inheritance' he describes goes back many thousands of years, to the early Bronze Age Harappan civilisation of the Indus Valley. Today, our understanding of the Harappan age has been very largely deciphered through the Indus Seals, which include references to Plakshagra, the mythical birthplace of the Sarasvati River; this has led some archaeologists to conclude that the *Rigveda* must have been in existence by 4000 BC. Where does that leave us? Even though the chronology is fragmented and incomplete, it is possible to piece together a picture of the Triveni Sangam as a place of cultural and spiritual importance that stretches far back to the very beginnings of human habitation in this part of the world, and with it the practice of pilgrimage and the hope of liberation. Here the *Rigveda* describes how

> Flower-like the heels of the wanderer,
> His body groweth and is fruitful;
> All his sins disappear,
> Slain by the toil of his journeying.

Is this what we mean when we think of pilgrimage as a quest for liberation? The setting aside of the burdens of guilt or regret, disappointment or longing that we accrue as we travel through life? Of course, there can be no single answer; the concept of freedom or liberty, like beauty, or love, is just a placeholder for something so complex and personal that it defies definition. We each know what we mean by it, even if we can't necessarily articulate it, and it means something uniquely different to each of us. For Nehru, it was wrapped up in the spirit of his ancient homeland and the desire to free it from British rule. We might flinch now at the power of the digital giants that dominate our data, our shopping, our photo albums, mail and address books, but in the eighteenth and nineteenth centuries, a commercial enterprise—the British East India Company—dominated almost every aspect of life in India, including trade, administration and defence. Pilgrimage was no exception. In 1806, the Company became responsible for the management of the Jagannath Temple in the east of India; from 1812 to 1840, it took over the collection of a pilgrim tax at a number of other important Hindu shrines. The Company passed a law in effect outlawing *sadhus*, turning holy men into criminals overnight. Imagine Google or Facebook taking over major shrines in today's religious landscape and taxing those who went there, and you can imagine that oppressing pilgrims might have proved to be an imperial step too far—the beginning of the end for unfreedom.

\* \* \*

Almost a century before the end finally came for the British Raj, a talented young employee of that imperialist administration was dreaming of his own liberty, and he was willing to go to great lengths to achieve it. Richard Burton formed the plan to go in disguise to Mecca, and his subsequent account of this expedition made his reputation. Over the course of his career Burton become one of the most noted explorers of his age and, like many habitual solo travellers, the freedom of the road enhanced rather than diminished his natural eccentricity. After a lifetime of expeditions, including one to find the source of the Nile, when the end came he was buried alongside his wife in a churchyard in Surrey, his stone tomb formed in the shape of a Bedouin tent decorated with the Islamic star and crescent moon. Peering through a glass at the rear, visitors can see two coffins and some dusty artefacts, including camel bells and a crucifix.

At the time of his journey to the Arabian Peninsula in 1853, Burton was employed by the British East India Company, and had requested and been refused permission by his employers to take extended leave to explore Arabia. They did, however, grant him a long furlough to undertake a diversion via Egypt on his way back to India from England—an extra leg ostensibly to master his Egyptian Arabic. He seized the opportunity to continue with his preparations to visit the Hijaz, albeit within a more constrained timeframe. Burton applied to the Royal Geographical Society for funds and was duly granted £200 to travel first to Medina and then on to Mecca. He had eleven months to complete the trip and return to his job as an officer of the East India Company, or risk being fired.

As we saw in Chapter Eight, one of the rituals of liberation for pilgrims through the ages has been the casting off of normal attire in favour of special clothing. But Burton went much further in donning the persona of a *hajji*, and before he set off had himself circumcised as a precaution, believing that discovery as an infidel would lead to certain death. He started as he meant to go on, embarking on the first leg of his voyage from Southampton to Alexandria in character as Shaykh Abdullah bin Yusef el Farangi (Abdullah, son of Joseph the foreigner)—a Persian scholar and medic who spoke little English. Burton spent the two-week sea voyage to Alexandria growing his beard and conversing in broken English with fellow passengers, using the several Eastern languages he'd learnt while working as an engineer in the 18th Sepoy Regiment in Sindh province.[8] He remarks that '[in] the matter of assuming an Oriental nationality, Nature has been somewhat propitious to me: golden locks and blue eyes, however per se desirable, would have been sad obstacles to progress in swarthy Arabia. And to what Nature had begun, Art contributed by long years of laborious occupation.'[9] Added to these natural advantages, Burton had a keen eye for behavioural detail, noting, for example, the way in which a devout Indian took a drink of water—from how he would raise the glass to his lips to how he would give thanks to God once his thirst was quenched.

Beyond the initial, heart-filling romance of Burton's vision of Oriental adventure, there was the more practical question of packing.[ii] In his account, he lists the few necessaries he acquired in Alexandria for the onward journey:

---

[ii] Many of the items he listed—waterproof, sleeping bag, water bottle, medicaments—can be found in many modern travel guides and indeed Burton's list more or less mirrored the contents of my and Constance's

A change or two of clothing, a substantial leather money belt to carry my gold, a little cotton bag for silver and small change for ready use in the breast pocket, a zemzemiyah, or water bag of goat-skin, a huge cotton umbrella of Cairene make, bright yellow, like an overgrown marigold, a coarse Persian rug, which acted [as] bed, table, chair, [a medicine chest] and lastly a *kafan*, or shroud, without which no person sets out for Mecca.[10]

He explains that, should a pilgrim get sick or wounded while on the Hajj, the caravan cannot wait for him. The patient is therefore ceremonially washed, wrapped up in his *kafan*, partly covered in sand, and left to his fate.

While Burton's journey to Mecca was not a true pilgrimage— he was, after all, an infidel—he was impelled by that same mix-ture of curiosity and risk-seeking that drives many pilgrims to cast off the comforts of their everyday selves in pursuit of some-thing greater and more profound, more free. Burton could not and did not claim to be the first European to enter Mecca, but only the first to do so in disguise, and to record everything of his journey in great detail.[11] In his written account of the trip, he reveals that he was 'curious to see what men are mostly content only to hear of—namely, Moslem inner life in a purely Mohammedan land—and longing to set foot within that myste-rious Mecca which no vacation tourist has yet measured, sketched, photographed and described.'[iii]

Burton's journey to the holy cities of Islam became one of the defining features of his reputation as an explorer and chronicler,

---

rucksacks on the road to Rome—although when C. succumbed to crip-pling blisters after 2 days of walking, I did not abandon her wrapped in a shroud at the side of the road.

[iii] As we saw with the Russian spy Tsybikov in Chapter 6, Burton was not alone in his choice of disguise as a pilgrim in the 19th century: Buddhists from Central or South-East Asia were the foreigners who could enter Tibet.

soldier and poet. His facility in learning foreign languages—he reputedly mastered twenty-nine in all, over the course of his life—meant that he was able to engage fully with his fellow travellers and record in detail what he saw and heard. Added to this, his prose style hooks the reader by the ear, so that even now we can feel for ourselves the heat of the road, the Damascus caravan 'dragging its slow length' across the desert between Medina and Mecca, where

> The filmy spray of the sand and the up-seething of the atmosphere, the heat-reek and the dancing of the air upon the baked surfaces of the bright yellow soil, blending with the dazzling blue above, invest the horizon with a broad band of deep dark green, and blurs the gaunt figures of the camels, which at a distance, appear strings of gigantic birds.

Not only did this false pilgrimage of Richard Burton contravene the provision forbidding non-believers from visiting the Holy Cities, but he wilfully misled his employers in order to get time away from work to make the trip. Ultimately, however, it was not his duplicity that would prove most troubling to his employers, but the contrary: his frank honesty. Travelling by steamer down the Mahmudiyah Canal and the Nile on his way to Suez, Burton had made friends with a former shawl and cotton merchant, Miyan Khudabaksh Namdar; as the caravanserais in Cairo were full, he had lodged with him for a fortnight. Their conversations had alerted Burton to the possibility of an Indian uprising against British rule, and he included this observation in his published account of the trip.[12] Burton was not alone, it seemed, in craving liberty, and his prediction, however unpalatable to his masters, was to prove accurate. Within two years of his account, in 1857, the Indian 'Mutiny' claimed the lives of hundreds of thousands of men, women and children, amongst both British and Indian communities.[iv]

---

[iv] The term 'Indian Mutiny' is fraught with controversy, implying a

Prior to the rebellion of 1857, the British authorities were already suspicious of the Hajj, seeing it as a threat to their interests on many fronts.[v] Indian Muslims would have been exposed to a different ideological framework in the holy cities, one in which the spiritual authority of 'faith' had primacy; on returning to India, they would naturally see imperial power in a new light: less omnipotent, less inevitable, less entitled to command obeisance. Added to these concerns around protecting Britain's political power and commercial interests were the wider considerations of security and responsibility. At the time that Burton was sailing to Alexandria, the British ruled over the greatest number of Muslims in the world; followers of Islam comprised the largest religious group in an Empire that reached across the world, from Canada to New Zealand, covering parts of Africa, Asia, the Middle East and the Caribbean.[13]

The fifth pillar of Islam, the duty to undertake the Hajj, falls to all Muslims healthy enough to travel and with the financial means to do so. In earlier centuries, the challenges of long-distance travel had meant that only the very wealthy, the very devout or those travelling on the charity of others were able to make the journey. Pilgrims coming from Nigeria and other parts of West Africa would have taken months to get to Mecca, and those coming from Central Asia, India and Indonesia had faced slow overland travel, followed by sea crossings made under sail. This all changed with the introduction of steamships from the 1830s, as well as the completion of the Suez Canal in 1869. These innovations not only helped to facilitate international trade

---

betrayal of trust and authority. Alternative terms include Rebellion of 1857, the Indian Uprising, Great Indian Mutiny, Sepoy Mutiny, Sepoy Rebellion and Sepoy War.

[v] In 1803, three Sumatran pilgrims returning from Mecca had instigated a jihad against the Dutch authorities which continued into the 1830s.

for the various European imperial powers—the new, faster routes to Arabia cut the journey time for pilgrims too. European shipping companies soon entered the pilgrim travel market, running lines from Bombay or Singapore to Jeddah, and the numbers making the Hajj each year grew exponentially.

The masses' newfound freedom to make the Hajj presented several challenges, both to the British administration in India, and to the Sharif of Mecca. Large numbers of people travelling together raised the possibility of epidemic disease, and indeed this occurred many times during the nineteenth and twentieth centuries, notably when an outbreak of cholera in 1865 killed 15,000 of the 90,000 pilgrims in the Hijaz at the time. As this epidemic spread across Europe, it claimed a further 200,000 lives.[14] This was a serious concern for the authorities in Mecca, but equally for the British, as India was identified as the seat of the epidemic. Quarantine centres were established in Egypt and Yemen for pilgrims from India in the years that followed. This was not the first intervention by the British in the matter of pilgrimage. In the early 1800s, the British authorities had prevented *sadhus* from collecting alms at *melas* in India, and had taken it upon themselves to exact a punitive tax of 1 rupee from each pilgrim wishing to enter the waters. By comparison, these quarantine centres could at least be interpreted as an act of public interest, albeit one informed by the Empire's ever-present fear of revolt. Whatever the motives behind the measure, it seemed to pit the natural liberation of pilgrimage against the constraints of an imperial bureaucracy struggling to maintain control.

While the British might have seen the growing number of pilgrims to Mecca as a threat to public health, or to law and order, commercial interests saw it as an opportunity. For many poor Indians, the new freedom to travel ended in bondage or death. Unscrupulous ship-owners driven by profit rather than piety packed in as many passengers as possible, and conditions aboard many of the pilgrim ships were truly grim. The poor were often confined below decks for the entire voyage, on limited water rations; even by the standards of the time, the inhumanity of the pilgrim trade was a scandal. The British attempted to address this by engaging Thomas Cook in 1883 as official agents. This appointment was in part a response to the fate of the pilgrim ship the *Jeddah*, which was wrecked off the coast of Aden close to the end of its voyage from Singapore. The court report from 1881 details how Captain Clark, his wife, his first mate and his third engineer all jumped into a lifeboat, abandoning almost a thousand men, women and children adrift in a vessel that was sinking. The court found that, had the Captain shown some leadership, the combined efforts of the crew and the able-bodied passengers could have averted the crisis.[15] As it was, the ship was rescued by a passing Dutch vessel, the *Antenor*, whose chief officer bravely boarded the sinking ship and led the pilgrims in pumping the water out of the hull until the *Jeddah* safely reached port.

The *Jeddah* reappears as the *Patna* in Joseph Conrad's novel *Lord Jim*, published a few years later.[16] Conrad describes the pilgrims streaming aboard an ancient vessel, 'as old as the hills, lean like a greyhound, and eaten up with rust worse than a condemned water-tank.' In Conrad's retelling of events, as the ship begins to take on water, Jim—the ship's chief officer—leaps into the lifeboat alongside the other crew, leaving the passengers to whatever fate awaited them. In abandoning his own vessel, Jim breaks the code of seamanship, thereby sacrificing his honour in order to save his life. *Lord Jim* is about fear and guilt, and it is clear that the British Empire of the late nineteenth century was plagued by both. The shadow of the Indian 'Mutiny' remained—fearing further revolt from its subjects, the Raj was torn between a policy of non-interference with the Hajj and its responsibility towards British Indian citizens, many of whom were destitute and dying on the streets of Mecca. In 1927, the Hajj attracted over 130,000 overseas pilgrims, and 5,000 destitute Indians applied for repatriation.[17]

In this period around the turn of the century, there were many who travelled to Mecca thanks to *zakat*—charity, the third pillar of Islam—but could not afford to return, exposing many who had completed the Hajj to a choice between destitution and exploitation. A plantation-owner based in Singapore called Sayyid Mohammed bin Alsagoff, whose shipping enterprises included the fated *Jeddah*, found a way to capitalise on this. Labour conditions on his estates were notoriously bad, leading to a shortage of willing workers. His scheme was simple: he shipped poor pilgrims stranded in the Hajj back to Singapore, and in return they worked off the debt on his plantations. For many trapped in indentured labour, the freedom of pilgrimage ended in near-slavery.

As the sun finally set on the British Empire, the full responsibility for the welfare and management of pilgrims transferred to the authorities in Saudi Arabia, and today it is not freedom to travel that constrains the faithful from making the Hajj, but sheer logistics. There are over 1.9 billion Muslims in the world today, projected to reach 2.76 billion by 2050,[18] and with the Hajj taking place only once a year, it is inevitable that many must wait several years before they are able to fulfil this important article of their faith. Consideration for public safety has necessitated the introduction of a quota system, with Hajj visas granted to 2 million or so Muslims each year.[vi] For some, the truly liberating aspect of the Hajj occurs as the individual enters the ocean of other people. The Hajj virtual project that accompanied a British Museum exhibition in 2012 recorded the

---

[vi] Quotas are set per the number of Muslims in each country. In some, visas are then distributed according to a lottery system; in others, they are allocated via the government or through specialist travel agencies.

accounts of many *hajjis*, including Zehra: 'Once you remove your [regular] clothes and all the signs which distinguish "you" as an individual, you may enter into the heart of the crowd.' Here, she tells us, the individual melts away, assuming a new form as part of 'mankind', and the group becomes a 'people'. Like the Hindu pilgrims at the Kumbh Mela, and so many others on the road to Rome or Jerusalem, the greatest liberation of all comes in the escape from the boundaries of the self.

* * *

Beyond the uplifting earthly joy of living faith, the achievement of national independence, the partying at Glastonbury, the freedom of the road to Rome, comes the final liberation that awaits us all. Varanasi, also known as Benares or Kashi, is the holiest of the Sapta Puri: India's seven holy cities. For many who come to Varanasi, their purpose is to die in this holiest of places, and by so doing to improve the chance to attain *moksha*—liberation from the self and from the cycle of rebirth. In his essay 'The Pilgrim's Guide', Mark Twain describes Varanasi as 'a big church, a religious hive in which every cell is a temple, a shrine, or mosque', noting that 'The Ganges itself, and every individual drop of water in it are temples.' Twain observes a Hindu man working for salvation by forming tiny deities no bigger than carpet tacks from a wad of clay, a grain of rice stuck into each to represent a *lingam*, a symbol of Shiva's life-force. 'Each day he makes 2,000 of these tiny figures and throws them into the sacred waters of the Ganges, attracting the homage of the pious and their loose change.'[19]

More than a century later, my friend Jo, who lived in India for many years, described Varanasi to me as 'an assault on the senses', a place where death is very normal and 'it isn't at all shocking or distressing to see dozens of bodies being carried through the streets on stretchers wrapped in white shrouds by the male relatives, whilst everyday life carries on around them.' She recalled the overwhelming smell and sounds of the city, even at night, when the streets thronged with 'thousands upon thousands of people and nearly as many cows'; and then the calm serenity of early morning, as pilgrims descended into the sacred river to pray. 'We took a boat and rowed along the Ganges at sunrise. This was one of my defining and most memorable moments from our five years in India. The boy-priests sitting meditating, and some chanting cross-legged on stone ledges high above the Ghats.'

For those pilgrims who come to die, the true focus is on the days and hours leading up to the moment when they will abandon their earthly form. There are many hospices in Varanasi, so-called *muktibhavans*, where the dying can stay under the care of their families as they prepare for the final liberation, and with it the hope of eternal salvation. In his study *Dying the Good Death*, Christopher Justice describes the scene as a rickshaw arrives at one such hospice carrying three men, their dying grandmother laid horizontally across their knees. It was clear she had come straight from hospital (the IV catheter still in place in her hand); by bringing her to Varanasi, her grandsons were ensuring that the very last thing to pass her lips would be the sacred waters of the Ganga. Calling in on the family the following morning, the author found that she had died soon after arrival and that 'by then she had been burned and her ashes were floating many miles down the Ganga.'[20]

* * *

Not all pilgrim deaths are so serenely liberating. In 2013, the Kumbh Mela attracted over 100 million, the crowd so vast that it could be seen by satellite—a sea of people as perilous in its unpredictability as any true ocean. Crowds on this scale can be truly catastrophic, and on this occasion a sudden surge near the railway station led to the death of forty-two pilgrims. In 2015, a panic in the crowd at Mecca caused a stampede in which 2,400 people perished. Looking for an answer to this problem, a team of scientists led by the University of Amsterdam embarked on a multi-year programme to build a dynamic computational model that could help with the management of extremely large crowds. The project combines geoinformatics and remote sensing to look for patterns and warning signs: electronic devices, including wrist-bands, smartphones, drones and other sources provide real-time data that can be used to predict how a massive crowd of millions of individuals on the move might shift and change at any moment.

We can imagine a time when digital and geospatial technologies such as these would make physical pilgrimage unnecessary; a time when we could, if we wished, make a pilgrimage without leaving home, our senses stimulated instead by a virtual reality headset, augmented by smell, heat or cold. Cyber-pilgrimage already exists in a basic form and more sophisticated virtual-reality experiences cannot be long in coming. For some, this may be enough, like the medieval penitents who paid others to make their pilgrimage for them, or the sensible folks watching Glastonbury Festival from the comfort of the sofa. But for many pilgrims, the very act of stepping outside the constraints of what is safe and certain brings with it the prospect of liberation. Surely no virtual reality technology, however sophisticated, can substitute for the freeing sensation of carrying everything you might need in one small backpack, as you set off along some ancient sacred path. At the close of Mark Twain's great odyssey, *Huckleberry Finn*, the eponymous narrator sums up the choice between the security of home and the freedom of the open road: 'I reckon I got to light out for the Territory ahead of the rest, because Aunt Sally she's going to adopt me and sivilize me, and I can't stand it. I been there before.'

10

# ENLIGHTENMENT

*'The happiest man is he who learns from nature the lesson of worship'*

Ralph Waldo Emerson[1]

The precise dates are unresolved, but sometime in the fifth century BCE, a princeling was born in Lumbini, Nepal. He was to become one of the world's great teachers. Siddhartha Gautama, later the Buddha, was the son of a leader of the Shakya clan. He was raised in a sheltered, courtly world of wealth and privilege, but from the very start he was destined for an entirely different path.

On the day of his birth, Asita—a great sage who dwelt on the side of a Himalayan mountain—beheld the gods and learnt that a child had been born who was bound for greatness. Along with his nephew Naradatta, Asita rose up like a royal swan and flew through the air, landing just outside the gates of the city of Kapilavatthu, and completing on foot his journey to see the boy's father, Suddhodana. Upon seeing the child, shining with the brilliance of a hundred merits and adorned with the thirty-two marks of a great man, Asita declared that he would follow one of two paths, and no other: if he dwelt within a house, he would become a great king; but if he went forth into the world, he would become a Tathagata, a fully enlightened Buddha. Asita then fell to the floor weeping, and Suddhodana, concerned that the sage had foreseen some danger for his son, asked what ailed him. But Asita was weeping for himself, realising that due to his own great age he would not live long enough to hear the Buddha's doctrine.

This is one of many versions of the opening scenes of the life of Buddha, a life exemplifying the idea of a physical outward journey in pursuit of an inner quest to understand the nature of existence. As we now know, young Siddhartha's journey took him along a path from being a bodhisattva (one who seeks enlightenment) to achieving the full state of Buddhahood or enlightenment—but his father had resolved to send him along the other path foreseen by Asita. With this intent, Suddhodana kept his son at home, making sure he received a good education in all intellectual matters, but ensuring that he saw nothing of the pains and ills of the world. In the Pali Canon, the standard collection of scriptures in the Theravada Buddhist tradition, Buddha gives an account of this period of his life:

> I was delicate, O monks, extremely delicate, excessively delicate. In my father's dwelling lotus-pools had been made, in one blue lotuses, in another red, in another white, all for my sake ... Night and day a white parasol was held over me so that I should not be touched by cold or heat, by dust or weeds or dew.[2]

He goes on to describe that he had three palaces: one for the hot season, one for the cold season and one where, in the four months of the rainy season, he was entertained by female minstrels. Siddhartha's father was determined that he should fulfil his destiny as a great king, a universal monarch, and throughout his development from boy to man, he was shielded from anything that might make him question the injustice or cruelty of the world. In his father's household, the Buddha tells us, even the slaves and workmen ate rice and meat, rather than the more usual sour gruel.

Once Siddhartha reached manhood, it was inevitable that he would encounter the realities of mortality: old age, sickness, sorrow, impurity and death. Aged twenty-nine, he was out for a ride in the park with his charioteer when he encountered an old man. The idea that old age and death awaited him truly horrified the poor naïf. He rushed home to his father, who seemingly responded by ordering more dancing girls to distract him. On subsequent outings, Siddhartha came across a sick man and a corpse, each time returning home in despair. Finally, coming face to face with a man who had abandoned all worldly matters, Siddhartha decided that he too would abandon the world. But this was also the day of birth of Siddhartha's own son, Rahula (meaning 'fetter'). He went to the chamber to find mother and child asleep on a bed strewn with jasmine. Old age, sickness, death, and now birth—Siddhartha had encountered the four truths of life. He considered picking up his infant son, but realised that if the child or the mother awoke then he could never leave. He turned around and departed. The day of the Great Renunciation had arrived, and Siddhartha was now a wandering ascetic, searching for meaning.

After years of meditation, and not a little suffering and hardship, the bodhisattva achieved his goal and became Buddha, 'the enlightened one'. He spent the rest of his life teaching the eight practices of the eightfold path: right view, right resolve, right speech, right conduct, right livelihood, right effort, right mindfulness, and right *samadhi* (meditative consciousness). At the end of his long life, Buddha declared that he could die happy in the knowledge that he had not kept a single teaching hidden in a closed hand. Most importantly, perhaps, he urged his disciples to follow their own guiding light, and look within themselves to find joy. In all the centuries since, people all over the world have lived by an ethos of finding their own truth, and going out to discover what lies within.

This ancient idea of embarking on a physical journey that is truly an inner journey re-emerged in the middle of the nineteenth century amongst the Transcendentalists of New England. The pre-eminent exponents of this philosophy were Ralph Waldo Emerson and Henry David Thoreau, and the epicentre of the movement was Concord, Massachusetts. Home to many other notable New Englanders of the 1800s, including the writers Louisa May Alcott and Nathaniel Hawthorne, Concord was also an important symbol of the freedom and autonomy of the New World. It was here that the American War of Independence had begun. Famously, Paul Revere rode through the night of 18 April 1775 to warn the people of Concord that the redcoats were coming, and the first shots were fired here when the local militia or 'minutemen' confronted the British troops. Strike out and pursue your own truth, live by your own beliefs and values—the guiding resolution that had led the Pilgrim Fathers to these shores in the seventeenth century drove the cause of independence in the eighteenth, and was born anew with Transcendentalism in the nineteenth. But this time it was about more than faith and taxes.

In June 1893, many years after both Emerson and Thoreau had passed into legend, the 'Wilderness Prophet' John Muir made a pilgrimage to Concord, to see the places where the two men had lived and died, and in particular to see Walden Pond, the place of Thoreau's retreat and meditation, by now firmly established as a shrine to the ideal of free will. Thoreau was the son of a modest Massachusetts pencil-maker and a mother who had made sacrifices to fund his education, but—in common with the young Siddhartha Gautama—he was destined to choose his own path. While this path ultimately led him to make a greater and more enduring impact on the world, its beginnings looked distinctly unpromising. Thoreau eschewed a conventional career in academia or business, preferring instead to work only when money was needed. He claimed to have as many trades as he had fingers, and turned his hand to boat-building, fence-building, surveying, grafting fruit trees, gardening and other tasks as necessity demanded. Thoreau long dreamt of living simply on the land, writing in his diary, 'I want to go soon and live away by the pond where I shall hear only the wind whispering among the reeds.'

He was to have his wish. After a failed attempt to buy a farm, Thoreau was given a piece of land by Ralph Waldo Emerson and here, on this sparsely wooded plot by Walden Pond, not far from his parents' house, he erected a small hut, bought from an Irish labourer who had worked on the construction of the nearby Fitchburg Railroad. This is the setting for *Walden*, Thoreau's account of his time on the Pond. A little way into the text, he sets out the profound rationale for his actions: 'I went to the woods because I wished to live deliberately, to front only the essential facts of life, and see if I could not learn what it had to teach, and not, when I came to die, discover that I had not lived.'[3]

First published in 1854, the book quickly captured the imagination of ordinary men and women shackled by working life in nearby Boston and other industrial cities. Over time, the site of Thoreau's hut became a place of pilgrimage, a shrine to the pastoral dream—that timeless desire to strip away the material world, to get back to the land, and to hold, if only for a moment, a true consciousness of what it is to exist. Thoreau's quest, to understand how to live and what to live for, is one for all ages, and this perhaps explains why his reputation has eclipsed that of Emerson, the man who inspired him.

Thoreau was nineteen years old and a student at Harvard College when Ralph Waldo Emerson, a leading figure in the Transcendental movement, published his influential essay 'Nature'. In this work, Emerson put forward the idea that God speaks to man through the phenomenon of nature, and that 'Nature is made to conspire with spirit to emancipate us'.[4] At the time of its publication in 1836, New England Puritans believed that theirs was the promised land, the New Jerusalem; that they were God's chosen people, that the Bible was law, and that man's knowledge of God came only through Scripture. As civil and ecclesiastical law was based on the exact word of Scripture, the government's authority in New England townships and communities was deemed to come straight from God. The Pilgrim Fathers might have found this 'direct rule' idea helpful in establishing a new colony in 1620, but 200 years later it had less utility. Newly independent and fresh-thinking was the order of the day in nineteenth-century Massachusetts.

Writing fifty-three years after the end of the War of Independence, Emerson protested that 'Our age is retrospective. ... The foregoing generations beheld God and nature face to face ... Why should not we have a poetry and philosophy of insight and not of tradition, and a religion by revelation to us, and not the history of theirs?' Emerson was born and raised in a brave new world, and now he was shaping the fundamental philosophy on which it would be built. In his 1841 essay 'Self-Reliance', Emerson advocates that

> A man should learn to detect and watch that gleam of light which flashes across his mind from within, more than the lustre of the firmament of bards and sages. Yet he dismisses without notice his thought, because it is his. In every work of genius we recognize our own rejected thoughts: they come back to us with a certain alienated majesty.[5]

His message was clear: look to yourself, trust your own senses and thoughts; the past is another country, the present belongs to you. Emerson stepped out from under the shadow of Puritanism to advocate a radical creed for a new generation, stating, 'The sun shines today also. There is more wool and flax in the fields. There are new lands, new men, new thoughts. Let us demand our own works and laws and worship.'⁶ Emerson's idea that we can understand the very meaning of existence through a direct experience of nature spurred Thoreau's ambition to live life on his own terms, setting out into the wilderness in search of that enlightenment.

Thoreau's creation in *Walden* was more than simply a book on living with nature or a treatise on individual liberty; it was a window into a highly spiritual existence in which life in the immediate present connected boundlessly with the unfathomably ancient world. Throughout his life, Thoreau turned to the *Bhagavad Gita* for inspiration, and in *Walden* he describes how every morning in his hut he would bathe his intellect in its 'stupendous and cosmogonal philosophy', before putting the book aside and going to the well for water, where 'lo! there I meet the servant of the Bramin, priest of Brahma and Vishnu and Indra, who still sits in his temple on the Ganges reading the Vedas, or dwells at the root of a tree with his crust and water jug'. Thus, amidst Thoreau's profound spiritual contemplation, 'the pure Walden water is mingled with the sacred water of the Ganges.'

While Thoreau was on retreat from the world, his writing inadvertently spun a mystique that would place this modest pond on the philosophical map of the modern age. Thoreau's account of his two years, two months and two days on Walden Pond touched a nerve with his readers: they too were looking for something more than work and money and church on Sunday, and they began to come—first by train from nearby Boston, and then from further afield—to see for themselves this monument to personal enlightenment. A distant place, a revered text, an exceptional spiritual person: Walden Pond had all the components of a pilgrim destination, and over a century after the initial publication of *Walden*, it was still attracting over half a million visitors a year.⁷ But even within living memory of Emerson and Thoreau, both Concord and Walden proved magnetic places. In

1904, Henry James wrote of his visit: 'not a russet leaf fell for me, while I was there, but fell with an Emersonian drop.'[8]

Like many canonised secular figures, before and since, Thoreau had the good grace to die young—in his case, at the age of forty-five from tuberculosis. Emerson gave the funeral address, which included the line 'He chose to be rich by making his wants few and supplying them himself.' At the time of the eulogy, Emerson was a major national intellectual figure, and Thoreau a minor local celebrity, but the appeal of *Walden* and Thoreau's untimely death, combined with Emerson's patronage, caused his reputation to rise posthumously, and public interest in him to grow.

Thoreau's descriptions of the changing seasons and the life around the pond contributed to his reputation as a natural historian, and he remains an important figure in today's environmental movement in the US. The chapter entitled 'The Pond in Winter' illustrates both the natural and spiritual dimensions of Thoreau's enterprise, as here we learn that

> Every winter the liquid and trembling surface of the pond, which was so sensitive to every breath, and reflected every light and shadow, becomes solid to the depth of a foot or a foot and a half ... I cut my way first through a foot of snow, and then a foot of ice, and open a window under my feet, where, kneeling to drink, I look down into the quiet parlor of the fishes, pervaded by a softened light as through a window of ground glass, with its bright sanded floor the same as in summer; there a perennial waveless serenity reigns as in the amber twilight sky, corresponding to the cool and even temperament of the inhabitants. Heaven is under our feet as well as over our heads.

When John Muir visited Concord in June 1893, some thirty years after Thoreau's death, he was already himself a distinguished thinker and writer on the natural world and an environmental activist. He had lived alone for two years in an isolated hut, not on the outskirts of a Boston suburb, but in the epic landscape of the Yosemite Valley. He had helped found the Sierra

Club, one of the most influential environmental campaigning groups in the US, then as now. He later inspired President Theodore Roosevelt to embark on a wide-ranging conservation programme that included establishing Yosemite National Park. But on this visit to rural Massachusetts, Muir was the *chela*, the disciple or follower, and he came to Concord with the open heart of a pilgrim, laying flowers on the graves of Thoreau and Emerson in Sleepy Hollow Cemetery.

On the question of Walden Pond, Muir was an enthusiast, and tactfully did not comment on its proximity to the road and the Fitchburg rail line. He wrote, 'No wonder Thoreau lived here two years. I could have enjoyed living here two hundred or two thousand', but Muir was not undiscerning, noting that the pond is 'only about one and a half or two miles from Concord, a mere saunter, and how people should regard Thoreau as a hermit on account of his little delightful stay here I cannot guess.'[9] I have to admit that I was equally baffled when I visited Walden Pond, but—as is so often the case—the potency of place can be hard to fathom unless seen through the eyes of those drawn to it.

John Muir was a true environmental pioneer and many places bear his name, including the John Muir Trail, which runs for over 200 miles through the Sierra Nevada of the western United States, and the Muir Woods in California, with their 2,000-year-old sequoia trees. In common with Walden Pond, Muir Woods has become a destination for both day-trippers and environmental and literary pilgrims. Muir's achievements were exceptional, soaring high above the reach of most of us. We can admire him, but we cannot aspire to achieve what he achieved. His spirit was forged in the harsh Scottish winters of his childhood and burnished under the skies of a nation in the making. By contrast, Thoreau was an 'everyman' looking for meaning in a life marked by its ordinariness, and we can all relate to that. Thoreau consciously relinquished his worldly needs, albeit briefly, in order to create the space in which to develop his intellectual and spiritual self—an approach many pilgrims will recognise. By contrast, Muir did not so much repudiate convention by taking time out from polite society, but rather embraced nature red in tooth and claw, braving the cold of Alaska and the remote solitude of Yosemite to find a way to live. In a letter to his friend Emily Pelton on 23 May 1865, he wrote, 'I never tried to abandon creeds or code of civilization; they went away of their own accord ... without leaving any consciousness of loss.'

Muir was raised in an intensely religious Scottish family and his use of language to describe the natural world at once reflects this, as well as the Transcendentalist precept that man experiences God through nature. Writing in October 1869 to his friend and spiritual mother, the botanist Mrs Ezra Carr, he declares that 'my summer in the third heaven of the Sierra is past'. The following month he declined her kind invitation to stay, writing, 'I must return to the mountains of Yosemite, I am told that the winter storms there will not easily be borne, but I am bewitched, enchanted and tomorrow I must start for the great temple, to listen to the winter songs and sermons preached and sung only there.'[10]

Out in this pristine wilderness, Muir's spiritual path deviated from the Christian creed expressed in the book of Genesis whereby God granted man 'dominion over the fish of the sea and the fowl of the air and over the cattle and over all the earth, and over every creeping thing that creepeth upon the earth.' Furthermore, when it came to man's relationship with nature, he rejected the European Enlightenment ideas of the previous two centuries—ideas that only heretics of modernity would have the temerity to challenge. The term 'Enlightenment' stood and still stands for a bursting portmanteau of radical scientific and social ideas and values, many of which we live by today, including the notion of fundamental human rights. But this great leap forward in ideas and invention coincided with an equally great era of trade and manufacturing, and it served the latter particular cause to believe that the Bible had it right, and that the earth existed as a resource for humanity. Writing in 1713, the Reverend William Derham, a scientist and a Christian, stated that man could 'travel to the farthest regions of this world, to acquire wealth, to increase our knowledge, or even only to please our eye and fancy', yet no matter what we did, or to what extent, 'still the Creation would not be exhausted'.[11]

By contrast, Muir advocated not only that we should respect the natural world, but that wilderness should be preserved for purposes greater than human use.[12] In this regard, Muir's sentiment is closer to the Zen Buddhist ideology: that nature has an intrinsic value, rather than simply being a tool or resource for the benefit of mankind. His is the enlightenment of a truly spiritual pilgrim, out in the natural world, looking for a way to live, breathing in creation, feeling the delicate balance of all things, and seeing the earth for what it is: our life support system. If we should ever doubt it, we might, as our ancestors once did, look up at the stars and the moon, and remind ourselves that at every given moment we are hurling through space.

\* \* \*

In the century or so since Muir died in 1914, aged seventy-six, society's concern for the natural world has expanded from the local to the systemic, and now includes the pressing question of what we can do to limit or prevent changes to the planet's climate. Expressed in many different ways and at all levels of society, from intergovernmental accords to citizen action, this reverence for the earth is not the cult of Gaia reborn for the modern age, but rather—like our earliest belief systems—founded on a recognition that our continued existence is subject to the forces of the universe. In California, water, that substance so fundamental to the

whole ecosystem, has become the subject of a pilgrimage centred on Mono Lake at the heart of Yosemite, which John Muir
helped preserve.

In this excerpt from his first summer there, Muir writes, 'Have
just returned from a fine wild excursion across the range to
Mono Lake, by way of the Mono or Bloody Cañon Pass ... The
glacier meadows that lay along my way served to soothe my
morning speed, for the sod was full of blue gentians and daisies,
kalmia and dwarf vaccinium, calling for recognition as old
friends, and I had to stop many times'.[13] Like fellow pilgrims
following other ancient routes, Muir recognised that he was
treading where many had gone before. He noted that the Pass
had long been used by wild animals and by the Native Americans,
well before its discovery by white men.

Today, the Walking Water project unites Native Americans,
faith groups, community activists and environmentalists under a
common purpose, expressed through the act of pilgrimage. Their
founding cause is one told many times in the history of human
habitation: that of the 'tragedy of the commons', in this case the
impact of industry, agriculture and human habitation on the
water resources of the Owens Valley and Mono Lake.[14] Despite
the deafening ring of conservationist alarm bells that have
sounded over many decades, water continues to be diverted from
the lake, lowering water levels and impacting its salinity; and, as
cattle continue to graze surrounding lands, bird habitat is
increasingly impacted. Added to this, California has experienced
several successive years of drought in the 2010s, putting additional pressure on all of the state's water resources.

In September 2015, just over a century after the first water
rights were purchased in the Owens Valley, a group of pilgrims
from around the world gathered to begin the first phase of a
walk that would take place over three successive autumns,
stretching 180 miles from Mono Lake to Los Angeles. The
Walking Water route followed the course of natural and man-

made waterways, and was not so much a protest against self-interest as a positive act of collaboration, designed to generate new thinking around issues of conservation. The organisers described their pilgrimage as 'bearing witness' to the water situation, and 'a celebration of the possibilities we have when we come together.'

Their passion and prayer were fuelled by the value of the collective stakes: Mono Lake, which sits between the Great Basin and the Sierra Nevada in the south-western United States, has an exceptional ecosystem. Trillions of tiny saltwater shrimp live in the saline waters of the lake, and the alkaline flies that live in the surrounding marshes provide food for millions of migrating birds.[15] Each summer, over 100,000 red-necked and Wilson's phalaropes descend upon Mono Lake before flying on to South America. The Audubon Society, dedicated to the protection of birds and their habitat in the US, records that 20,000 sandpipers and 10,000 avocets were once counted here in a single day.[16] Every year, millions of eared grebes pass through this habitat on their way south for the winter. As it continues to be eroded through lower water levels and cattle farming, the ecosystem on which these migrating species depend looks increasingly at risk.

Many species depend for their survival on a complex balance of factors, from habitat to insect life, climate and predation, and in this sense they really are the 'canaries in the coalmine' when it comes to the impacts of environmental degradation on the natural world more generally. The 2019 US Audubon Society's report predicts that, of the 588 North American bird species studied, two-thirds are likely to be negatively impacted by a range of factors including land-use change, expanding agriculture, increased wildfire risk, warmer springs, drought, and excess precipitation. For a bigger picture view, we could usefully turn to NASA, America's National Aeronautics and Space Administration. It is the Pythia that pronounces on the future of this planet, and if the question is 'Are we are in trouble unless we take action?', their answer is unequivocally 'Yes.' We cannot always see what we have, even when it is right in front of us, and Walking Water exists to open our eyes before it is too late.

Siri Gunnarson, one of the pilgrims, wrote on the Walking Water blog of her hopes for the pilgrimage:

> We have been walking with the water, walking with the stories, walking with inquiry, collecting questions and listening deeply ... it is about reconciliation of relationship between people, between organizations, between the human species and water. What if all the stakeholders, all those impacted by and caring for these waters, came together in a cohesive vision for reconciliation and restoration? ... Each year we have water activists joining us from all over the world, sharing their stories from India, Bolivia, Israel–Palestine, Kenya [and] we see connection in the struggles, and [in the] dedication to a new way of stewardship.

The action of Walking Water was not simply a protest, but a deeply spiritual act: setting out each morning, the pilgrims began in silence, their outer journey and their inner journey keeping in step through hours of meditative walking. Gunnarson has written that these 'moments of walking with water bring me more deeply into myself, and [after] the first year I felt water began to walk me, bringing me more deeply into the study and research of water...' As well as the common pilgrim themes of healing and solace, her account also touched on how her pilgrim experience had helped her to grow up, by giving herself up to something bigger. As demonstrated by Muir, Thoreau and others before and since, being out in the natural world, walking and thinking, creates the possibility of insight that cannot be had anywhere else, not even alone at home. As Emerson noted, 'To go into solitude, a man needs to retire as much from his chamber as from society. I am not solitary whilst I read and write, though nobody is with me. But if a man would be alone, let him look at the stars.'[17]

# EPILOGUE

'When we try to pick out anything by itself, we find it hitched to
everything else in the Universe.'

John Muir, *My First Summer in the Sierra*

While Walking Water chose pilgrimage as a way to address an
environmental crisis, elsewhere the growing interest in pilgrimage is part of the problem itself. Our individual enterprise; our
fear and adoration of the forces that govern the universe; our
search for survival, kinship, faith, wonder, solace, redemption,
hope, gratitude, liberation, enlightenment—it all adds up. Every
year, staggering numbers of feet are marching devotedly to the
world's major shrines, both religious and secular. And each of
these pilgrimages has an environmental footprint.

In November 2010, over the course of six days, pilgrims making
the Hajj to Mecca disposed of an estimated 100 million plastic
water bottles. One hundred million. This startling fact is reported
in *The Green Guide for Hajj*. Launched by the charities Global One
and The Eco Muslim, this publication offers guidance to pilgrims
on how to reduce their environmental impact both during the
festival and after they return home. The *Guide* interweaves the
principles of environmental stewardship with the sayings of the
Prophet Muhammad and verses from the Quran, thereby making

respect for Earth and respect for God one and the same: 'All creation prostrates to Allah, all creation must be respected, and Muslims must protect Allah's creation—Allah's environment and ecosystems ... Allah ... made us [custodians] of the Earth and as such we are instructed to care for the Earth.' The *Guide* reminds pilgrims that their behaviour towards the environment during their Hajj is in part what will gain Allah's pleasure.[1]

At a very practical level, a waste-recycling project recently introduced for the Hajj ties the act of recycling to *zakat*, one of the five pillars of the Islamic faith. Next in importance to prayer, Muslims have a religious obligation to give a portion of their income to charity. By demonstrating that the proceeds from the waste recycling will fund charitable causes, the project encourages pilgrims to see recycling as part of their religious duty. This link between religious observance and care for the environment is a powerful one; but Islam is by no means alone in addressing the scale of waste from pilgrimage, or in harnessing the mass audience of the faithful to communicate more widely on the question of our relationship with the natural world.

In 2015, Pope Francis issued the first ever papal document dedicated exclusively to the environment. While this did not specifically address the issues of green pilgrimage, it was timed to influence the international talks on climate change that were then taking place in Paris. Taking its title from the words of St Francis of Assisi, *Laudato Si'* (praise be to You), the Pope's encyclical letter sets out the problem of our relationship with the earth: 'We have come to see ourselves as her lords and masters, entitled to plunder her at will.' The encyclical ran to 184 pages, setting out a comprehensive case for why faith and care for the environment are indivisible.

Glastonbury, a place that seems to have been exceptionally agile in responding to cultural shifts over the millennia, is now securing its legitimacy once again in this age of environmental consciousness. In 2017, more than 60 tonnes of paper and card, 32 tonnes of glass, 40 tonnes of plastic bottles and 45 tonnes of cans were recycled after the festival. That same year, 132 tonnes of food waste were composted and 4,500 litres of cooking oil converted into biofuel.[2] By 2019 the organisers of Glastonbury Festival had banned the sale of plastic bottles, urging festival-goers to bring reusable water bottles and other items in a bid to cut down on the waste generated at the event.

Elsewhere, EcoSikh, founded in 2009, works to ensure that 'our deep reverence for all creation remain a central part of the Sikh way of life.' The first target of EcoSikh was to help gurd-waras introduce greener practices in their community kitchens, thereby bringing these principles right into the heart of Sikhism. Other EcoSikh action programmes include EcoAmritsar, which brings a range of stakeholders together to make Amritsar 'a greener city, because it is a holy city'. An estimated 13 million pilgrims visit Amritsar each year,[3] and the aim of EcoSikh is to help Amritsar reduce waste, conserve water, and expand greenery projects; but beyond that, the programme also wants pilgrims to Amritsar to see the city as a model for other parts of India, and to return home with 'a sense that being faithful is being gentle to the planet'. It seems to be working: with new water stations installed around the Golden Temple, the consumption of bottled water in the city is already significantly reduced from the levels at the time the organisation was founded. In 2019, EcoSikh launched its Million Tree Project. Rajwant Singh, who is behind the worldwide tree-planting project, said he hoped it would motivate Sikhs to improve their relationship with nature and would be seen as 'a gift to the entire planet.'

Much of the impetus for this link between faith, pilgrimage and the environment began in 1986 at a gathering in Assisi, when the Duke of Edinburgh—then president of the World Wide Fund for Nature—invited leaders of five major religions (Judaism,

Buddhism, Christianity, Islam and Hinduism) to consider how they could support the goals of conservation. Soon afterwards, WWF began working with each of these faith groups to create programmes that could deliver change, and within a few years a new organisation was created to manage this work: the Alliance of Religions and Conservation (ARC). The original five were soon joined by the Daoist, Shinto, Sikh, Zoroastrian, Bahai and Jain faiths; through the common thread of humanity's dependence on the natural world, ARC found a way to work with each, in line with their own core teaching, beliefs and practices.

One of ARC's early research projects considered how Daoism could protect the ecology of the sacred mountains that play such an important role in Daoist pilgrimage practices. Compiled at some time between the late sixth and late fourth centuries BCE, the Daoist *Book of the Way*, or *Dao De Jing*, describes a world in which nature and man are one: 'Dao is the mother that has given birth to the world, which as the child, is rooted in Dao. Man is a creature of nature, and as such he is rooted in nature, which is rooted in Dao. Dao–nature–man–nature–Dao forms the great chain of being.'[4] The Daoist world is one where each season gives way to the next in a cycle of renewal, and where change is the universal phenomenon governing all things: the duality of heaven and humanity does not exist; all is one. This idea of the oneness of creation suggests the imperative of humanity's responsibility to the natural world, and in 2006 a group of Daoist monks and nuns got together to discuss how to mobilise their community to protect the environment in and around their temples.

The much-adapted saying 'A journey of a thousand miles starts beneath one's feet' comes from the *Dao De Jing* and the monks and nuns soon took the first step from thought to action. It was agreed that solar panels would be installed on Daoist temples across China, with an undertaking to carry out environmental impact assessments at all sites. Perhaps most importantly of all, it was proposed that the great sage Laozi, said to be the author of the *Dao De Jing*, be adopted as the 'Daoist God of Ecological Protection'. In 2007, the first green Daoist temple was built in China's Shaanxi province, on the pilgrimage mountain Taibaishan, and the *Daoist Ecological Temple Handbook* was published. It opens with this passage from Chapter Fifty-One of the *Dao De Jing*:

> Everything streams from the Dao (the way),
> Everything is nurtured by De (virtue).
> Everything is made out of substance.
> Everything is created by the Dao of Nature
> — and from everything on earth that surrounds it.
> So every living thing should bow to the Dao and the De
> Because they are what it is.[5]

Twenty-five years after that first meeting in Assisi, ARC launched the Green Pilgrimage Network, recognising the impact of the growing practice of pilgrimage on the cities and sites that receive these purposeful travellers. The organisation estimates global pilgrim numbers to be in excess of 300 million annually, and believes that protecting the environment and reducing the 'pilgrim footprint' should be an essential expression of faith. The list of projects initiated or influenced through the Green Pilgrimage Network is wide-ranging, from protecting biodiversity along pilgrim routes, to the reclamation of 400 acres of desert around the Coptic Orthodox Monastery of St Pishoy in Egypt to grow organic crops to feed monks and pilgrims. By greening pilgrim routes and destinations and raising environmental awareness amongst the vast flow of pilgrims at sites like Amritsar and Mecca, these grassroots programmes are leveraging the convening power of religion and pilgrimage sites to change the way we think about the natural world in all its fragility. These new initiatives from the 2010s give us a taste of a future in which we are able to bridge the secular–religious divide to collaborate in securing our sacred commonwealth. There can be little doubt that the green pilgrim movement is likely to grow in step with both our eco-consciousness and with our increasing appetite for ritual journeys of meaning.

Many first-hand pilgrim accounts talk of stepping outside normal life, to get a different perspective; a view from the edge. Nowhere is this truer in the literal sense than for those who have ventured beyond the pale of the earth's atmosphere. At the time of writing, the NASA astronaut Don Pettit had spent 369 days, 16 hours and 41 minutes in space; he is very familiar with viewing this blue marble from a distance. He describes how, looking back from the heavens,

> The most amazing aspect of this view is how thin this life-preserving blanket is when compared to the full extent of the planet. Like an orbital eggshell, our atmosphere looks so frail that it might crack and be gone in an instant, rendering Earth as barren and lifeless as any other baked hunk of rock orbiting the sun.[6]

This observation bears a striking resemblance to one made by John Muir 100 years earlier: 'When we contemplate the globe as one great dew drop, striped and dotted with continents and islands, flying through space with other stars all singing and shining together as one, the whole universe appears as an infinite storm of beauty.'[7]

\* \* \*

Some 11,000 years ago, small bands of nomads came together at their summer hunting grounds in southern Anatolia to quarry the rocks that would be used to build what is thought to have been an immense pilgrimage site at Göbekli Tepe. Christians and Blackfoot tribes were amongst those who left stones to mark the route of a sacred journey, and in the remote, arid desert of the Hijaz, a black stone, very possibly the result of a meteorite shower from the heavens, marks a place that has drawn pilgrims since before its history was written.

At the advent of agriculture, the ancients created the Eleusinian Mysteries, a pilgrim festival to celebrate that profound moment when humans first planted seed that they hoped would grow into food months hence. Over the millennia that followed, we have celebrated this same miracle with harvest festivals such as the Jewish Passover and the Shinto pilgrimage to the Ise shrine—to give thanks for crops reaped, and help secure those yet to come.

The heliacal rising of the Pleiades constellation marked the beginning of the pilgrim season for the Ancient Greeks, and the magnetic moon, with its influence on the tides, still determines the festival calendar for Christians, Hindus, Jews and Muslims, whose great annual Hajj pilgrimage is scheduled according to the lunar cycle. Water plays its part too, from Lourdes to the Pushkar Lake and the thousands of other sacred sources found across the world, not forgetting the largest single pilgrimage event on Earth: the Kumbh Mela, where Hindus wash away their sins at the confluence of the Ganges, Yamuna and mystical Sarasvati Rivers.

From the sacred cedars of Humbaba in the *Epic of Gilgamesh*, to the oak of Dodona and the sacred Bodhi Fig Tree under which Buddha attained enlightenment, to the Maypoles that once marked spring festivals across Europe, trees have formed part of our pilgrim rites since the earliest time. And, last but not least, there are the mountains. For over 5,000 years, pilgrims of successive creeds have been making their way up Croagh Patrick in the west of Ireland; and at the other side of the world, in China's Shandong province, for generations emperors made a pilgrimage to Mount Tai, to pay respect to the mountain. Here, as in each of the main pilgrimage sites around the world—whether it be Jerusalem or Mecca, Delphi or Glastonbury, Rome or Varanasi—the veil between this world and the realms that lie beyond our knowing seems more transparent. And, as we take the first step of our pilgrimage, to give thanks, to repent, to pray, or to express awe at the wonder of existence, we have—since the beginning of recorded time—stepped outside of our everyday lives and experienced what it is to be part of something more.

On 4 August 2018, a warm, starlit night, I was being driven across Lebanon with my friend Miriam. We were travelling from our retreat at the Qozhaya Maronite Monastery to the ancient city of Baalbek, also known as Heliopolis: from monotheism to paganism in a single journey, on the quest for enlightenment. As we ascended over the ridge of the Lebanon Mountains, Mars came into view. This low red glow in the velvet dark appeared to be floating over the Bekaa Valley, so close that one might have snared it with a single deft throw of the lasso. Down we went, through the valley and into Heliopolis, where the sounds of a festival were pulsing out from the ruins of temples dedicated to three more planets: Venus, Jupiter and Mercury.[8] Looking up at these cosmic bodies that once charted the seasons for our ancient Bronze Age ancestors, it seemed to me that humankind has come full circle in recognising that we depend on the natural world for our survival. Whatever our creed, we know that we are part of something greater than ourselves.

Is it possible that, 12,000 years ago, Neolithic pilgrims looking up at the cosmos through the soaring pillars of Göbekli Tepe came to that self-same realisation?

# NOTES

## PROLOGUE

1. James Hutton, eighteenth-century geologist.

## 1. SURVIVAL

1. In spring 2009, radar technology research logged some 11 million painted ladies entering the UK, with 26 million departing that autumn. Taking up to six generations to complete the journey, each butterfly must stop to lay eggs; when they hatch into caterpillars, they must first grow and then pupate, during which time almost every cell is dissolved into a fluid within the cocoon. From this DNA soup the next-generation butterfly is created and continues on with the migration. How this newly formed being knows where it must then fly to and why is a mystery, but it appears to be inherent.
2. Chaucer, Geoffrey. *The Canterbury Tales*, trans. David Wright, Oxford: OUP, 1985.
3. Göbekli Tepe dates from the period known as the Pre-Pottery Neolithic.
4. Magli, Giulio. 'Sirius and the Project of the Megalithic Enclosures at Gobekli Tepe', *Nexus Network Journal* 18.2 (2016): 337–46.
5. Lang, Caroline, Joris Peters, Nadja Pöllath, Klaus Schmidt & Gisela Grupe. 'Gazelle behaviour and human presence at early Neolithic Göbekli Tepe, south-east Anatolia', *World Archaeology* 45.3 (2013): 410–29.
6. Garfinkel, Yosef. 'The Earliest Dancing Scenes in the Near East', *Near Eastern Archaeology* 66.3, special edition 'Dance in the Ancient World' (September 2003): 84–95.

7. Barsh, Russel Lawrence and Chantelle Marlor. 'Driving Bison and Blackfoot Science', *Human Ecology* 31.4 (2003): 571–93.

8. Dillon, M. *Pilgrims and Pilgrimage in Ancient Greece*, London: Routledge, 1997.

9. Excavated in the late nineteenth and very early twentieth centuries by a team from the French Archaeological School of Athens, under the direction of Théophile Homolle.

10. Flacelière, Robert. *Greek Oracles*, London: Elek Books, 1965.

11. Eade, John and Michael J. Sallnow (eds). *Contesting the Sacred: The Anthropology of Christian Pilgrimage*, London: Routledge, 1991.

12. Parke, H.W. *A History of the Delphic Oracle*, Oxford: Basil Blackwell, 1939.

13. Pausanias, *Description of Greece* 7.22.2, available at https://hellenismo-saionios.wordpress.com/2015/08/17/oracle-of-hermes-agoraios/ [accessed 22/11/2019].

14. Lawler, Andrew. 'Erbil Revealed', *Archaeology* 67.5 (2014): 38–43.

## 2. KINSHIP

1. Homer. *The Odyssey*, trans. R. Fitzgerald, New York: Everyman, 1910, pp. 58–9.

2. Sumption, J. *Pilgrimage: An Image of Mediaeval Religion*, London: Faber, 1975.

3. Bredon, J. and I. Mitrophanow. *The Moon Year*, Shanghai: Kelly & Walsh, 1927.

4. Qingming also marks the start of the spring rains: the very best teas, designated as 'pre-Qingming', are picked in the short period between the emergence of new spring growth in late March and 5 April; they command a much higher price than those picked after the festival.

5. Burkhardt, Valentine Rodolphe. *Chinese Creeds and Customs*. London: Kegan Paul China Library, 2006.

6. Köhler-Rollefson, Ilse. 'The Raika Dromedary Breeders of Rajasthan', *Nomadic Peoples* 30 (1992): 74–83.

7. Catholic Church for England and Wales. *Pilgrim Catholic: Newsletter of the Gypsy and Traveller Support Network*, March 2006.

8. Badone, Ellen. 'Pilgrimage, tourism and *The da Vinci code* at Les-Saintes-Maries-De-La-Mer, France,' *Culture and Religion* 9.1 (2008): 23–44.

9. Franz de Ville, *Tziganes. Témoins des temps*, Brussels: Office de Publicité, 1956.

10. The Tanakh is the canonical collection of Jewish texts, also a textual source for the Christian Old Testament. It includes the Torah, Nevi'im and Ketuvim, and is also known as the Mikra.

11. Jericho was the locus of Natufian culture, which dates back to around 12,500 BCE.

12. One of the five books which make up the Pentateuch, Exodus is thought variously to have been revealed to Moses, or written by a number of unknown authors living between 950 and 450 BCE.

13. Deuteronomy 16.16, 16.17.

14. Titus Flavius Josephus. *The Wars of the Jews, or History of the Destruction of Jerusalem*, trans. William Whiston, Project Gutenberg, 2013.

15. Gurevich, David. 'The Water Pools and the Pilgrimage to Jerusalem in the Late Second Temple Period', *Palestine Exploration Quarterly* 149.2 (2017): 103–34.

16. Montefiore, Simon Sebag. *Jerusalem: The Biography*, London: Weidenfeld & Nicolson, 2011, p. 87.

3. FAITH

1. Conrad, Joseph. *Lord Jim*, London: Everyman, 1992.

2. Afsaruddin, Asma. *The First Muslims: History and Memory*, Oxford: Oneworld, 2008, pp. 13–14.

3. Malcolm X, 'The Pilgrimage to Makkah', letter from Mecca, available at http://islam.uga.edu/malcomx.html [accessed 22/11/2019].

4. Clingingsmith, David, Asim Ijaz Khwaja and Michael Kremer. 'Estimating the Impact of the Hajj: Religion and Tolerance in Islam's Global Gathering', *Quarterly Journal of Economics* 124.3 (2009): 1133–70.

5. Syed, Insiya. '"Shall I Feed My Daughter, or Educate Her?"', Human Rights Watch, 12 November 2018, https://www.hrw.org/report/2018/11/12/shall-i-feed-my-daughter-or-educate-her/barriers-girls-education-pakistan [accessed 22/11/2019].

6. British Museum, Virtual Hajj project, 2012.

7. 'Indeed, the first House [of worship] established for mankind was that at Makkah—blessed and a guidance for the worlds.' Quran 3.96.

8. Thomsen, Elsebeth. 'New Light on the Origin of the Holy Black Stone of the Ka'ba', *Meteoritics* 15.1 (1980): 87–91.

9. Sardar, Ziauddin. *Mecca: The Sacred City*, London: Bloomsbury, 2014, pp. 64–7.

10. Probably by Eustorgius I, Bishop of Milan and later Saint.

11. Source: Confraternity of St James.

12. Catedral de Santiago, Oficina de Acogida al Peregrino. 'Informe estadístico: Año 2018', available at http://oficinadelperegrino.com/wp-content/uploads/2016/02/peregrinaciones2018.pdf [accessed 22/11/2019].

## 4. WONDER

1. Hardy, Thomas. Quoted in *The Personal Notebooks of Thomas Hardy* (ed. Richard H. Taylor), London: Macmillan, 1978.

2. Jutla, Rajinder S. 'The Evolution of the Golden Temple of Amritsar into a Major Sikh Pilgrimage Center', *AIMS Geosciences* 2.3 (2016): 259–72.

3. Alliance of Religions and Conservation, 'Pilgrim numbers', last updated June 2014, http://www.arcworld.org/projects.asp?projectID=500 [accessed 22/11/2019].

4. Singh Khalsa, Pritpal. 'Guruka Langar', Sikh Dharma International, 22 September 2015, https://www.sikhdharma.org/guruka-langar/ [accessed 22/11/2019].

5. Erasmus, Desiderius. *Pilgrimages to Saint Mary of Walsingham and Saint Thomas of Canterbury* (trans. John Gough Nichols), London: J. Bowyer Nichols & Son, 1849.

6. Collinson, Patrick. 'The Protestant Cathedral 1541–1660', in Collinson, Patrick, Nigel Ramsay and Margaret Sparks, *A History of Canterbury Cathedral*, Oxford: OUP, 1995.

7. Stewart, Aubrey (ed., trans.). *The Book of Wanderings of Brother Felix Fabri*, London: Palestinian Pilgrim's Text Society, 1896.

8. Hölbl, Günther. *A History of the Ptolemaic Empire*, London: Routledge, 2002.

9. McKenzie, Judith S., Sheila Gibson, and A. T. Reyes. 'Reconstructing the Serapeum in Alexandria from the Archaeological Evidence', *The Journal of Roman Studies* 94 (2004): 73–121.

10. Wilkinson, Toby A. H. *The Rise and Fall of Ancient Egypt: The History of a Civilisation from 3000 BC to Cleopatra*. London: Bloomsbury, 2010.

11. Jobson, Christopher. 'The Shaolin Flying Monks Temple Blasts Monks Into the Sky Above a Mountainside Amphitheater', Colossal, 13 March 2017, https://www.thisiscolossal.com/?s=shaolin+flying+monks+ [accessed 04/12/2019].

12. Lu, Zhouxiang. *A History of Shaolin: Buddhism, Kung Fu and Identity*. New York: Routledge, Taylor & Francis Group, 2019.

13. Officially, in China, the sporting version of the martial art 'kung-fu' is known as *wushu*.

## 5. SOLACE

1. Psalm 137, common to both Jewish and Christian faiths, laments the time when Nebuchadnezzar II, King of Babylon, besieged Jerusalem and sent its people into exile and captivity.

2. Kerouac, Jack. *Selected Letters, 1940–1956* (ed. Ann Charters), New York/London: Viking, 1995.

3. As we learn in Kerouac's book, *The Dharma Bums*, New York/London: Viking, 1958.

4. Kerouac, Jack. *Desolation Angels*, London: Andre Deutsch, 1966.

5. Ibid.

6. The complete haiku reads: 'Has spring come/or has the year gone?/second-to-last-day'.

7. Matsuo, Bashō. *Basho's Journey: The Literary Prose of Matsuo Basho* (trans. David Landis Barnhill), New York: State University of New York Press, 2005.

8. By comparison, the Colossus of Rhodes stood at just 33 metres, and lasted for a mere 54 years before being brought down by an earthquake in 226 BCE.

9. As retold in Llewelyn Morgan's *The Buddhas of Bamiyan* (London: Profile Books, 2012).

10. Mahallati, Amineh. 'Women as Pilgrims: Memoirs of Iranian Women Travelers to Mecca', *Iranian Studies* 44.6 (2011): 831–49.

11. Derks, Sanne, and Meike Heessels. 'Battered Women Venerating a

Vicious Virgin: Reconsidering Marianismo at a Bolivian Pilgrimage Shrine', *Culture and Religion* 12.3 (2011): 303–16.

12. Albro, Robert. 'Neoliberal Ritualists of Urkupiña: Bedeviling Patrimonial Identity in a Bolivian Patronal Fiesta', *Ethnology* 37.2 (1998): 133–64.

13. Brooke, Rupert. 'Dust', 1908–11.

## 6. REDEMPTION

1. Wordsworth, William. 'I travelled among unknown men', 1807.

2. McKenna, Catherine. 'Performing Penance and Poetic Performance in the Medieval Welsh Court', *Speculum* 82.1 (2007): 70–96.

3. Roach, A. 'Penance and the Making of the Inquisition in Languedoc', *The Journal of Ecclesiastical History*, 52.3 (2001): 409–33.

4. Sebald, W. G. *The Rings of Saturn*, London: New Directions Books, 1998.

6. Published in German as *Die Ringe des Saturn: Eine englische Wallfahrt—Rings of Saturn—An English Pilgrimage*.

6. Letter from Joseph Conrad to Marguerite Paradowska, 23–25 March 1890, quoted by John Cant in his *Notes on the Ring of Saturn*, work in progress, September 2012.

7. Hamburger, Michael and Peter Dale. *Michael Hamburger in Conversation with Peter Dale*. London: Between the Lines, 1998.

8. In 'Afterthoughts on the Mug's Game' (*Irish Pages* 3.1, 2005: 220–36), M.H. describes how he never stepped inside a synagogue until he was in his 30s or 40s.

9. Ambitiously subtitled '*Relations of the World and the Religions Observed in all Ages and Places Discovered from the Creation unto this Present*', the little-travelled country parson Samuel Purchas's work was compiled out of stories gleaned from seafarers and from the texts of historical travellers, such as Marco Polo's account of the Mongolian city of Xanadu. Purchas himself lived close to the English port of Leigh-on-Sea.

10. Quoted from: Adair, Patricia. 'Lowes', in *The Waking Dream: A Study of Coleridge's Poetry*, London: Edward Arnold, 1967.

11. Anna Pincus works to support people held in immigration detention and the volunteers who visit them weekly. Her co-organiser David

Herd is Professor of Modern Literature at the University of Kent. See: Refugeetales.org [accessed 10/01/2020].

12. Relief & Reconciliation for Syria. See: http://www.reliefandreconcil-iation.org.

13. Andreyev, Alexander. 'Russian Buddhists in Tibet, from the End of the Nineteenth Century—1930', *Journal of the Royal Asiatic Society* 11.3 (2001): 349–62.

## 7. HOPE

1. 'Untitled haiku' (trans. Jane Hirshfield), 'Seeing Through Words: An Introduction to Basho and Haiku', in Hirshfield, Jane. *Ten Windows: How Great Poems Transform the World*, New York: Knopf, 2015.

2. Bede. *Bede's Ecclesiastical History of the English Nation: A New Translation* (trans. Rev. Lewis Gidley, James Parker and Co.), Oxford: James Parker & Co., 1870.

3. Bede. *The Venerable Bede's Ecclesiastical History of England: Also the Anglo-Saxon Chronicle* (ed. J. A. Giles), London: George Bell, 1894.

4. This annual record of events began in the ninth century during the reign of King Alfred the Great. Providing a systematic year-by-year account of English history, it was maintained and added to by generations of anonymous scribes until the middle of the twelfth century.

5. Harris, Ruth. *Lourdes: Body and Spirit in a Secular Age*, London: Allen Lane, 1999, p. 258.

6. Eade, John. 'Order and Power at Lourdes: Lay helpers and the organization of a pilgrimage shrine', in Eade, John and Michael J. Sallnow (eds), *Contesting the Sacred: The Anthropology of Christian Pilgrimage*, London/New York: Routledge, 1991.

7. Eade and Sallnow. *Contesting the Sacred*.

8. Stark, Laura. *Peasants, Pilgrims and Sacred Promises; Ritual and the Supernatural in Orthodox Karelian Folk Religion*, Helsinki: Studia Fennica, 2002.

9. Dowden, Ken. 'Grades in the Eleusinian Mysteries', *Revue de l'histoire des religions* 197.4 (1980): 409–27.

10. *Homeric Hymn to Demeter* (trans. Gregory Nagy), Center for Hellenic Studies, Harvard University; available at: https://chs.harvard.edu/CHS/article/display/5292 [accessed 09/12/2019].

11. Dillon, Matthew. *Pilgrims and Pilgrimage in Ancient Greece*, London: Routledge, 2007.

12. Quoted from Bede.

13. Gombrich, Richard F. *Theravāda Buddhism: A Social History from Ancient Benares to Modern Colombo*, London/New York: Routledge/ Kegan Paul, 1988.

14. *Maha Parinibbana Sutta* Chapter 5 (trans. Thanissaro Bhikkhu, 1998). Available at https://www.accesstoinsight.org/tipitaka/dn/dn.16.5–6. than.html#chap5 [accessed 09/12/2019].

## 8. GRATITUDE

1. Muir, John. 'An Unpublished Journal of John Muir', *The North American Review* 245.1 (1938): 24–51.

2. Bradley, Ian. *Pilgrimage: A Spiritual and Cultural Journey*, Oxford: Lion Hudson, 2009.

3. Johnson, Mira C. *The Croagh Patrick Pilgrimage: Identity Construction and Spiritual Expereince at Ireland's Holy Mountain*, MA thesis, University of Oregon, June 2011, available at https://scholarsbank.uoregon.edu/ xmlui/bitstream/handle/1794/11497/Johnson_Mira_C_ma2011sp.pdf; jsessionid=DCE844D8F7D9AAC6597E9D48E42F7C0D?sequence=1 [accessed 09/12/2019].

4. Jones, Prudence and Nigel Pennick. *A History of Pagan Europe*, London: Routledge, 1995.

5. Breen, John, and Mark Teeuwen. *A New History of Shinto*, Blackwell Brief Histories of Religion, Chichester: Wiley-Blackwell, 2010.

6. A survey carried out amongst 363 university students in 1988 reported extreme contempt for organised religion amongst 92 per cent of those surveyed. Reader, Ian. *Religion in Contemporary Japan*, Basingstoke: Macmillan, 1991.

7. Ibid., p. 14.

8. Glazebrook, Diana and Mohammad Jalal Abbasi-Shavazi. 'Being Neighbors to Imam Reza: Pilgrimage Practices and Return Intentions of Hazara Afghans Living in Mashhad, Iran', *Iranian Studies* 40.2 (2007), 187–201.

## 9. LIBERATION

1. Letter to sister Sarah Galloway, 3 September 1873, available in *The Writings of John Muir: The Life and Letters of John Muir* (trans. William Frederic Badè), 1924.
2. Largely thanks to the publication of Geoffrey of Monmouth's *History of the Kings of Britain*, which retold the Arthurian legend as true history.
3. His pilgrimage inspired the sixteenth-century/Ming Dynasty tale *Journey to the West*, one of the great works of Chinese literature.
4. Khonde, Nitesh and Sunil Kumar Singh, D. M. Maurya, Vinai K. Rai, L. S. Chamyal and Liviu Giosan. 'Tracing the Vedic Saraswati River in the Great Rann of Kachchh', *Scientific Reports*, 7.5476 (2017).
5. Nehru, Jawaharlal. *A Bunch of Old Letters: Written Mostly to Jawaharlal Nehru and Some Written by Him*, Bombay: Asia House, 1958.
6. Bhisma. Verses 4–12, 9.15, in *Mahabharata* (trans. Alex Cherniak), New York: NYU Press, 2008.
7. Nehru, *A Bunch of Old Letters*.
8. Lovell, Mary S. *A Rage to Live: A Biography of Richard and Isabel Burton*, New York/London: W. W. Norton, 1998.
9. Burton, Richard and John Hayman and Henry E. Huntington Library Art Gallery. *Sir Richard Burton's Travels in Arabia and Africa: Four Lectures from a Huntington Library Manuscript*, San Marino CA: Huntington Library, 1990.
10. Ibid.
11. As above—he cites accounts by Ludovico di Bartema in 1503, Joseph Pitts of Exeter in 1680, Giovanni Finati of Ferrara in 1811, and 'the excellent Swiss Traveller' Burckhardt in 1814.
12. Included in Burton's account *A Pilgrimage to Medinah and Mecca* (1855).
13. Slight, John. *The British Empire and the Hajj, 1865–1956*, Cambridge MA: Harvard University Press, 2015.
14. Ibid.
15. Board of Trade Wreck Report for Jeddah (No. 896). 'Report of a Court of Inquiry held at Aden into the cause of the abandonment of the steamship "JEDDAH,"', 1881, Port Cities Southampton, available at https://plimsoll.southampton.gov.uk/SOTON_Documents/Plimsoll/14642.pdf [accessed 09/12/2019].

16. Conrad, Joseph. *Lord Jim*, in *The Works of Joseph Conrad*. London: J. M. Dent & Sons, 1923.

17. Slight, J. *The British Empire and the Hajj*, Cambridge MA: Harvard University Press, 2015, p. 242.

18. Pew Research Center. 'The Future of World Religions: Population Growth Projections, 2010–2050', 2 April 2015, https://www.pewforum.org/2015/04/02/religious-projections-2010–2050/ [accessed 09/12/2019].

19. Twain, Mark. *A Tramp Abroad; Following the Equator; Other Travels* (ed. Roy Blount), New York: Library of America, 2010.

20. Justice, Christopher J. S. *The Good Death in Kashi: Process and Experience of the Pilgrimage to Die in the Hindu Holy City*, 1994.

10. ENLIGHTENMENT

1. Emerson, Ralph Waldo. *Nature*, Boston MA: James Munroe, 1836.

2. Thomas, Edward J. *The Life of Buddha as Legend and History*, 3rd Edition, London: Routledge & Kegan Paul, 1969.

3. Thoreau, Henry David. *Walden*. Boston/Cambridge: Houghton, Mifflin and Company/The Riverside Press, 1881.

4. Labriola, Patrick. 'Ralph Waldo Emerson's "Nature": Puritan Typology and German Idealism', in *The Concord Saunterer*, New Series, Vol. 10 (2002): 124–33.

5. Emerson, Ralph Waldo. *Self-reliance*. New York: Thomas Y. Crowell, 1911.

6. Emerson, *Nature*, Boston MA: James Munroe, 1836.

7. Buell, Lawrence. 'The Thoreauvian Pilgrimage: The Structure of an American Cult', *American Literature* 61.2 (1989): 175–99.

8. James, Henry. 'The American Scene' and 'Concord and Salem' (1907) in *Henry James: Collected Travel Writings*, Vol. 2, New York: Library of America, 1993, pp. 565–78.

9. Muir, John. 'Trees and Travel 1891–1897', in *The Writings of John Muir: The Life and Letters of John Muir* (trans. William Frederic Badè), Vol. 10, Part 2, Boston MA: Houghton Mifflin, 1924.

10. Muir, John. *Letters to a Friend: Written to Mrs. Ezra S. Carr, 1866–1879*, Houghton Mifflin Company, 1915.

11. Porter, Roy. *Enlightenment: Britain and the Creation of the Modern World*, London: Allen Lane, 2000, p. 299.

12. Branch, Michael P. 'John Muir's *My First Summer in the Sierra* (1911)', *Interdisciplinary Studies in Literature and Environment* 11.1 (2004): 139–52.

13. Muir, John. *My First Summer in the Sierra*, Boston MA: Houghton Mifflin, 1911.

14. 'Tragedy of the commons' was first coined by economist William Forster Lloyd in 1833 to describe the behaviours that so often led to overgrazing of cattle on common land in England.

15. Mono Lake Committee. 'Archived: Birds and Other Wildlife Sightings, 2007–2008', www.monolake.org/birds [accessed 09/12/2019].

16. The Audubon Society is America's leading organisation for bird conservation: www.audubon.org.

17. Emerson, Ralph Waldo. *Nature*, Boston MA: James Munroe, 1836.

EPILOGUE

1. Supported by the Alliance of Religions and Conservation and the UN Development Program (2015). The original 2011 guide is available here: https://globalone.org.uk/wp-content/uploads/2017/12/Green_Guide_for_Hajj.pdf [accessed 09/12/2019].

2. Herbert, Tom. 'Glastonbury plastic bottles ban 2019: Has Glasto gone plastic free? Which single use plastics has the festival banned?', *Evening Standard*, 25 June 2019, https://www.standard.co.uk/futurelondon/the-plasticfreeproject/glastonbury-plastic-bottles-ban-single-use-plastic-free-festival-a4175076.html [accessed 09/12/2019].

3. Alliance of Religions and Conservation figures vary from 13 to 30 million.

4. Chen, Ellen Marie. 'The Meaning of Ge in the Tao Te Ching: An Examination of the Concept of Nature in Chinese Taoism', *Philosophy East and West* 23.4 (1973): 457–70.

5. 'Daoist Ecological Temple Handbook', available via the Alliance of Religions and Conservation: http://www.arcworld.org/downloads/Daoist-Eco-Handbook-Eng.pdf [accessed 09/12/2019].

6. Don Pettit was a science officer on the International Space Station in

2002–3. Quoted in Nelson, Craig. *Rocket Men*, London: John Murray, 2009.

7. Muir, John and Marion Randall Parsons. *Travels in Alaska*, Boston MA: Houghton Mifflin, 1915.

8. Kropp, Andreas J. M. 'Jupiter, Venus and Mercury of Heliopolis (Baalbek): The Images of the "Triad" and its Alleged Syncretisms', *Syria* 87 (2010): 229–64.

# INDEX

# INDEX

# INDEX

# INDEX

# INDEX

# INDEX

# INDEX

# INDEX

# INDEX

# INDEX

# INDEX

# INDEX

# INDEX

# INDEX

# INDEX

# INDEX

# INDEX

# INDEX

# INDEX

# INDEX

# INDEX

# INDEX

# INDEX

# INDEX